CONTENTS

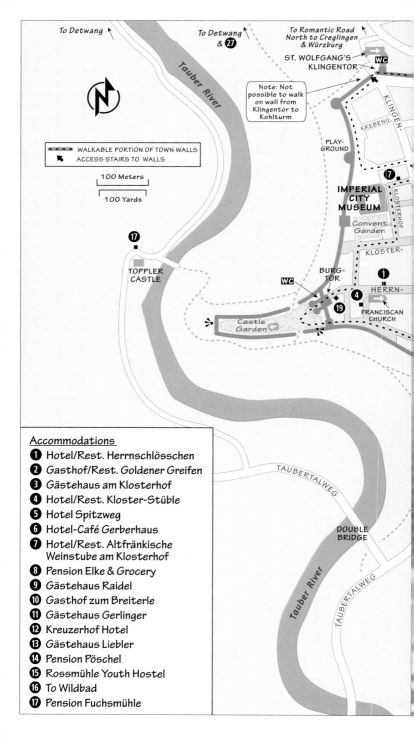

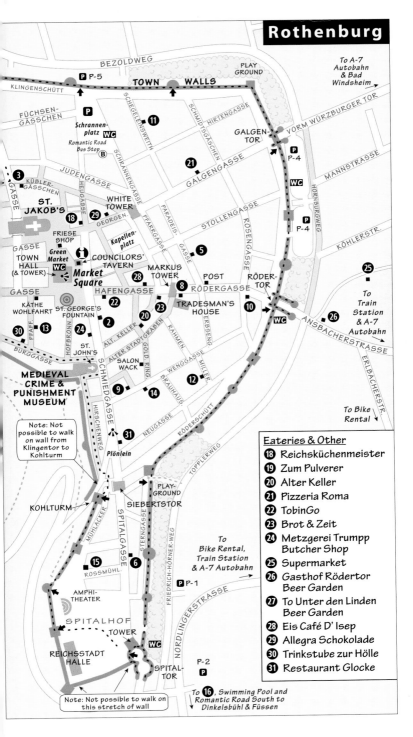

Rothenburg

Eateries & Other

⑱ Reichsküchenmeister
⑲ Zum Pulverer
⑳ Alter Keller
㉑ Pizzeria Roma
㉒ TobinGo
㉓ Brot & Zeit
㉔ Metzgerei Trumpp Butcher Shop
㉕ Supermarket
㉖ Gasthof Rödertor Beer Garden
㉗ To Unter den Linden Beer Garden
㉘ Eis Café D' Isep
㉙ Allegra Schokolade
㉚ Trinkstube zur Hölle
㉛ Restaurant Glocke

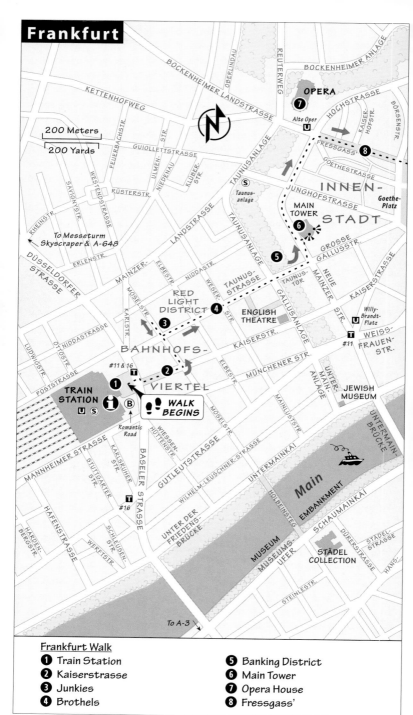

Frankfurt

200 Meters
200 Yards

To Messeturm
Skyscraper & A-648

WALK BEGINS

To A-3

Frankfurt Walk
1. Train Station
2. Kaiserstrasse
3. Junkies
4. Brothels
5. Banking District
6. Main Tower
7. Opera House
8. Fressgass'

OPERA
Alte Oper
INNEN-STADT
Goethe-Platz
MAIN TOWER
RED LIGHT DISTRICT
ENGLISH THEATRE
BAHNHOFS-VIERTEL
TRAIN STATION
Romantic Road
Main
EMBANKMENT
MUSEUM
JEWISH MUSEUM
STÄDEL COLLECTION
UNTERMAIN BRÜCKE

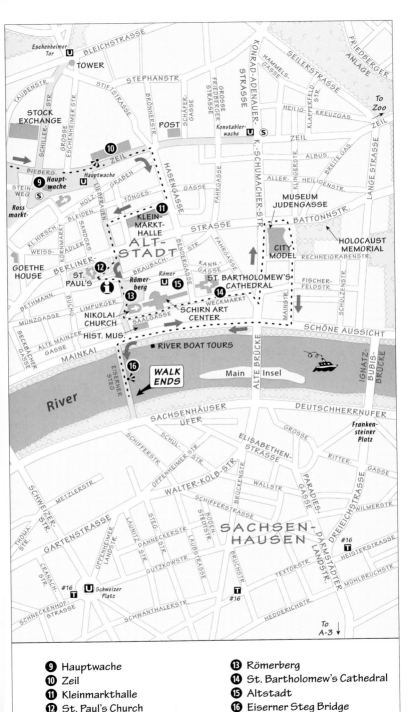

9 Hauptwache

10 Zeil

11 Kleinmarkthalle

12 St. Paul's Church

13 Römerberg

14 St. Bartholomew's Cathedral

15 Altstadt

16 Eiserner Steg Bridge

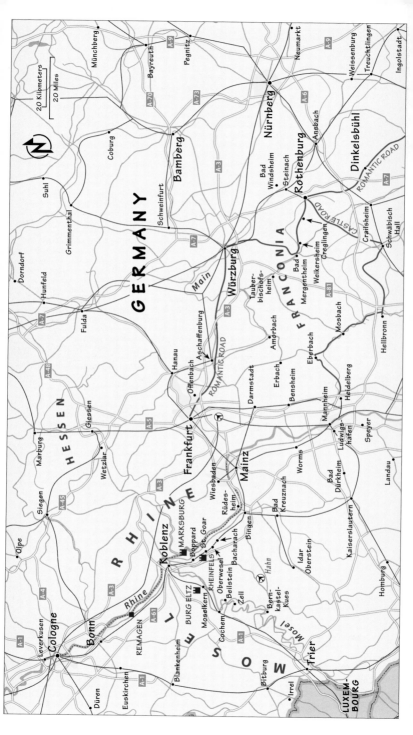

INTRODUCTION

This Snapshot guide, excerpted from my guidebook *Rick Steves Germany*, introduces you to some of the most romantic and historic parts of Germany—including the medieval walled town of Rothenburg ob der Tauber and the most picturesque stretch of the mighty Rhine River.

In Rothenburg, you can immerse yourself in the Middle Ages. Wander the town's mysterious and well-preserved ramparts, marvel at its churches' grand Gothic altarpieces, shudder at its creatively sadistic Medieval Crime and Punishment Museum, and do some of the best souvenir shopping in Germany. Along the Rhine, you can enjoy a self-guided tour of this scenic stretch of river—whether you're on a speedy train or the deck of a slow steamboat—as you compare stately castles and silly legends. Listen for the intoxicating songs of the mythical Mädchen at the Loreley cliff. Hike to a pair of the best castles high above the river: the evocative ruins of Rheinfels Castle, and the well-preserved, fully furnished Marksburg Castle.

Then explore the other delights of this region. Würzburg is a university town with an impressive, fun-to-tour Residenz palace (with manicured gardens and a dazzling Rococo chapel), a hilltop fortress, atmospheric wine bars, and a bridge that's perfect for strolling at sunset. Frankfurt is the country's bustling banking center, with a skyscraping skyline, giving you a good look at modern Germany. The Mosel River Valley, near the Rhine Valley, harbors wine-loving cobbled towns, such as handy Cochem and tiny, quaint Beilstein. Nestled within a forest is my favorite European castle, Burg Eltz, which feels lived in, because it is. And busy Cologne, on the Rhine River, has a spectacular Gothic cathedral looming over its train station, making it a rewarding, quick stop that's especially convenient for train travelers.

To help you have the best trip possible, I've included the following topics in this book:

• **Planning Your Time,** with advice on how to make the most of your limited time

• **Orientation,** including tourist information (abbreviated as TI), tips on public transportation, local tour options, and helpful hints

• **Sights** with ratings:

      ▲▲▲—Don't miss

      ▲▲—Try hard to see

      ▲—Worthwhile if you can make it

      No rating—Worth knowing about

• **Sleeping and Eating,** with good-value recommendations in every price range

• **Connections,** with tips on trains, buses, and driving

Practicalities, near the end of this book, has information on money, staying connected, hotel reservations, transportation, and more, plus German survival phrases.

To travel smartly, read this little book in its entirety before you go. It's my hope that this guide will make your trip more meaningful and rewarding. Traveling like a temporary local, you'll get the absolute most out of every mile, minute, and dollar.

Gute Reise!

ROTHENBURG & THE ROMANTIC ROAD

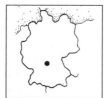

The Romantic Road takes you through Bavaria's medieval heartland, a route strewn with picturesque villages, farmhouses, onion-domed churches, Baroque palaces, and walled cities. The route, which runs from Würzburg to Füssen, is the most scenic way to connect Frankfurt with Munich. No trains run along the full length of the Romantic Road, but Rothenburg (ROH-tehn-burg), the most interesting town along the way, is easy to reach by rail. Drivers can either zero in on Rothenburg or take some extra time to meander from town to town on the way. For nondrivers, a tour bus travels the Romantic Road once daily in each direction.

Countless travelers have searched for the elusive "untouristy Rothenburg." There are many contenders (such as Michelstadt, Miltenberg, Bamberg, Bad Windsheim, and Dinkelsbühl), but none holds a candle to the king of medieval German cuteness. Even with crowds, overpriced souvenirs, Japanese-speaking night watchmen, and, yes, even *Schneeballen*, Rothenburg is best. Save time and mileage and be satisfied with the winner.

Rothenburg ob der Tauber

In the Middle Ages, when Berlin and Munich were just wide spots on the road, Rothenburg ob der Tauber was a "free imperial city" beholden only to the Holy Roman Emperor. During Rothenburg's heyday, from 1150 to 1400, it was a strategic stop on the trade routes between northern and southern Europe. Because of its privileged position, along with the abundant resources of its surrounding countryside (textile-producing sheep and fertile farmlands), Rothenburg thrived. With a whopping population of 6,000, it was one of Germany's largest towns. But as with many of Europe's best time-warp towns, Rothenburg's fortunes tumbled suddenly. (In this case, it was an occupation/ransacking during the Thirty Years' War, and a plague that followed soon after, that did the town in.) With no money to fix up its antiquated, severely leaning buildings, the town was left to languish in this state. Today, it's the country's best-preserved medieval walled town, enjoying tremendous tourist popularity without losing its charm.

Rothenburg's great trade these days is tourism: Two-thirds of the 2,500 people who live within its walls are employed to serve you. While roughly 2 million people visit each year, most come only on day trips. Rothenburg is yours after dark, when the groups vacate and the town's floodlit cobbles wring some romance out of any travel partner.

Too often, Rothenburg brings out the shopper in visitors before they've had a chance to see the historic town. True, this is a fine place to do your German shopping. But appreciate Rothenburg's great history and sights, too.

Germany has several towns named Rothenburg, so make sure you're going to Rothenburg ob der Tauber (not "ob der" any other river); people really do sometimes drive or ride the train to nondescript Rothenburgs by accident.

PLANNING YOUR TIME

Rothenburg in one day is easy. If time is short, you can make just a two- to three-hour midday stop in Rothenburg, but the town is really best appreciated after the day-trippers have gone home. Ideally, spend at least one night in Rothenburg (hotels are cheap and good).

With two nights and a full day, you'll be able to see more than the essentials and actually relax a little. I'd suggest starting your day with my self-guided town walk, including a visit to St. Jakob's Church (for the carved altarpiece) and the Imperial City Museum (historic artifacts). Then spend the afternoon visiting the Medieval Crime and Punishment Museum and taking my "Schmiedgasse-Spitalgasse Shopping Stroll," followed by a walk on the wall (from Spitaltor to Klingentor). Cap your day with the entertaining Night Watchman's Tour (at 20:00). Locals love *Die blaue Stunde* (the blue hour)—the time just before dark when city lamps and the sky hold hands. Be sure to be out enjoying the magic of the city at this time.

For nature lovers, there are plenty of relaxing walks and bike rides in the forested environs around the town.

Rothenburg is very busy through the summer and in the Christmas Market month of December. Spring and fall are a joy, but it's pretty bleak in November and from January through March—when most locals are hibernating or on vacation. Legally, shops are only allowed to remain open 40 Sundays a year; this means that many close on Sundays during the slow off-season months.

Orientation to Rothenburg

To orient yourself in Rothenburg, think of the town map as a human head. Its nose—the castle garden—sticks out to the left, and the skinny lower part forms a neck, with the youth hostel and a recommended hotel being the Adam's apple. The town is a delight on foot. No sights or hotels are more than a 15-minute walk from the train station or each other.

Most of the buildings you'll see were in place by 1400. The city was born around its long-gone castle fortress—built in 1142, destroyed in 1356—which was located where the castle garden is now. You can see the shadow of the first town wall, which defines the oldest part of Rothenburg, in its contemporary street plan. Two gates from this wall still survive: the Markus Tower and the White Tower. The richest and biggest houses were in this central part. The commoners built higgledy-piggledy (read: picturesque) houses farther from the center but still inside the present walls.

Although Rothenburg is technically in Bavaria, the region around the town is called—and strongly identifies itself as—"Franken," one of Germany's many medieval dukedoms ("Franconia" in English).

ROTHENBURG

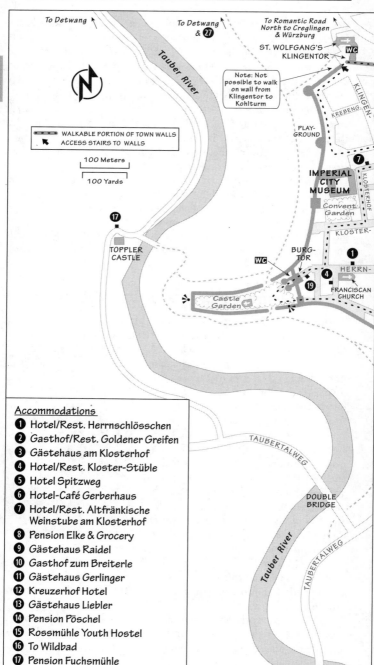

To Detwang

To Detwang
& **27**

To Romantic Road
North to Creglingen
& Würzburg

ST. WOLFGANG'S
KLINGENTOR

WC

KLINGEN-

KREBENG-

Tauber River

Note: Not
possible to walk
on wall from
Klingentor to
Kohlturm

PLAY-
GROUND

7

IMPERIAL
CITY
MUSEUM

KLOSTERHOF

Convent
Garden

KLOSTER-

17

TOPPLER
CASTLE

WC

BURG-
TOR

4

19

1

HERRN-

FRANCISCAN
CHURCH

Castle
Garden

N

⬥⬥⬥ WALKABLE PORTION OF TOWN WALLS
↖ ACCESS STAIRS TO WALLS

100 Meters
100 Yards

TAUBERTALWEG

DOUBLE
BRIDGE

Tauber River

TAUBERTALWEG

Accommodations
1. Hotel/Rest. Herrnschlösschen
2. Gasthof/Rest. Goldener Greifen
3. Gästehaus am Klosterhof
4. Hotel/Rest. Kloster-Stüble
5. Hotel Spitzweg
6. Hotel-Café Gerberhaus
7. Hotel/Rest. Altfränkische
   Weinstube am Klosterhof
8. Pension Elke & Grocery
9. Gästehaus Raidel
10. Gasthof zum Breiterle
11. Gästehaus Gerlinger
12. Kreuzerhof Hotel
13. Gästehaus Liebler
14. Pension Pöschel
15. Rossmühle Youth Hostel
16. To Wildbad
17. Pension Fuchsmühle

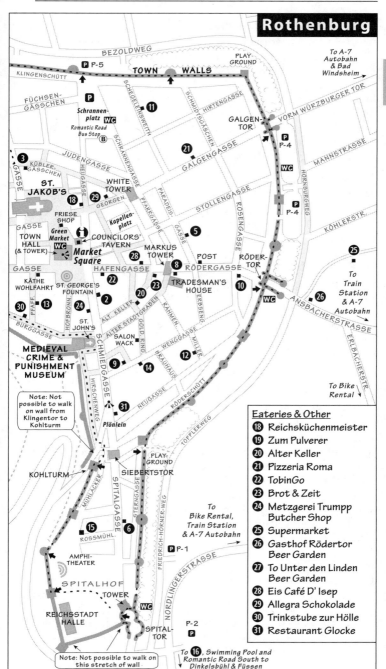

Rothenburg

ROTHENBURG

BEZOLDWEG

KLINGENSCHÜTT

TOWN WALLS

PLAY GROUND

To A-7 Autobahn & Bad Windsheim

FÜCHSEN-GÄSSCHEN

P P-5

Schrannen-platz WC

Romantic Road Bus Stop B

SCHEGELENSBWETH

SCHMIDTSGASSCHEN

HIRTENGASSE

VORM WÜRZBURGER TOR

GALGEN-TOR

11

MANNSTRASSE

P P-4

HORNBURGWEG

WC

KÜBLER-GÄSSCHEN

3

JUDENGASSE

HEUGASSE

SCHRANNENGASSE

GALGENGASSE

21

ST. JAKOB'S

GASSE

WHITE TOWER

18 29

GEORGEN.

PARADEIS

STÖLLENGASSE

ROSENGASSE

KÖHLERSTR.

P P-4

FRIESE SHOP

Green Market

Kapellen-platz

PFARRGASSE

TOWN HALL (& TOWER)

GASSE

WC

i

Market Square

COUNCILORS' TAVERN

5

25

To Train Station & A-7 Autobahn

28

MARKUS TOWER

GASSE

POST

RÖDER-TOR

8

RÖDERGASSE

KÄTHE WOHLFAHRT

HAFENGASSE

22

TRADESMAN'S HOUSE

26

ANSBACHERSTRASSE

ERKLBACHERSTR

30 13

PFAFF.

ST. GEORGE'S FOUNTAIN

24

2

20

23

10

WC

HOFBRONN

BURGGASSE

ST. JOHN'S

ALT. KELLER

ALTER STADTGRABEN

RAHMEN.

ERDSEN.

MILLER.

To Bike Rental

MEDIEVAL CRIME & PUNISHMENT MUSEUM

Note: Not possible to walk on wall from Klingentor to Kohlturm

SALON WACK

9

14

GOLD RING

BRAUHAUS

WENGGASSE

12

RÖDERSCHÜTT

TOPPLERWEG

31

Plönlein

HIRSCHENWEG

NEUGASSE

KOHLTURM

SCHMIEDGASSE

SIEBERTSTOR

PLAY-GROUND

To Bike Rental, Train Station & A-7 Autobahn

MÜHLACKER

SPITALGASSE

TERNGASSE

FRIEDRICH-HÖRNER-WEG

15

6

P P-1

ROSSMÜHL.

AMPHI-THEATER

SPITALHOF

TOWER

WC

NORDLINGERSTRASSE

P P-2

REICHSSTADT HALLE

SPITAL-TOR

Note: Not possible to walk on this stretch of wall

To 16, Swimming Pool and Romantic Road South to Dinkelsbühl & Füssen

Eateries & Other

18 Reichsküchenmeister

19 Zum Pulverer

20 Alter Keller

21 Pizzeria Roma

22 TobinGo

23 Brot & Zeit

24 Metzgerei Trumpp Butcher Shop

25 Supermarket

26 Gasthof Rödertor Beer Garden

27 To Unter den Linden Beer Garden

28 Eis Café D' Isep

29 Allegra Schokolade

30 Trinkstube zur Hölle

31 Restaurant Glocke

TOURIST INFORMATION

The TI is on Market Square (May-Oct and Dec Mon-Fri 9:00-18:00, Sat-Sun 10:00-17:00; off-season Mon-Fri until 17:00, Sat until 13:00, closed Sun; Marktplatz 2, tel. 09861/404-800, www.rothenburg.de/tourismus, run by Jörg Christöphler). If there's a long line, just raid the rack where they keep all the free pamphlets. The free city map comes with a walking guide to the town. The *Events* booklet covers the basics in English. They offer a variety of themed tours; ask when you arrive or check their website in advance. Also look for current concert-listing posters here (and at your hotel).

A fun pictorial town map, which also helpfully indicates some walking paths in the countryside beyond the town walls, is available for free when you show this book at the Friese shop, two doors west from the TI (toward St. Jakob's Church; see "Shopping in Rothenburg," later).

ARRIVAL IN ROTHENBURG

By Train: It's a 10-minute walk from the station to Rothenburg's Market Square (following the brown *Altstadt* signs, exit left from station, walk a block down Bahnhofstrasse, turn right on Ansbacher Strasse, and head straight into the Middle Ages). Taxis wait at the station (€10 to any hotel). Day-trippers can leave luggage in lockers on the platform. Free WCs are behind the Speedy snack bar on track 1. If killing time, you can pay to get online on one of the computers in the station's Spielothek gaming room (long hours daily).

By Car: Driving and parking rules in Rothenburg change constantly—ask your hotelier for advice. In general, you're allowed to drive into the old town to get to your hotel. Otherwise, driving within the old walled center is discouraged. Some hotels offer private parking (either free or paid). To keep things simple, park in one of the lots—numbered P-1 through P-5—that line the outside of the town walls (€5/day, buy ticket from *Parkscheinautomat* machines and display, 5- to 10-minute walk to Market Square).

For tips on getting here from Frankfurt, see "Route Tips for Drivers" on page 41.

HELPFUL HINTS

Festivals: For one weekend each spring (during Pentecost), beer gardens spill out into the street and Rothenburgers dress up in medieval costumes to celebrate Mayor Nusch's **Meistertrunk** victory (June 7-10 in 2019, www.meistertrunk.de). The **Reichsstadt festival** every September celebrates Rothenburg's history (Sept 6-8 in 2019), and the town's **Weindorf**

festival celebrates its wine (mid-Aug). Check the TI website for specifics.

Christmas Market: Rothenburg is dead for much of the winter except in December (its busiest month), when the entire town cranks up the medieval cuteness with concerts and costumes, shops with schnapps, stalls filling squares, hot spiced wine, giddy nutcrackers, and mobs of ear-muffed Germans. Christmas markets are big all over Germany, and Rothenburg's is considered one of the best. The market takes place each year during Advent. Try to avoid Saturdays and Sundays, when big-city day-trippers really clog the grog.

Wi-Fi: Free Wi-Fi (Network: rothenburg.freifunk.net) is available at varying strengths around town. As it requires no password, it's not a secure signal—use it to look up info (train schedules, museum hours) but not to check email or make purchases.

Mailing Your Goodies Home: You can get handy yellow €2.50 boxes at the old town **post office** (Mon-Fri 9:00-13:00 & 14:00-17:30 except closed Wed afternoon, Sat 9:00-12:00, closed Sun, inside photo shop at Rödergasse 11). The main post office is in the shopping center across from the train station.

Bike Rental: A ride through the nearby countryside is enjoyable on nice days (follow route described on page 31). **Rad & Tat** rents bikes for €14 for a 24-hour day (otherwise €10/6 hours, electric bike-€28/day; Mon-Fri 9:00-18:00, Sat until 13:00, closed Sun; Bensenstrasse 17, tel. 09861/87984, www.mietraeder.de). To reach it, leave the old town toward the train station, take a right on Erlbacher Strasse, cross the tracks, and look across the street from the Lidl supermarket.

Taxi: For a taxi, call 09861/2000 or 09861/7227.

Haircuts: At **Salon Wack** (pronounced "vahk," not "whack"), Horst and his team speak English and welcome both men and women (Tue-Fri 8:00-12:00 & 13:30-18:00, Sat 8:30-14:00, closed Sun-Mon; off Wenggasse at Goldene Ringgasse 8, tel. 09861/7834).

Swimming: Rothenburg has a fine swimming complex, with a heated outdoor pool *(Freibad)* from mid-May to mid-Sept (when the weather's good), and an indoor pool and sauna the rest of the year. It's about a 15-minute walk south of Spitaltor along the main road toward Dinkelsbühl (€3.50, kids-€2; outdoor pool daily 9:00-20:00; indoor pool Tue-Thu 9:00-21:00, Fri-Sun until 18:00, Mon 14:00-21:00; Nördlinger Strasse 20, tel. 09861/4565).

ROTHENBURG

Tours in Rothenburg

▲▲Night Watchman's Tour

This tour is flat-out the most entertaining hour of medieval wonder anywhere in Germany and the best evening activity in town. The Night Watchman (a.k.a. Hans-Georg Baumgartner) jokes like a medieval John Cleese as he lights his lamp and takes tourists on his rounds, telling slice-of-gritty-life tales of medieval Rothenburg (€8, teens-€4, free for kids 12 and under, mid-March-Dec nightly at 20:00, in English, meet at Market Square, www. nightwatchman.de). What's almost as entertaining as the tour is watching the parade of tourists following this pied piper through town each night.

▲Old Town Historic Walk

The TI offers engaging 1.5-hour guided walking tours in English (€8, Easter-Oct and Dec daily at 14:00, departs from Market Square). Just show up and pay the guide directly—there's always room. Take this tour for the serious side of Rothenburg's history, and to make sense of the town's architecture; you won't get as much of that on the fun—and completely different—Night Watchman's Tour. Taking both tours is a smart way to round out your overall Rothenburg experience.

Local Guides

A local historian can really bring the ramparts alive. Reserve a guide by emailing the TI (info@rothenburg.de; more info at www. tourismus.rothenburg.de—look under "Guided Tours"; €75/1.5 hours, €95/2 hours). I've had good experiences with **Martin Kamphans** (tel. 09861/7941, www.stadtfuehrungen-rothenburg.de, kamphans@posteo.de) and **Daniel Weber** (to get rates listed above ask for Rick Steves discount, mobile 0795-8311, www.toot-tours. com, mail@toot-tours.com).

Town Wall Walk

It's free to walk along Rothenburg's town wall, and 20 info plaques provide good English descriptions. (Ask at the TI for a pamphlet with narrated walk.) For details, see "Walk the Wall" on page 28.

Walks in Rothenburg

My self-guided circular "Rothenburg Town Walk" weaves the town's top sights together, takes about an hour without stops, and starts and ends on Market Square. (Note that this is roughly the same route followed by city guides on their daily Old Town Historic Walk, described earlier.) It flows into my "Schmiedgasse-Spitalgasse Shopping Stroll," which traces a straight shot from Market Square to Spitaltor, passing traditional shops and eateries on the way. Both walks are shown on the "Walks in Rothenburg" map.

∩ Download my free Rothenburg Town Walk audio tour.

ROTHENBURG TOWN WALK

This loop walk, worth ▲▲▲, links Market Square to St. Jakob's Church, the Imperial City Museum, the castle garden, and Herrngasse.

• *Start the walk on Market Square.*

Market Square Spin-Tour

Stand in front of the fountain at the bottom of Market Square (watch for occasional cars) and spin 360 degrees clockwise, starting with the Town Hall tower. Now do it again,

this time more slowly to take in some details:

Town Hall and Tower: Rothenburg's tallest spire is the Town Hall tower (Rathausturm). At 200 feet, it stands atop the old Town Hall, a white, Gothic, 13th-century building. Notice the tourists enjoying the best view in town from the black top of the tower (see "Sights in Rothenburg" for details on climbing the tower). After a fire in 1501 burned down part of the original building, a new Town Hall was built alongside what survived of the old one (fronting the square). This half of the rebuilt complex is in the Renaissance style from 1570. The double eagles you see decorating many buildings here are a repeated reminder that this was a "free imperial city" belonging directly to the (Habsburg) Holy Roman Emperor, a designation that came with benefits.

Meistertrunk Show: At the top of Market Square stands the proud Councilors' Tavern (clock tower from 1466). In its day, the city council—the rich guys who ran the town government—drank here. Today, it's the **TI** and the focus of most tourists' attention when the little doors on either side of the clock flip open and the wooden figures (from 1910) do their thing. Be on Market Square at the top of any hour (between 10:00 and 22:00) for the ritual gath-

ROTHENBURG

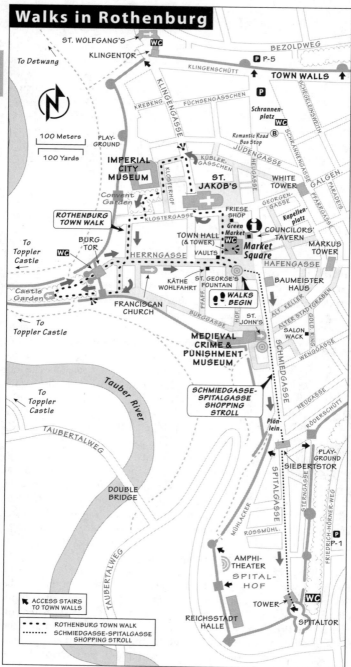

Walks in Rothenburg

ering of the tourists to see the less-than-breathtaking reenactment of the Meistertrunk ("Master Draught") story:

In 1631, in the middle of the Thirty Years' War, the Catholic army took this Protestant town and was about to do its rape, pillage, and plunder thing. As was the etiquette, the mayor had to give the conquering general a welcoming drink. The general enjoyed a huge tankard of local wine. Feeling really good, he told the mayor, "Hey, if you can drink this entire three-liter tankard of wine in one gulp, I'll spare your town." The mayor amazed everyone by drinking the entire thing, and Rothenburg was saved. (While this is a nice story, it was dreamed up in the late 1800s for a theatrical play designed—effectively—to promote a romantic image of the town. In actuality, if Rothenburg was spared, it had likely bribed its way out of the jam.) The city was occupied and ransacked several times in the Thirty Years' War, and it never recovered—which is why it's such a well-preserved time capsule today.

For the best show, don't watch the clock; watch the open-mouthed tourists gasp as the old windows flip open. At the late shows, the square flickers with camera flashes.

Bottom of Market Square: As this was the most prestigious address in town, it's ringed by big homes with big carriage gates. One of the finest is just downhill from the bottom end of the square—the **Baumeister** ("master builder") **Haus,** where the man who designed and built the Town Hall lived. It features a famous Renaissance facade with statues of the seven virtues and the seven vices. The statues are copies; the originals are in the Imperial City Museum (described later on this walk). While "Gluttony" is easy to find, see if you can figure out what his companions represent.

Behind you, take in the big 17th-century **St. George's fountain.** Its long metal gutters could slide to deposit the water into villagers' buckets. It's part of Rothenburg's ingenious water system: Built on a rock, the town had one real source above, which was plumbed to serve a series of fountains; water flowed from high to low through Rothenburg. Its many fountains had practical  functions beyond providing drinking water—some were stocked with fish on market days and during times of siege, and their water was useful for fighting fire. Because of its plentiful water supply—and its policy of requiring relatively wide lanes as fire breaks—the town never burned entirely, as so many neighboring villages did.

Two fine half-timbered buildings behind the fountain show

the old-time lofts with warehouse doors and pulleys on top for hoisting. All over town, lofts like these were filled with grain. A year's supply was required by the city so it could survive any siege. The building behind the fountain is an art gallery showing off work by members of the local artists' association. To the right is Marien Apotheke, an old-time pharmacy mixing old and new in typical Rothenburg style.

The broad street running under the Town Hall tower is **Herrngasse.** The town originated with its castle fortress (built in 1142 but now long gone; a lovely garden now fills that space). Herrngasse connected the castle to Market Square. The last leg of this circular walking tour will take you from the castle garden up Herrngasse and back here.

For now, walk a few steps down Herrngasse and stop by the arch under the Town Hall tower (between the new and old town halls). On the wall to the left of the gate are the town's measuring rods—a reminder that medieval Germany was made of 300 independent little countries, many with their own weights and measures. Merchants and shoppers knew that these were the local standards: the rod (4.3 yards), the *Schuh* ("shoe," roughly a foot), and the *Ell* (from elbow to fingertip—four inches longer than mine... climb up and try it). The protruding cornerstone you're standing on is one of many all over town—intended to protect buildings from careening horse carts. In German, going recklessly fast is called "scratching the cornerstone."

• *Careen around that stone and under the arch to find the...*

▲Historical Town Hall Vaults (Historiengewölbe)

The vaults house an eclectic and grade-schoolish little museum that gives a waxy but interesting look at Rothenburg during the Catholics-vs.-Protestants Thirty Years' War. Popping in here can help prep your imagination to filter out the tourists and picture ye olde Rothenburg along the rest of this walk. With helpful English descriptions, it offers a look at "the fateful year 1631," a replica of the mythical Meistertrunk tankard, an alchemist's workshop, and a dungeon—used as a bomb shelter during World War II—complete with three dank cells and some torture lore.

Cost and Hours: €3.50, daily 9:30-17:30, shorter hours Nov-April, closed Jan, weekends only Feb, tel. 09861/86751, www.meistertrunk.de.

• *Leaving the museum, turn left (past a venerable and much-sketched-and-photographed door) and find a posted copy of a centuries-old map showing the territory of Rothenburg.*

Map of Rothenburg City Territory

In 1537 Rothenburg actually ruled a little country—one of about

300 petty dukedoms like this that made up what is today's Germany. The territory spanned a 12-by-12-mile area (about 400 square kilometers), encompassing 180 villages—a good example of the fragmentation of feudal Germany. While not to scale (Rothenburg is actually less than a mile wide), the map is fun to study. In the 1380s, Mayor Toppler purchased much of this territory. In 1562 the city sold off some of its land to neighboring dukes, which gave it the money for all the fine Renaissance buildings that embellish the town to this day.

• *Continue through the courtyard and into a square called...*

Green Market (Grüner Markt)

Once a produce market, this parking lot fills with Christmas stands during December. Notice the clay-tile roofs. These "beaver tail" tiles became standard after thatched roofs were outlawed to prevent fires. Today, all the town's roofs are made of these. The little fences stop heaps of snow from falling off the roof and onto people below. A free public WC is on your left, and the recommended Friese gift shop (see listing under "Shopping in Rothenburg," later) is on your right.

• *Continue straight ahead to St. Jakob's Church. Study the exterior first, then pay to go inside.*

▲▲St. Jakob's Church (St. Jakobskirche)

Rothenburg's main church is home to Tilman Riemenschneider's breathtaking, wood-carved *Altar of the Holy Blood.*

Cost and Hours: €2.50, daily April-Oct 9:00-17:00, Dec 10:00-16:45, off-season 10:00-12:00 & 14:00-16:00, on Sun wait to enter until services end at 10:45.

Tours and Information: A free, helpful English info sheet is available. Concerts and a tour schedule are posted near the door. Guided tours in English run on Sat at 15:30 (April-Oct) for no extra charge. Or get the worthwhile audioguide (€2, 45 minutes) to tailor your education with dual commentary—historical and theological—for a handful of important stops in the church.

Visiting the Church: Start by viewing the exterior. Next, enter the church, where you'll see the main nave first, then climb above the pipe organ (in the back) to finish with the famous carved altar.

Exterior: Outside the church, under the little roof at the base of the tower, you'll see 14th-century statues (mostly original) showing Jesus praying at Gethsemane, a common feature of Gothic churches. The sculptor is anonymous—in the Gothic age (pre-Albrecht Dürer), artists were just nameless craftspeople working only for the glory of God. Five yards to the left (on the wall), notice the nub of a sandstone statue—a rare original, looking pretty bad after 500 years of weather and, more recently, pollution. Most original statues are now in the city museum. The better-preserved statues you see on the church are copies. Also outside the church is a bronze model of the city. Look closely to appreciate the detail, including descriptions in braille.

Before entering, notice how the church was extended to the west and actually built over the street. The newer chapel was built to accommodate pilgrims and to contain the sumptuous Riemenschneider carved altarpiece.

If it's your wedding day, take the first entrance—marked by a very fertile Eve and, around the corner, Adam showing off an impressive six-pack. Otherwise, head toward the church's second (downhill) door. Before going inside, notice the modern statue at the base of the stairs. This is **St. James** (a.k.a. Sankt Jakob in German, Santiago in Spanish, and Saint-Jacques in French). You can tell this important saint by his big, floppy hat, his walking stick, the gourd on his hip (used by pilgrims to carry water), and—most importantly—the scallop shell in his hand. St. James' remains are entombed in the grand cathedral of Santiago de Compostela, in the northwestern corner of Spain. The medieval pilgrimage route called the Camino de Santiago passed through here on its way to that distant corner of Europe. Pilgrims would wear the scallop shell as a symbol of their destination (where that type of marine life was abundant). To this day, the word for "scallop" in many languages carries the name of this saint: *Jakobsmuschel* in German, *coquille Saint-Jacques* in French, and so on.

Inside the Church: Built in the 14th century, this church has been Lutheran since 1544. The interior was "purified" by Romantics in the 19th century—cleaned of everything Baroque or not original and refitted in the Neo-Gothic style. (For example, the baptismal font—in the middle of the choir—and the pulpit above the second pew *look* Gothic but are actually Neo-Gothic.) The stained-glass windows behind the altar, which are most colorful in the morning light, are originals from the 1330s. Admiring this church, consider what it says about the priorities of a town of just a few thousand people, who decided to use their collective wealth to build such a place. The size of a church is a good indication of the town's wealth when it was built. Medallions and portraits of Rothenburg's leading families and church leaders line the walls above the choir in the front of the church.

The **main altar,** from 1466, is by Friedrich Herlin. Below Christ are statues of six saints—including St. James (a.k.a. Jakob), with the telltale shell on his floppy hat. Study the painted panels—ever see Peter with spectacles (below the carved saints)? Go around the back of the altarpiece to look at the doors. In the upper left, you'll see a painting of Rothenburg's Market Square in the 15th century, looking much like it does today, with the exception of the full-Gothic Town Hall (as it was before the big fire of 1501). Notice Christ's face on the white "veil of Veronica" (center of back side, bottom edge). It follows you as you walk from side to side—this must have given the faithful the religious heebie-jeebies four centuries ago.

The **Tabernacle of the Holy Eucharist** (just left of the main altar—on your right as you walk back around) is a century older. It stored the wine and bread used for Holy Communion. Before the Reformation this was a Roman Catholic church, which meant that the bread and wine were considered to be the actual body and blood of Jesus (and therefore needed a worthy repository). Notice the unusual Trinity: The Father and Son are bridged by a dove, which represents the Holy Spirit. Stepping back, you can see that Jesus is standing on a skull—clearly "overcoming death."

Now, as pilgrims did centuries ago, climb the stairs at the back of the church that lead up behind the pipe organ to a loft-like chapel.

Here you'll find the artistic highlight of Rothenburg and perhaps the most wonderful wood carving in all of Germany: the glorious 500-year-old, 35-foot-high *Altar of the Holy Blood.* Tilman Riemenschneider, the Michelangelo of German woodcarvers, carved this from 1499 to 1504 (at the same time Michelangelo was working on his own masterpieces). The altarpiece was designed to hold a rock-crystal capsule—set in the cross you see high above—that contains a precious scrap of tablecloth stained in the shape of a cross by a drop of communion wine considered to be the actual blood of Christ.

The altar is a realistic commotion, showing that Riemenschneider—a High Gothic artist—was ahead of his time. Below, in the scene of the Last Supper, Jesus gives Judas a piece of bread, marking him as the traitor, while John lays his head on Christ's lap. Judas, with his big bag of cash, could be removed from the scene (illustrated by photos on the wall nearby), as was the tradition for the four days leading up to Easter.

Everything is portrayed exactly as described in the Bible. In the relief panel on the left, Jesus enters the walled city of Jerusalem.

Notice the exacting attention to detail—down to the nails on the horseshoe. In the relief panel on the right, Jesus prays in the Garden of Gethsemane.

Before continuing on, take a moment to simply linger over the lovingly executed details: the curly locks of the apostles' hair and beards, and the folds of their garments; the delicate vines intertwining above their heads; Jesus' expression, at once tender and accusing.

• *After leaving the church, walk around the corner to the right and under the chapel (built over the road). Go two blocks down Klingengasse and stop at the corner of the street called Klosterhof. Looking farther ahead of you down Klingengasse, you see the...*

Klingentor

This cliff tower was Rothenburg's water reservoir. From 1595 until 1910, a 900-liter (240-gallon) copper tank high in the tower provided clean spring water—pumped up by river power—to the privileged. To the right of the Klingentor is a good stretch of wall rampart to walk. To the left, the wall is low and simple, lacking a rampart because it guards only a cliff.

Now find the shell decorating a building on the street corner next to you. That's once again the symbol of St. James, indicating that this building is associated with the church.

• *Turn left down Klosterhof, passing the shell and, on your right, the colorful, recommended Altfränkische Weinstube am Klosterhof pub. As you approach the next stop, notice the lazy Susan embedded in the wall (to the right of the museum door), which allowed cloistered nuns to give food to the poor without being seen.*

▲▲Imperial City Museum (Reichsstadt-Museum)

You'll get a vivid and artifact-filled sweep through Rothenburg's history at this excellent museum, housed in a former Dominican convent. The highlight for many is the painted glass mug said to have prompted the myth of the Meistertrunk.

Cost and Hours: €6; daily 9:30-17:30, Nov-March generally 13:00-16:00; pick up English info sheet at entrance, Klosterhof 5, tel. 09861/939-043, www.reichsstadtmuseum.rothenburg.de.

Visiting the Museum: As you follow the *Rundgang/Tour* signs to the left, watch for the following highlights:

Immediately inside the entry, a glass case shows off the 1616 Prince Elector's colorful glass tankard (which inspired the famous legend of the Meistertrunk, created in 1881 to drive tourism) and a set of golden Rothenburg coins. Down the hall, find a modern city model and trace the city's growth, its walls expanding like rings on a big tree. Before going upstairs, you'll see medieval and Renaissance sculptures, including original sandstone statues from St. Jakob's Church and original statues that once decorated the Baumeister Haus near Market Square. Upstairs in the nuns' dormitory are craftsmen's signs that once hung outside shops (see if you can guess the craft before reading the museum's label), ornate locks, tools for various professions, and a valuable collection of armor and weapons. You'll then go through two levels of rooms showcasing old furniture, housewares, and the Baroque statues that decorated the organ loft in St. Jakob's Church from 1669 until the 19th century, when they were cleared out to achieve "Gothic purity." Take time to enjoy the several rooms and shop fronts outfitted as they would have been centuries ago.

The painting gallery is lined with Romantic paintings of Rothenburg, which served as the first tourist promotion and give visitors today a chance to envision the city as it appeared in centuries past. Look for the large, gloomy work by Englishman Arthur Wasse (labeled *"Es spukt"*)—does that door look familiar?

Back downstairs near where you entered, circle left around the cloister to see a 14th-century convent kitchen *(Klosterküche)* with a working model of a lazy Susan (the kind that nuns would have used to share food with the poor outside the convent—go ahead, give it a swing) and a massive chimney (step inside and look up). Continue around to an exhibit of Jewish culture in Rothenburg through the ages *(Judaika)*, then see the grand finale (in the *Konventsaal*), the *Rothenburger Passion*. This 12-panel series of paintings showing scenes leading up to Christ's Crucifixion—originally intended for the town's Franciscan church (which we'll pass later)—dates from 1492.

• *Leaving the museum, go around to the right and into the Convent Garden (when locked at night, continue straight to the T-intersection and turn right).*

Convent Garden

This spot is a peaceful place to work on your tan...or mix a poisoned potion. Monks and nuns—who were responsible for concocting herbal cures in the olden days, finding disinfectants, and coming up with ways to disguise the taste of rotten food—often tended herb gardens. Smell (but don't pick) the *Pfefferminze* (peppermint), *Heidewacholder* (juniper/gin), *Rosmarin* (rosemary), *Lavandel* (lavender), and the tallest plant, *Hopfen* (hops...monks were the great medieval brewers). Don't smell the plants that are poisonous (potency indicated by the number of crosses, like stars indicating spiciness on a Thai food menu). Appreciate the setting, taking in the fine architecture and expansive garden—all within the city walls, where land was at such a premium. It's a reminder of the power of the pre-Reformation Church.

• *Exit opposite from where you entered, angling left through the nuns' garden, leaving via an arch along the far wall. Then turn right and go downhill to the...*

Town Wall

This part of the wall takes advantage of the natural fortification provided by the cliff (view through bars, look to far right) and is therefore much shorter than the ramparts.

• *Angle left along the wall. Cross the big street (Herrngasse, with the Burgtor tower on your right—which we'll enter from outside soon) and continue downhill on Burggasse until you hit another section of the town wall. Turn right, go through a small tower gate, and park yourself at the town's finest viewpoint.*

Castle Garden Viewpoint

From here enjoy a fine view of fortified Rothenburg. You're looking at the Spitaltor end of town (with the most interesting gate and

the former hospital). After this walk, you can continue with my "Schmiedgasse-Spitalgasse Shopping Stroll," which leads from Market Square down to this end of town, known as Plönlein, and then enter the city walls and walk the ramparts 180 degrees to the Klingentor tower (which we saw earlier on our walk, in the distance just after St. Jakob's Church). The droopy-eyed building at the far end of town (today's youth hostel) was the horse mill—which provided grinding power when the water mill in the valley below was not working (during drought or siege). Stretching below you is the fine park-like land around the Tauber River, nicknamed the "Tauber Riviera."

• *Now explore deeper into the park.*

Castle Garden (Burggarten) and the Burgtor Gate

The park before you was a castle fortress until it was destroyed in the 14th century. The chapel (50 yards straight into the park, on the left) is the only surviving bit of the original castle. In front of the chapel is a memorial to local Jews killed in a 1298 slaughter. A few steps beyond that is a flowery trellis that provides a fine picnic spot. If you walk all the way out to the garden's far end, you'll find another great viewpoint (well past the tourists, and considered by local teenagers the best place to make out).

When you're ready to leave the park, approach the Burgtor, the ornate fortified gate flanked by twin stubby towers, and imagine being locked out in the year 1400. (There's a WC on the left.) The tall tower behind the gate was accessed by a wooden drawbridge—see the chain slits above the inner gate, and between them the "pitch" mask with holes designed to allow defenders to pour boiling Nutella on attackers. High above is the town coat of arms: a red *(roten)* castle *(Burg)*.

As you go through the gate, study the big wooden door with the tiny "eye of the needle" door cut into it. If you were trying to enter town after curfew, you could have bribed the guard to let you through this door, which was small enough to keep out any fully armed attackers. Note also the square hole on the right and imagine the massive timber that once barricaded the gate.

• *Now climb up the big street, Herrngasse, as you return to your starting point.*

Herrngasse

Many towns have a Herrngasse, where the richest patricians and merchants (the *Herren*) lived. Predictably, it's your best chance to see the town's finest old mansions. Strolling back to Market Square, you'll pass, on the right, the **Franciscan Church** (from 1285—the oldest in town). Across the street, the mint-green house at #18 is the biggest patrician house on this main drag. The front door was big enough to allow a carriage to drive through it; a human-sized door cut into it was used by those on foot. The family, which has lived here for three centuries, has disconnected the four tempting old-time doorbells. The gift shop at #11 (Hornburghaus, on the right) offers a chance to poke into one of these big landowners' homes and appreciate their structure: living quarters in front above carriage-sized doors, courtyard out back functioning as a garage, stables, warehouse, servants' quarters, and a private well.

Farther up, also on the right, is Hotel Eisenhut, Rothenburg's fanciest hotel and worth a peek inside. Finally, passing the Käthe Wohlfahrt Christmas headquarters/shop (described under "Shopping in Rothenburg," later), you'll be back at Market Square, where you started this walk.

• *From here, you can continue walking by following my "Schmiedgasse-Spitalgasse Shopping Stroll," next. This stroll ends at the city gate called Spitaltor, a good access point for a walk on the town walls.*

▲▲SCHMIEDGASSE-SPITALGASSE SHOPPING STROLL

After doing the basic town walk and visiting the town's three essential interior sights (Imperial City Museum, Medieval Crime and Punishment Museum, and St. Jakob's Church), your next priority might be Rothenburg's shops and its town wall. I'd propose this fun walk, which goes from Market Square in a straight line south (past the best selection of characteristic family-run shops) to the city's most impressive fortification (Spitaltor).

Standing on Market Square, with your back to the TI, you'll see a street sloping downward toward the south end of town. That's where you're headed. This street changes names as you walk, from **Obere Schmiedgasse** (upper blacksmith street) to **Spitalgasse** (hospital street), and runs directly to the **Spitaltor** tower and gate. From Spitaltor you can access the town wall and walk the ramparts 180 degrees around the city to the Klingentor tower.

As you stroll down this delightful lane, feel welcome to pop in and explore any shop along this cultural and historical scavenger hunt. I've provided the street number and "left" or "right" to indicate the side of the street (see the "Walks in Rothenburg" map, earlier).

Market Square to Burggasse

The facade of the fine Renaissance **Baumeister Haus** at #3 (left) celebrates a secular (rather than religious) morality, with statues representing the seven virtues and the seven vices. Which ones do you recognize?

At #5 (left), **Gasthof Goldener Greifen** was once the home of the illustrious Mayor Toppler (d. 1408). By the looks of its door (right of the main entrance), the mayor must have had an impressive wine cellar. Note the fine hanging sign (much nicer than "hanging out your shingle") of a gilded griffin. Business signs in a mostly illiterate medieval world needed to be easy for all to read. The entire street is ornamented with fun signs like this one. Nearby, a pretzel marks the bakery, and the crossed swords advertise the weapon-maker.

Shops on both sides of the street at #7 display examples of *Schneeballen* gone wild. These "snowballs," once a humble way to bake extra flour into a simple treat, are now iced and dolled up a million ways—none of which would be recognizable to the kids who originally enjoyed them. Long ago locals used a fork to pierce the middle, but today's tourists eat them like an apple. Watch them crumble.

Waffenkammer, at #9 (left), is "the weapons chamber," where Johannes Wittmann works hard to make a wonderland in which young-at-heart tourists can shop for (and try out) medieval weapons, armor, and clothing. Fun photo ops abound, especially downstairs—where you can try on a set of chain mail and pose with a knight in shining armor (ask about Rick Steves discount).

At #18 (right), **Metzgerei Trumpp,** a top-end butcher, is a carnivores' heaven. Check out the endless wurst offerings in the window—a reminder that in the unrefrigerated Middle Ages meat needed to be smoked or salted. Locals who love bacon opt for fat slices of pork with crackling skins.

Burggasse to Plönlein

At the next corner, with **Burggasse,** find the Catholic St. John's Church. The Medieval Crime and Punishment Museum (just down the lane to the right) marks the site of Rothenburg's first town wall. Below the church (on the right) is an old fountain. Behind and below that find a cute little dog park complete with a doggie WC.

The **Jutta Korn** shop, on the right at #4, showcases the work of a local artisan who designs her own jewelry. She's been a jewelry master here for more than 30 years. At #6 (right), **Leyk** sells "lighthouses" made in town, many modeled after local buildings. The **Kleiderey,** an offbeat clothing store at #7 (left), is run by Tina, the Night Watchman's wife. The clothing is inspired by their southeast Asian travels.

At #13 (left), look opposite to find a narrow lane (**Ander Eich**) that leads to a little viewpoint in the town wall. Overlooking the "Tauber Riviera," it's a popular romantic perch in the evening.

The **Sumiko Ishii** souvenir shop, on the corner on the left, is a reminder that tourism from Asia is big business, and German shops are learning to cater to that crowd.

Continuing along, at #17 (left), the **Lebe Gesund Vegetarian** shop is all about healthy living. This charming little place (run by tasty-sample-dealing Universalist Christians who like to think of Jesus as a vegan) seems designed to offer forgiveness to those who loved the butcher's shop but are ready to repent.

On the right at #18, the **Da Vinci Lounge** café is decorated as if out of *Clockwork Orange*. Its modern interior is a stark contrast to this medieval city.

The **Käthe Wohlfahrt** shop at #19 (left) is one of the six Wohlfahrt stores around town, all owned by a local family and selling German clichés with gusto. Also on the left, at #21, the **An Ra** shop is where Annett Perner designs and sells her flowery clothes. You can pop in to see the actual work in the back. (There's more of An Ra across the street at #26.) Annett was behind a recent initiative, called "Handmade in Rothenburg," that formed a coalition between 10 local business owners who make everything from chocolate to jewelry to ceramics. They meet once a week to support each other and collaborate on ideas to strengthen the community, an example of the special bond of Rothenburg's town members.

At this point, stop and take a moment to notice the "vernacular architecture" (developed to meet local needs), with the cute gables and higgledy-piggledy rooflines, tiny doors closing narrow slits between homes, and the fountain that's hooked into pipes plumbed in the 1590s. In the Middle Ages, nothing was standard. Everything was built to order.

At #29 (left), **Glocke Weinladen am Plönlein** is an inviting shop of wine glasses and related accessories. The **Gasthof Glocke**, next door, with its wine-barrel-sized cellar door just waiting for some action, is a respected restaurant and home to the town's last vintner—a wonderful place to try local wines, as they serve a flight of five tiny glasses (several different flights: half-dry, dry, red, and sweet dessert wines) for those ready to appreciate this production.

Plönlein to Spitalhof

The corner immediately to your right is dubbed **Plönlein** and is famously picturesque. Plönlein is named for the carpenter's plumb line—a string that dangles exactly straight down when anchored by a plumb (a lead weight; the Latin word for lead is *plumbum*). The line helps carpenters build things straight, but of course, here, nothing is made "to plumb." If this scene brings you back to your childhood, that's because Rothenburg was  the inspiration for the village in the 1940 Disney animated film *Pinocchio*.

Walk a few more yards and look far up the lane **(Neugasse)** to the left. You'll see some cute pastel buildings with uniform windows and rooflines—clues that the buildings were rebuilt after WWII bombings hit that part of town. Straight ahead, the **Siebertstor Tower** marks the next layer of expansion to the town wall. Continue through the tower. The former tannery is now a pub featuring **Landwehr Bräu,** the local brew.

Farther along, at #14 (right), **Antiq & Trödel,** which smells like an antique shop should, is fun to browse through.

Still farther down, on the left at #25, **Hotel-Café Gerberhaus** is a fine stop for a coffee and cake, with a delicate dining room and a peaceful courtyard hiding out back under the town wall.

Spitalhof and Spitaltor

From here, the town runs out of energy and the remaining stretch is a bit glum. This is Spitalhof—the former Hospital Quarter—with some nice architecture and the town's retirement home. Stick with me and continue a few blocks to Spitaltor, the gate with the tall tower marking the end of town (and a good place to begin a ramparts ramble, if you're up for it).

In any walled city, the gate—made of wood—was the weak point. A bastion is an architectural shield, built beyond the wall proper to protect its wooden doors from cannon fire. Spitaltor is a double bastion, built around 1600 with the advent of stronger artillery. Walk through the gate (taking note of the stairs to the right—that's where you could begin your wall walk). Notice how the entry is curved: Any cannon that got past the first door and tried to blow the second door down would be vulnerable to cannon fire from the ramparts and arrows from the slits above.

Outside the fortified gate is the ditch that kept artillery at a distance (most medieval moats were dry like this one; water and alligators were mostly added by Hollywood). Standing outside the wall, ponder this sight as if approaching the city 400 years ago. The wealth of a city was shown by its walls and towers. (Stone was costly—in fact, the German saying for "filthy rich" is "stone rich.")

Circle around to the right. Look up at the formidable tower. The guardhouse atop it, one of several in the wall, was manned 24/7. Above the entry gate, notice the emblem: Angels bless the double eagle of the Holy Roman Emperor, which blesses the town (symbolized by the two red towers).

Cross the wooden bridge ahead and take a right. Past the first arch, you can access the cannon gallery upstairs in the double bastion—with stone ramps rather than stairs so that horse-drawn caissons bearing ammunition could make deliveries easily (free, always open, worth exploring but very dark). To the right of the second arch are the stairs that lead to the ramparts (from where you can start your ramparts walk around the east side of town; see "Walk the Wall" on page 28). Or you can hike back up the street you just walked down to return to the town center.

Sights in Rothenburg

ON AND NEAR MARKET SQUARE
▲Town Hall Tower

From Market Square you can see tourists on the crow's nest capping the Town Hall's tower. For a commanding view from the town's tallest perch, climb the steps of the tower. It's a rigorous but interesting 214-step climb that gets narrow and steep near the top—watch your head. Be here during the first or last hour of the day to avoid day-tripping crowds.

Cost and Hours: €2.50, pay at top, daily in season 9:30-12:30 & 13:00-17:00, enter from the grand steps overlooking Market Square.

▲▲Medieval Crime and Punishment Museum (Mittelalterliches Kriminalmuseum)

Specializing in everything connected to medieval criminal justice, this exhibit (well described in English) is a cut above all the tacky

and popular torture museums around Europe. Nearly everything on display here is an actual medieval artifact. In addition to ogling spiked chairs, thumbscrews, and shame masks, you'll learn about medieval police and criminal law. The museum is more eclectic than its name and includes exhibits on general history, superstition, biblical art, and so on. The museum is undergoing renovations in 2019, which may affect some areas when you visit.

A thoughtfully curated **Luther and the Witches** exhibit, created for the 500th anniversary of the Protestant Reformation, should still be on display when you visit. In the same building as the museum's café, you can explore two floors of original artifacts and multimedia displays on the history and lore of witchcraft, sorcery, and medieval and early Renaissance Christianity.

Cost and Hours: €7, includes Luther exhibit; daily 10:00-18:00, Nov and Jan-Feb 14:00-16:00, Dec and March 13:00-16:00; last entry 45 minutes before closing, fun cards and posters, Burggasse 3-5, tel. 09861/5359, www.kriminalmuseum.eu.

Visiting the Museum: It's a one-way route. Just follow the yellow arrows and you'll see it all. Keep an eye out for several well-done interactive media stations that provide extra background on the museum's highlights.

From the entrance, head downstairs to the **cellar** to see some enhanced-interrogation devices. Torture was common in the Middle Ages—not to punish, but to extract a confession (medieval "justice" required a confession). Just the sight of these tools was often enough to make an innocent man confess. You'll see the rack, "stretching ladder," thumb screws, spiked leg screws, and other items that would make Dick Cheney proud. Medieval torturers also employed a waterboarding-like technique—but here, the special ingredient was holy water.

Upstairs, on the **first and second floors,** the walls are lined with various legal documents of the age, while the dusty glass cases show off law-enforcement tools—many of them quite creative. Shame was a big tool back then. The town could publicly humiliate those who ran afoul of the law by tying them to a pillory in the main square and covering their faces in an iron mask of shame. Fanciful mask decorations indicated the crime: Chicken feathers meant promiscuity, horns indicated that a man's wife slept around (i.e., cuckold), and a snout suggested that the person had acted piggishly. A gossip might wear a mask with giant ears (heard everything), eyeglasses (saw everything), and a giant, wagging tongue (couldn't keep her mouth shut). The infamous "iron maiden" started out as more of a "shame barrel"; the internal spikes were added to play up popular lore when it went on display for 18th-century tourists. For more serious offenses, criminals were branded—so that even if they left town, they'd take that shame with them for the rest of their lives. When all else failed, those in charge could always turn to the executioner's sword.

To safely capture potential witches, lawmen used a device resembling a metal collar—with spikes pointing in—that was easy to get into but nearly impossible to get out of. A neck violin—like a portable version of a stock—kept the accused under control. (The double neck violin could be used to lock together a quarrelsome couple to force them to work things out.) The chastity belts were used to ensure a wife's loyalty (giving her traveling husband peace of mind) and/or to protect women from rape, then a commonplace crime.

The exit routes you through a courtyard garden to a **last building** with temporary exhibits (see "Luther and the Witches," earlier) and a café. If you must buy a *Schneeball,* consider doing it here. A recent blind taste test among the town's tour guides deemed these the best. They're inexpensive; they come in regular, medium, and bite-sized; and you'll support the museum.

▲German Christmas Museum (Deutsches Weihnachtsmuseum)

This excellent museum, in a Disney-esque space upstairs in the giant Käthe Wohlfahrt Christmas Village shop, tells the history of Christmas decorations. There's a unique and thoughtfully de-scribed collection of tree stands, mini trees sent in boxes to WWI soldiers at the front, early Advent calendars, old-time Christmas cards, Christmas pyramids, and a look at the evolution of Father Christmas as well as tree decorations through the ages—including the Nazi era and when you were a kid. The museum is not just a ploy to get shoppers to spend more money but a serious collection managed by professional curator Felicitas Höptner.

Cost and Hours: €4 most of the year, €2.50 low-season rate available to my readers year-round with this book; daily 10:00-17:30, shorter and irregular hours Jan-March; Herrngasse 1, tel. 09861/409-365, www.christmasmuseum.com.

▲Tradesman's House (Alt-Rothenburger Handwerkerhaus)

If all the higgledy-piggledy buildings make you curious about how people lived way back when, stop into this restored 700-year-old home to see the everyday life of a Rothenburger in the town's heyday. You'll crouch under low ceilings as you explore a house that doesn't seem to have a single right angle—kitchen (with soot-blackened ceilings); tight, shared bedrooms; and attic workshop. Ponder the rugged reality of medieval *Bürger* life. While the house itself is fascinating, information (in any language) is scarce; pick up the free, paltry English handout, or shell out some cash for a little more background.

Cost and Hours: €3, daily 11:00-17:00, closed Nov-Easter except in early Dec, two blocks east of Market Square, near Markus Tower at Alter Stadtgraben 26.

ALONG THE WALL
▲▲Walk the Wall

Just longer than a mile and a half around, providing great views and a good orientation, this walk can be done by those under six feet tall in less than an hour. The hike requires no special sense of balance. Much of the walk is covered and is a great option in the rain. Photographers will stay very busy, especially before breakfast or at sunset, when the lighting is best and the crowds are gone. You can enter or exit the ramparts at nearly every tower.

While the ramparts circle the city, some stretches aren't walkable per se: Along much of the western side of town, you can't walk atop the wall, but you can walk right along-side it and peek over or through it for great views outward from street level. Refer to the "Rothenburg" map at the start of this chapter to see which portions of the wall are walkable.

If you want to make a full town circuit, Spitaltor—at the south end of town, with the best fortifications—is a good starting place. From here it's a counterclockwise walk along the eastern and northern ramparts. After exiting at Klingentor you can still follow the wall for a bit, but you'll have to cut inland, away from the wall, when you hit the Imperial City Museum and again near the Medieval Crime and Punishment Museum. At the Kohlturm tower, back at the southern end of town, you can climb the stairs and walk atop the remaining short stretch of wall to the Spitalhof quarter, where you'll need to exit again. Spitaltor, where you started, is just a *Schneeball*'s toss away.

The TI has installed a helpful series of English-language plaques at about 20 stops along the route. The names you see along the way belong to people who donated money to rebuild the wall after World War II, and those who've more recently donated €1,200 per meter for the maintenance of Rothenburg's heritage.

▲The Allergic-to-Tourists Wall and Moat Walk

For a quiet and scenic break from the tourist crowds and a chance to appreciate the marvelous fortifications of Rothenburg, consider this hike: From the Castle Garden, go right and walk outside the wall to the Klingentor. At the Klingentor, climb up to the ramparts and walk on the wall past the Galgentor to the Rödertor. Then descend, leave the old town, and hike through the park (once the moat) down to Spitaltor. Explore the fortifications here before hiking a block up Spitalgasse, turning left on Rossmühlgasse to pass the youth hostel, popping back outside the wall, and heading along the upper scenic reaches of the river valley and above the vineyards back to the Castle Garden. Note that on the west (cliff-top) side of town, some of the outside-the-wall sections are steeper and harder to hike than the wall-top walkway.

St. Wolfgang's Church

This fortified Gothic church (which feels like a pale imitation of St. Jakob's) is built into the medieval wall at the Klingentor. While it sounds intriguing—and looks striking from the outside—its dungeon-like passages and shepherd's-dance exhibit are pretty lame.

Cost and Hours: €2, July-Aug Wed-Mon 11:00-13:00 & 14:00-17:00, closed Tue; April-Oct Fri-Sat 9:30-17:00, Sun 9:30-13:00, closed Mon-Thu; closed Nov-March.

ROTHENBURG

NEAR ROTHENBURG
▲▲A Walk in the Countryside

This pleasant stroll—easy and downhill at the start, with an uphill return at the end—takes you through the tranquil countryside below Rothenburg, including stops at a characteristic little "castle-ette," a *Biergarten,* and a historic church.

From the *Burggarten* (castle garden), head into the Tauber Valley. As you come through the Burgtor into the castle garden, veer left to find the path that leads out of the garden (via the archway below and to the left of the chapel). At the fork just beyond the arch, keep right and head down and around, keeping the castle garden on your right. A few minutes later, at the next big fork, continue downhill (the level path on the right leads around and back into the castle garden). From here the trail becomes quite steep, taking you down to the wooden covered bridge on the valley floor. Across the bridge, the road goes left to Toppler Castle (5 minutes away) and right (downstream, with a pleasant parallel footpath) to Detwang (20 minutes).

Tiny **Toppler Castle** (Topplerschlösschen) is cute, skinny, sky-blue, and 600 years old. It was the castle/summer home of the medieval Mayor Toppler. The tower's top looks like a house—a sort of tree fort for grownups. It's in a farmer's garden, and while generally closed to visitors these days, it's still worth a look from the outside (open to groups of at least 5 people—call ahead, €3 each, one mile from town center at Taubertalweg 100, tel. 09861/7358).

People say the mayor had this valley-floor escape built to get people to relax about leaving the fortified town...or to hide a mistress. After leaving the "castle," you can continue straight along the same road to reach the big bridge in the valley just below town; from here, various roads and paths lead steeply back up into town.

Or, to extend your stroll, walk back to the small footbridge and follow the river downstream (passing the recommended Unter den Linden beer garden) to the peaceful village of **Detwang.** One of the oldest villages in Franconia, Detwang dates from 968. Like Rothenburg, it has a Riemenschneider altarpiece in its **Church of Sts. Peter and Paul.** Founded more than a millennium ago, this church has a dimly lit Romanesque interior with some Gothic frills. Riemenschneider's *Altar of the Holy Cross* depicts the moment when Christ, up on the cross, takes his last breath. While the central figures carry the same level of detail and emotion as any of

Riemenschneider's work, the side panels (praying in Gethsemane on the left, the Resurrection on the right) exhibit a bit less mastery than the altarpiece in St. Jakob's. Originally carved for a church in Rothenburg, the altar was later trimmed to fit this smaller space. Notice the soldier on the right looking at an angle into thin air. Before being scooted in, his gaze fell on the dying Christ. Angels and other figures were cut out entirely.

From Detwang, it's a reasonably steep 15-minute hike back up into Rothenburg (arriving at the northern edge of town), or backtrack to the wooden footbridge—or all the way to Toppler Castle—and head up from there.

Franconian Bike Ride

To get a fun, breezy look at the countryside around Rothenburg, rent a bike (see "Helpful Hints," earlier). For a pleasant 10.5-mile, half-day pedal, do the first portion of the 60-mile "Delightful Tauber Valley" bike route. Escape the old town through the Rödertor, bike along Topplerweg to Spitaltor, and follow the curvy road down into the river valley. Turn right at the yellow *Leutzenbronn* sign to cross the double-arcaded bridge. From here a peaceful road follows the river downstream to Detwang, passing the cute Toppler Castle (described earlier). From Detwang, follow the main road to the old mill, and turn left to follow the *Liebliches Taubertal* bike path signs as far up the Tauber River (direction: Bettwar) as you like. About 5.2 miles from Rothenburg (and 2.5 miles after Detwang), you'll arrive in the sleepy farming town of Bettwar, where you can claim a spot among the chickens and the apple trees for a picnic or have a drink at one of the two restaurants in town. Ride back the way you came to return to Rothenburg.

Franconian Open-Air Museum
(Fränkisches Freilandmuseum)

A 20-minute drive from Rothenburg—in the undiscovered "Rothenburgy" town of Bad Windsheim—is an open-air folk museum that, compared with others in Europe, is a bit humble. But it tries very hard and gives you a good look at traditional rural Franconia.

Cost and Hours: €7, Tue-Sun 9:00-18:00, shorter hours Nov-Feb, check website for schedule, last entry one hour before closing, tel. 09841/66800, www.freilandmuseum.de.

Shopping in Rothenburg

Take note...Rothenburg is one of Germany's best shopping towns. Do it here and be done with it. Lovely prints, carvings, wine glasses, Christmas-tree ornaments, and beer steins are popular. Rödergasse is the old town's everyday shopping street. There's also a modern shopping center across the street from the train station.

To find local artisans, pick up the *Handmade in Rothenburg* pamphlet at the TI or visit the group's website (www.rothenburg-handmade.com).

For an appealing string of family-run shops, follow my "Schmiedgasse-Spitalgasse Shopping Stroll" (described earlier, under "Walks in Rothenburg"). Below are two shops not on that walk:

Käthe Wohlfahrt Christmas Headquarters

Rothenburg is the headquarters of the Käthe Wohlfahrt Christmas trinkets empire, which has spread across the half-timbered reaches of Europe. Rothenburg has six Wohlfahrts. Tourists flock to the two biggest, just below Market Square (Herrngasse 1 and 2). Start with the **Christmas Village** (Weihnachtsdorf) at Herrngasse 1. This Christmas wonderland is filled with enough twinkling lights (196,000—mostly LEDs) to require a special electrical hookup. You're greeted by instant Christmas mood music (best appreciated on a hot day in July) and tourists hungrily filling little woven shopping baskets with goodies to hang on their trees (items handmade in Germany are the most expensive). With this book, you'll get 10 percent off official wooden KW products (look for the *Käthes Original* tag; must show book to receive discount).

Let the spinning, flocked tree whisk you in, and pause at the wall of Steiff stuffed animals, jerking uncontrollably and mesmerizing little kids. Then head downstairs to find the vast and sprawling "made in Germany" section, surrounding a slowly spinning 15-foot tree decorated with a thousand glass balls. The fascinating **Christmas Museum** upstairs is described earlier, under "Sights in Rothenburg." The smaller shop (across the street at Herrngasse 2) specializes in finely crafted wooden ornaments. Käthe opened her first storefront here in Rothenburg in 1977. The company is now run by her son Harald, who lives in town (Christmas Village open Mon-Sat 9:00-18:00, Sun from 10:00 beginning in late April; shorter hours at other locations).

Friese Shop

Cuckoo with friendliness, trinkets, and reasonably priced souvenirs, the Friese shop has been open for more than 90 years—and they've been welcoming my readers for more than 30 of those years. They give shoppers with this book tremendous service: a 10 percent discount off all items and a free pictorial map. Run for many years by Anneliese Friese, it's now lovingly run by her son, Bernie, with help from his daughter Amber, nieces Dolores and Nicole, and their friend Elizabeth. They let tired travelers leave their bags in the back room for free (Mon-Sat 9:00-17:00, Sun from 10:00,

20 steps off Market Square at Grüner Markt 8—around the corner from TI and across from free public WC, tel. 09861/7166).

Sleeping in Rothenburg

Rothenburg is crowded with visitors, but most are day-trippers. Except for the rare Saturday night and during festivals (see page 8), finding a room is easy. Competition keeps quality high. If you want to splurge, you'll snare the best value by paying extra for the biggest and best rooms at the hotels I recommend. In the off-season (Nov and Jan-March), hoteliers may be willing to discount.

Train travelers save steps by staying in the Rödertor area (east end of town). Hotels and guesthouses will sometimes pick up tired heavy-packers at the station. If you're driving, call ahead to get directions and parking tips. Save some energy to climb the stairs: Only one of my recommended hotels has an elevator.

Keep your key when out late. As Rothenburg's hotels are small and mostly family-run, they often lock up early (at about 22:00) and take one day a week off, so you'll need to let yourself in at those times.

For locations, see the "Rothenburg" map at the beginning of this chapter.

IN THE OLD TOWN

$$$$ Hotel Herrnschlösschen prides itself on being the smallest (8 rooms) and most exclusive hotel in Rothenburg. If you're looking for a splurge, this is your best bet. This 1,000-year-old building has a beautiful Baroque garden and every amenity you'd ever want (including a sauna), but you'll pay for them (Herrngasse 20, tel. 09861/873-890, www.herrnschloesschen.de, info@ herrnschloesschen.de).

$$$ Gasthof Goldener Greifen, once Mayor Toppler's home, is a big, traditional, 650-year-old place with 14 spacious rooms and all the comforts. It's run by a helpful family staff and creaks with rustic splendor (family rooms, free loaner bikes for guests, free and easy parking, half a block downhill from Market Square at Obere Schmiedgasse 5, tel. 09861/2281, www.gasthof-greifen-rothenburg.de, info@gasthof-greifen-rothenburg.de; Brigitte, daughter Ursula, and Klingler family). The family also runs a good restaurant, serving meals in the back garden or dining room.

$$$ Gästehaus am Klosterhof, offering four apartments with kitchenettes, provides splurge-worthy comfort. Three apartments are outfitted in contemporary German style and one in charming Bavarian decor. Breakfast at the Altfränkische Weinstube (listed below and run by the same people) is included for the three contemporary apartments but is extra for the Bavarian one (Klingengasse 8, tel. 15151/086-047, www.am-klosterhof.de, info@am-klosterhof.de).

$$ Hotel Kloster-Stüble, deep in the old town near the castle garden, is one of my classiest listings. Twenty-one rooms, plus two apartments, each with its own special touches, fill two medieval buildings connected by a modern atrium (family rooms, just off Herrngasse at Heringsbronnengasse 5, tel. 09861/938-890, www. klosterstueble.de, hotel@klosterstueble.de, energetic Erika).

$$ Hotel Spitzweg is a rustic-yet-elegant 1536 mansion (never bombed or burned) with 10 big rooms, new bathrooms, open beams, and endearing hand-painted antique furniture. It's run by gentle Herr Hocher, whom I suspect is the former Wizard of Oz—now retired and in a very good mood (apartment, inviting old-fashioned breakfast room, free but limited parking, Parade-isgasse 2, tel. 09861/94290, www.hotel-spitzweg.de, info@hotel-spitzweg.de).

$$ Hotel Gerberhaus mixes modern comforts into 20 bright and airy rooms—some with four-poster *Himmel* beds—that maintain a sense of half-timbered elegance. Enjoy the pleasant garden in back and the delightful breakfast buffet. It's just inside the town wall, a five-minute walk to the main square (family rooms, apartment, pay parking, pay laundry, Spitalgasse 25, tel. 09861/94900, www.gerberhaus.rothenburg.de, info@hotelgerberhaus.com, Inge).

$$ Hotel Altfränkische Weinstube am Klosterhof is *the* place for well-heeled bohemians. Mario and Hanne rent eight cozy rooms above their dark and evocative pub in a 650-year-old building. It's an upscale *Lord of the Rings* atmosphere, with modern plumbing, open-beam ceilings, and some canopied four-poster beds (off Klingengasse at Klosterhof 7, tel. 09861/6404, www. altfraenkische.de, altfraenkische-weinstube@web.de). Their pub is a candlelit classic—and a favorite with locals, serving hot food to Hobbits (see listing later, under "Eating in Rothenburg"). It also hosts the Wednesday evening English Conversation Club (see "Meet the Locals" on page 40).

$ Pension Elke, run by spry Erich Endress and his son Klaus, rents 12 comfy rooms above the family grocery store. Guests who jog are welcome to join Klaus on his half-hour run around the city every evening at 19:30 (RS%, cheaper rooms with shared bath, cash only; reception in grocery store until 19:00, otherwise go around back and ring bell at top of stairs; near Markus Tower at Rödergasse 6, tel. 09861/2331, www.pension-elke-rothenburg.de, info@pension-elke-rothenburg.de).

$ Gästehaus Raidel rents eight rooms in a 500-year-old house filled with beds and furniture all handmade by friendly, soft-spoken Norry Raidel. The ramshackle ambience makes me want to sing the *Addams Family* theme song, but the place has a

rare, time-passed family charm. Norry, who plays in a Dixieland band, has invented a fascinating hybrid saxophone/trombone called the Norryphone... and loves to jam (family rooms, cash only, pleasant terrace with small garden, Wenggasse 3, tel. 09861/3115, Norry asks you to use the reservations form at www.romanticroad.com/raidel).

$ Gasthof zum Breiterle offers 23 comfortable rooms with wooden accents above their spacious breakfast room near the Rödertor. Because the inn sits on a busy street, light sleepers may want to request a room not facing Wenggasse (apartment, reception in restaurant, pay parking, Rödergasse 30, tel. 09861/6730, www.breiterle.de, info@breiterle.de, Mike and Nicole).

$ Gästehaus Gerlinger, a fine value, has five comfortable rooms in a pretty 16th-century house with a small terrace for guests (family apartment, cash only, easy parking, Schlegeleinsweth 10, tel. 09861/87979, mobile 0171-690-0752, www.pension-gerlinger. de, info@pension-gerlinger.de, Hermann).

$ Kreuzerhof Hotel offers 11 decent rooms surrounding a courtyard on a quiet side street near the Rödertor (family rooms, pay parking in courtyard, Millergasse 2, tel. 09861/3424, www. kreuzerhof.eu, info@kreuzerhof.eu, Heike and Walter Maltz).

$ Gästehaus Liebler, run by Frau Liebler, rents two large, modern, ground-floor rooms with kitchenettes. They're great for those looking for real privacy close to the action. On the top floor is an attractive two-bedroom apartment (RS%, no breakfast but café nearby, cash only, behind Christmas shop at Pfäffleinsgässchen 10, tel. 09861/709-215, www.gaestehaus-liebler.de, info@gaestehaus-liebler.de). Frau Liebler has three more apartments a couple blocks away.

$ Pension Pöschel is simple, with six plain rooms in a concrete but pleasant building and an inviting garden out back. Five rooms have shared baths; one pricier room has a private shower and toilet (cash only, Wenggasse 22, tel. 09861/3430, mobile 0170-700-7041, www.pensionpoeschel.de, pension.poeschel@t-online. de, Bettina).

¢ Rossmühle Youth Hostel rents 182 beds in two institutional yet charming buildings. Reception is in the huge building with droopy dormer windows—formerly a horse-powered mill, it was used when the old town was under siege and the river-powered mill was inaccessible (private rooms available, all-you-can-eat dinner-€6.50, membership required, close to P-1 parking lot, entrance on Rossmühlgasse, tel. 09861/94160, www.rothenburg. jugendherberge.de, rothenburg@jugendherberge.de).

OUTSIDE THE WALL

$$ **Wildbad** provides a tranquil escape on the edge of the Tauber River. Built into the hillside and offering 58 stylish rooms, this historic building occupies the site of a former 10th-century spa. The owners promote mixing and mingling of guests (including pilgrims walking the Camino de Santiago)—TVs are found in common areas only. The vast park surrounding the hotel, replete with walking trails, offers free summer concerts and Sunday *Kaffee und Kuchen* on the terrace. There's even a covered *Kegeln* lane where you can rent 19th-century wooden pins and try your hand at ninepin bowling. An elevator covers the first seven floors, but you'll have to walk to the eighth, where there's a tiny chapel and library (family rooms, free parking, Taubertalweg 42, tel. 09861/9770, www. wildbad.de, info@wildbad.de). While it's walkable to town, those arriving by train can take a taxi for around €7.

$ **Pension Fuchsmühle** is charmingly located in a renovated old mill on the river below the castle end of Rothenburg, across from Toppler Castle. It feels rural but is a pleasant (though steep) 15-minute hike from Market Square or a €12 taxi ride from the train station. Alex and Heidi Molitor, a young couple with kids, offer eight bright, modern, light-wood rooms. The building's electric power comes from the millwheel by the entrance, with excess sold to the municipal grid (family rooms, healthy farm-fresh breakfast, free parking, Taubertalweg 101, tel. 09861/92633, www. fuchsmuehle.de, info@fuchsmuehle.de).

Eating in Rothenburg

My recommendations are all within a five-minute walk of Market Square. While all survive on tourism, many still feel like local hangouts. Your choices are typical German or ethnic. You'll see regional Franconian *(fränkische)* specialties advertised, such as the German ravioli called *Maultaschen* and Franconian bratwurst (similar to other brats, but a bit more coarsely ground, with less fat, and liberally seasoned with marjoram). Many restaurants take a midafternoon break and stop serving lunch at 14:00; dinner may end as early as 20:00.

For locations, see the "Rothenburg" map at the beginning of this chapter.

TRADITIONAL GERMAN RESTAURANTS

$$$ **Reichsküchenmeister**'s interior is like any forgettable big-hotel restaurant's, but on a balmy evening, its pleasant tree-shaded

terrace overlooking St. Jakob's Church and reliably good dishes are hard to beat, including the *Flammkuchen*—southern German flatbread (daily 11:30-22:30, reservations smart, Kirchplatz 8, tel. 09861/9700, www.hotel-reichskuechenmeister-rothenburg.de).

$$$ **Hotel Restaurant Kloster-Stüble,** on a small street off Herrngasse near the castle garden, is a classy place for delicious and beautifully presented traditional cuisine, including homemade *Maultaschen.* Chef Rudi cooks while head waitress Erika makes sure communication goes smoothly. Choose from their shaded terrace, sleek-and-stony modern dining room, or woody traditional dining room (daily 18:00-20:30, Sat-Sun also 12:00-14:30, Heringsbronnengasse 5, tel. 09861/938-890).

$$ **Gasthof Goldener Greifen,** in a historic building with a peaceful garden out back, is just off the main square. The Klingler family serves quality Franconian food at a good price...and with a smile. The wood is ancient and polished from generations of happy use, and the ambience is practical rather than posh (affordable kids' meals, Wed-Mon 11:30-21:00, closed Tue, Obere Schmiedgasse 5, tel. 09861/2281, Ursula).

$$ **Altfränkische Weinstube am Klosterhof** seems designed for gnomes to celebrate their anniversaries. At this very dark pub, classically candlelit in a 650-year-old building, Mario whips up gourmet pub grub (hot food served Wed-Mon 18:00-21:30, closed Tue, off Klingengasse at Klosterhof 7, tel. 09861/6404). If you'd like dinner company, drop by on Wednesday evening, when the English Conversation Club has a big table reserved from 18:30 on (see "Meet the Locals," page 40). You'll eat well and with new friends—both travelers and locals.

$$ **Zum Pulverer** ("The Powderer") is a very traditional *Weinstube* (wine bar) just inside the Burgtor gate that serves a menu of affordable and well-executed regional fare, some with modern flourishes. The interior is a cozy wood-hewn place that oozes history, with chairs carved in the shape of past senators of Rothenburg (daily 17:00-23:00 except Sat-Sun from 12:00, closed Tue, Herrengasse 31, tel. 09861/976-182).

$$ **Alter Keller** is a modest, tourist-friendly restaurant with an extremely characteristic interior and outdoor tables on a peaceful square just a couple blocks off Market Square. The menu has German classics at reasonable prices—*Spätzle,* schnitzel, and roasts—as well as steak (Wed-Sun 11:30-15:00 & 17:30-21:00, closed Mon-Tue, Alter Keller 8, tel. 09861/2268, Markus and Miriam).

A NON-FRANCONIAN SPLURGE

$$$$ **Hotel Restaurant Herrnschlösschen** is the local favorite for gourmet presentation and a departure from Franconian fare. They offer a small menu of international and seasonal dishes with a

theme. There's always a serious vegetarian option and a €50 fixed-price meal with matching wine. It's perhaps the most elegant dining in town, whether in the classy dining hall or in the shaded Baroque garden out back. Reservations are a must (Herrngasse 20, tel. 09861/873-890, Ulrika, www.hotel-rothenburg.de).

BREAKS FROM PORK AND POTATOES

$$ Pizzeria Roma is the locals' favorite for pizza and pastas, with good Italian wine. The Magrini family moved here from Tuscany in 1968 (many Italians immigrated to Germany in those years), and they've been cooking pasta for Rothenburg ever since (Thu-Tue 11:30-23:00, closed Wed and mid-Aug-mid-Sept, Galgengasse 19, tel. 09861/4540, Riccardo).

$ TobinGo, just off Market Square, serves cheap and tasty Turkish food to eat in or take away. Their *döner kebab* must be the best €4.20 hot meal in Rothenburg. For about €1 more, try a less-bready *dürüm döner*—same ingredients but in a warm tortilla (daily 10:00-22:00, Hafengasse 2).

SANDWICHES AND SNACKS

$ Brot & Zeit (a pun on *Brotzeit*, "bread time," the German term for snacking), conveniently located a block off Market Square, is like a German bakery dressed up as a Starbucks. In a bright, modern atmosphere just inside the super-picturesque Markus Tower gate, they sell takeaway coffee, sandwiches, and a few hot dishes, making it a good one-stop shop for grabbing a meal to go or to eat inside or outside at its few small tables (Mon-Sat 6:00-18:30, Sun 7:30-18:00, Hafengasse 24, tel. 09861/936-8701).

Bakery and Butcher Sandwiches: While any bakery in town can sell you a sandwich for a couple of euros, I like to pop into **$ Metzgerei Trumpp,** a high-quality butcher shop serving up cheap and tasty sausages on a bun with kraut to go (Mon-Fri 7:30-18:00, Sat until 16:00, usually closed Sun, a block off Market Square at Schmiedgasse 18).

Grocery Stores: A small grocery store is in the center of town at Rödergasse 6. Larger supermarkets are outside the wall: Exit the town through the Rödertor, turn left through the cobbled gate, and cross the parking lot to reach the **Edeka** supermarket; or head to the even bigger **Kaufland** across from the train station (grocery stores generally open Mon-Sat until 20:00, closed Sun).

BEER GARDENS

Rothenburg's beer gardens can be great fun, but they're open only when the weather is balmy. My first listing is just outside the gate; the second is a hike away in the valley.

$$ Gasthof Rödertor, just outside the wall through the

Rödertor, runs a backyard *Biergarten* that's popular with locals. It's great for a rowdy crowd looking for pizza, classic beer garden fare, and good beer. Their passion is potatoes—the menu is dedicated to spud cuisine. Try a plate of *Schupfnudeln*—potato noodles with sauerkraut and bacon (May-Sept Tue-Sat 17:30-22:00, Sun until 21:00, closed Mon and in bad weather, table service only—no ordering at counter, Ansbacher Strasse 7, look for wooden gate, tel. 09861/2022). If the *Biergarten* is closed, their indoor restaurant, with a more extensive menu, is a good value (Tue-Sun 11:30-14:00 & 17:30-21:00, closed Mon).

$$ Unter den Linden is a family-friendly (with sandbox and swing), slightly bohemian *Biergarten* in the valley along the river. It's worth the 20-minute hike on a pleasant evening, or on Sunday morning for the breakfast buffet (in season with decent weather open Wed-Sun 10:00-22:00, Mon-Tue from 14:00, good food and good beer, order at the kiosk and they'll yell your name when it's ready, Kurze Steige 7, tel. 09861/5909). As it's in the valley on the river, it's cooler than Rothenburg; bring a sweater. Take a right outside the Burgtor, then a left on the footpath toward Detwang; it's at the bottom of the hill on the left.

DESSERT

Eis Café D'Isep, with a pleasant "Venetian minimalist" interior, has been making gelato in Rothenburg since 1960, using family recipes that span four generations. They proudly serve up cakes, drinks, fresh-fruit ice cream, and fancy sundaes. Their sidewalk tables are great for lazy people-watching (daily 10:00-22:00, closed early Oct-mid-Feb, one block off Market Square at Hafengasse 17, run by Paolo and Paola D'Isep and son Enrico).

The **Allegra Schokolade** chocolate shop is run by delightful Alex, a pastry chef-turned-chocolatier who trained in Switzerland. He makes artisan chocolates with local ingredients like mint, hazelnuts, and even beer, and can arrange group workshops for you to create your own chocolate Santa or animal (Tue-Sat 10:00-18:00, Sun from 11:00, closed Mon; workshops from €10, minimum 4 people, 1.5 hours, arrange in advance; Georgengasse 9, tel. 9861/688-0293, www.allegra-schokolade.de, info@allegra-schokolade.de).

Pastries: Rothenburg's **bakeries** *(Bäckereien)* offer succulent pastries, pies, and cakes...but skip the bad-tasting *Rothenburger Schnee-ballen.* Unworthy of the heavy promotion they receive, *Schneeballen* are bland

Rothenburger Spezialität Schneeballen

pie crusts crumpled into a ball and dusted with powdered sugar or frosted with sticky-sweet glop. If the curiosity is too much to bear, avoid the slick places on the busier tourist avenues—instead, try a fresh *(frisch)*, handmade *(handgemacht)* one from a smaller bakery or a sweet mini-*Schnee* at the Medieval Crime and Punishment Museum's café. There's little reason to waste your appetite on a *Schneeball* when you can enjoy a curvy *Mandelhörnchen* (almond crescent cookie), a triangular *Nussecke* ("nut corner"), a round *Florentiner* cookie, a couple of fresh *Krapfen* (like jelly doughnuts), or a soft, warm German pretzel.

WINE-DRINKING IN THE OLD CENTER

$$$ Trinkstube zur Hölle ("Hell") is dark and foreboding, offering a thick wine-drinking atmosphere, pub food, and a few main courses. It's small and can get painfully touristy in summer (Mon-Sat 17:00-24:00, food until 22:00, closed Sun, a block past Medieval Crime and Punishment Museum on Burggasse, look for the devil hanging out front, tel. 09861/4229).

Altfränkische Weinstube am Klosterhof (listed earlier, under "Traditional German Restaurants") is the liveliest place and a clear favorite with locals for an atmospheric drink or late meal. When every other place is asleep, you're likely to find good food, drink, and energy here.

$$ Restaurant Glocke, a *Weinstube* (wine bar) with a full menu, is run by Rothenburg's oldest and only surviving winemakers, the Thürauf family. The very extensive wine list is in German only because the friendly staff wants to explain your options in person. Their special €5.60 flight lets you sample five Franconian white wines (Mon-Sat 11:00-21:00, Sun until 14:00, Plönlein 1, tel. 09861/958-990).

MEET THE LOCALS WEDNESDAY NIGHTS

For a rare chance to mix it up with locals who aren't selling anything, bring your favorite slang and tongue twisters to the **English Conversation Club** at Mario's Altfränkische Weinstube am Klosterhof (Wed 18:30-24:00, restaurant listed earlier). This group of intrepid linguists has met more than 1,000 times. Hermann the German and his sidekick Wolfgang are regulars.  Consider arriving early for dinner, or after 21:00, when the beer starts to sink in, the crowd grows, and everyone seems to speak that second language a bit more easily.

Rothenburg Connections

BY TRAIN

If you take the train to or from Rothenburg, you'll transfer at Stein-ach. A tiny branch train line shuttles back and forth hourly between Steinach and Rothenburg (15 minutes, generally departs Steinach at :35 and Rothenburg at :06). Train connections in Steinach are usually quick and efficient (trains to and from Rothenburg gener-ally use track 5; use the conveyor belts to haul your bags smartly up and down the stairs).

Note that the last train from Steinach to Rothenburg departs at about 22:30. But all is not lost if you arrive in Steinach after the last train: A subsidized taxi service runs to Rothenburg (cheaper for the government than running an almost-empty train). To use this handy service, called AST *(Anrufsammeltaxi),* make an ap-pointment with a participating taxi service (call 09861/2000 or 09861/7227) at least an hour in advance (2 hours ahead is better), and they'll drive you from Steinach to Rothenburg for the cost of train fare (€4.70/person) rather than the regular €30 taxi fare.

The Rothenburg station has ticket machines for fare and schedule information and ticket sales. If you need extra help, visit the combined ticket office/travel agency in the station (€1-3 sur-charge for most tickets, Mon-Fri 10:00-18:00, Sat 9:00-13:00, closed Sun, tel. 09861/7711). The station at Steinach is entirely un-staffed but has ticket machines. Train info: www.bahn.com.

From Rothenburg (via Steinach) by Train to: Würzburg (hourly, 70 minutes), **Cochem** (every 1-2 hours, 6 hours, 4 chang-es), **Nürnberg** (hourly, 1.5 hours, change in Ansbach), **Munich** (hourly, 3.5 hours, 2-3 changes), **Füssen** (hourly, 5 hours, often with changes in Treuchtlingen and Augsburg), **Frankfurt** (hourly, 3 hours, change in Würzburg), **Frankfurt Airport** (hourly, 3.5 hours, change in Würzburg), **Berlin** (hourly, 5.5 hours, 3 changes).

BY BUS

The **Romantic Road bus** stops in Rothenburg once a day (mid-April-mid-Oct) on its way from Frankfurt to Munich and Füssen (and vice versa). The bus stop is at Schrannenplatz, a short walk north of Market Square. See the schedule and tour description at the end of this chapter.

ROUTE TIPS FOR DRIVERS

The three-hour autobahn drive from **Frankfurt Airport** (and other points north) to Rothenburg is something even a jet-lagged zombie can handle. It's a 75-mile straight shot to Würzburg on the A-3 autobahn; just follow the blue autobahn signs toward *Würzburg.* Then turn south on A-7 and take the *Rothenburg o.d.T.* exit (#108).

For a back-roads alternative, consider driving along the Romantic Road—see "From Würzburg (or Frankfurt) to Rothenburg," below.

The Romantic Road

The countryside between Frankfurt and Munich is Germany's medieval heartland. Walls and towers ring half-timbered towns, and flowers spill over the win-dowsills of well-kept houses. Glockenspiels dance from town halls by day, while night watchmen still call the hours after dark. Many travelers bypass these small towns by fast train or autobahn. But consider an extra day or two to take in the slow pace of small-town German life. With a car, you can wander through quaint hills and rolling villages and stop wherever the cows look friendly or a town fountain beckons.

In the 1950s, towns in this region joined together to work out a scenic driving route for visitors that they called the Romantic Road (*Romantische Strasse*, www.romantischestrasse.de). Because local train service was poor, they also organized a bus along the route for tourists, from Würzburg in the north to Füssen in the south.

The Romantic Road is the oldest and most famous of Germany's two dozen signposted scenic routes. Others celebrate toys, porcelain, architecture (Swabian Baroque or brick Gothic), clocks, and baths—and there are even two separate *Spargelstrassen* (asparagus roads). The "Castle Road" that runs between Rothenburg and Mannheim sounds intriguing, but it's nowhere near as interesting.

Now that the A-7 autobahn parallels the old two-lane route, the Romantic Road itself has become less important, but its destinations are still worthwhile. For drivers, the Romantic Road is basically a set of scenic stepping stones to Rothenburg, which is the most exciting town along the way. You can make a day out of the drive between Würzburg (or Frankfurt) and Rothenburg, stopping in the small towns along the Tauber River valley. If linking Rothenburg and Munich, stop in Dinkelsbühl and/or Nördlingen. The drive from Rothenburg to Füssen on two-lane roads makes for a full day, but it's possible to squeeze in a quick visit to Dinkelsbühl, Nördlingen, the Wieskirche, or Landsberg am Lech, hop-

The Romantic Road

Romantic Road Bus Route

Other Buses

Note: Not all rail lines are shown

ping on the autobahn to speed up parts of the trip. If you're driving with limited time, just zero in on Rothenburg by autobahn.

A confusing web of roads crisscrosses the Romantic Road region, and drivers will find that the official, signposted route is rarely the fastest option. Using GPS or a mapping app to find your way is confusing, as you'll usually be routed to the nearest highway or autobahn. This is smart if your time is tight and you want to focus on a few carefully selected stopovers. But if your goal is to meander and explore, skip the GPS, get a good map, and follow the brown *Romantische Strasse* signs.

For those without a car, the tour bus that still runs along the Romantic Road route once a day during the summer is a way to connect Rothenburg with Frankfurt, Würzburg, and Munich, or to go between Munich and Füssen, while seeing more scenery than you'd get on the train.

Sights Along the Romantic Road

I've divided the Romantic Road into three sections. The stretch from Würzburg (or Frankfurt) to Rothenburg runs up the Tauber River valley, offering pleasant views. Rothenburg to Augsburg is fairly flat and dull. From Augsburg south to Füssen, the route follows the Lech River up to where the Alps begin, and the scenery gets more exciting at every turn. To help you find your way, I've included some driving directions. While you can reach some of these destinations by public transit, most aren't worth the hassle without a car (try the Romantic Road bus, though the schedule can be sparse—see end of chapter).

FROM WÜRZBURG (OR FRANKFURT) TO ROTHENBURG

To follow this scenic back-road approach from Frankfurt, take A-3, then turn south on A-81, get off at the Tauberbischofsheim exit, and track signs for *Bad Mergentheim*. Or stay on A-3 to the Heidingsfeld-Würzburg exit and follow *Stuttgart/Ulm/Road 19* signs south to Bad Mergentheim. From Würzburg, follow *Ulm/Road 19* signs to Bad Mergentheim.

Bad Mergentheim

This town, one of the less romantic stops along this route, holds a unique footnote in Germanic history: In 1525, the Teutonic Knights (called the *Deutschorden*, or "German Order") lost their lands in East Prussia (today's Poland) and the Baltic states. The order's leadership retreated to their castle at Bad Mergentheim, which became their headquarters for the next three centuries.

Today the building houses the **German Order Museum**—practically a pilgrimage for German historians but underwhelming for casual visitors, who will find it dry and with limited English (www.deutschordensmuseum.de).

Leaving Bad Mergentheim, continue east. Turn into Weikersheim off the main road, following *Stadtmitte* and *Schloss* signs, then bear right to park in the large free lot. From there it's a couple minutes' walk to the town square.

▲Weikersheim

This picturesquely set town, nestled between hills, has a charming little main square offering easy access to a fine park and an impressive palace.

Weikersheim's **palace** (Schloss Weikersheim), across a moat-turned-park from the main square, was built in the late 16th century as the Renaissance country estate of a local count. With its bucolic location and glowing sandstone texture, it gives off a *Downton Abbey* vibe. The palace interior boasts an unusual triangular floor plan but is only viewable by a guided tour in German (tel. 07934/992-950, www.schloss-weikersheim.de).

I'd skip the tour and instead focus on exploring the palace's fine Baroque **gardens.** From the ticket office, cut through the courtyard and pop out at the finely manicured gardens, originally laid out in the early 18th century and populated by an army of whimsical stony statues (most of them mythological figures). Along the balustrade separating the palace from the gardens are the most photographed statues, the so-called "Dwarves' Gallery." At the far end of the complex is an orangery, offering fine views back over the gardens to the palace.

The **rose garden,** to the right as you face the palace, is free (but likely not at its best, as it's been recovering from an infestation). A gate off the rose garden leads to a spooky "alchemy garden" with plants used by medieval witches.

If you have time after your garden visit, Weikersheim's pleasant **town square** and cobbled old town are worth exploring. The **city park** (*Stadtpark,* enter off town square) is a fine picnic spot, and from it you can peer over the hedge into the palace gardens.

Creglingen

While Creglingen itself isn't worth much fuss (TI tel. 07933/631, www.creglingen.de), two quick and rewarding sights sit across the road from each other a mile south of town.

The peaceful 14th-century **Herrgottskirche Church,** worth ▲, is graced with Tilman Riemenschneider's greatest carved altarpiece, completed sometime between 1505 and 1510. The church was built on the site where a local farmer found a seemingly miraculous communion host in a field. Centuries later, Riemenschneider graced the space with an impressive altar nearly 30 feet high—tall enough that its tip pokes up between the rafters. While

Riemenschneider's altars in Rothenburg and Detwang (see pages 15, 17, and 30) are focused on Jesus, the star here is Mary, captured in the moment she ascends to heaven. Angels—with their angular wings jutting out in all directions—whisk Mary off into the sky as the 12 apostles watch in wonder. Just above Mary, appreciate the remarkably intricate tangle of vines. Higher up is the heavenly coronation of Mary, who is surrounded by God and Jesus (distinguished by the bushiness of their beards) and the Holy Spirit. The side panels show important scenes from Mary's life. The church's other,
colorful (non-Riemenschneider) altars are also worth a peek (tel. 07933/338, www.herrgottskirche.de).

The **Fingerhut Museum,** showing off thimbles (literally, "finger hats"), is far more interesting than it sounds. You'll step from case to case to squint at the collection, which numbers about 4,000 (but still fits in a single room) and comes from all over the world; some pieces are centuries old. Owner Thorvald Greif got a head start from his father, who owned a thimble factory (tel. 07933/370, www.fingerhutmuseum.de).

FROM ROTHENBURG TO AUGSBURG

Dinkelsbühl and Nördlingen (via B-25) are the main attractions between Rothenburg and Augsburg. From Donauwörth, taking the B-2 highway (which parallels the Romantic Road here) can speed up your trip.

▲Dinkelsbühl

Rothenburg's little sister is cute enough to merit a short stop. A moat, towers, gates, and a beautifully preserved medieval wall all surround this town. Dinkelsbühl is pretty, and a bit less touristy than Rothenburg, but also less exciting. Still, it's a delight to simply stroll for an hour or two. Park at one of the free lots outside the town walls, which are well signed from the main road (parking inside the town is limited to one hour).

To orient yourself, head for the tower of **St. Georg's Cathedral,** at the center of town. This 15th-century church has a surprisingly light, airy interior and fine carved altarpieces. On good-weather summer weekends, you can climb to the top of the tower.

Back outside the church, follow the signs around the corner (first into Ledermarkt, then Altrathausplatz) to the **TI,** which offers a free "Tour of the Town" brochure (tel. 09851/902-440, www.dinkelsbuehl.de). In the TI, take a minute to watch the TV monitor showing the stork nest on top of the old Town Hall (also visible at www. storch24.de). Dinkelsbühl offers an evening Night Watchman Tour similar to Rothenburg's, but it's in German only (details at TI).

The TI doubles as the ticket office for the fine **City History Museum** (Haus der Geschichte) in the same building. This shiny, up-to-date museum fills three floors. Learn about Dinkelsbühl's location along important north-south travel routes in early times, its role in the Thirty Years' War, and how the tug-of-war between Catholics and Protestants ended in a power-sharing agreement and the loss of the town's medieval prosperity. The self-service movie theater shows short film clips about Dinkelsbühl. On the top floor is the large, recently restored town model (Stadtschaue) with only the walls and a few key buildings set up on a medieval street plan. There's also a kids' play area.

Sleeping in Dinkelsbühl: Dinkelsbühl has a good selection of hotels, many of them lining the main drag in front of the church (though more choices and lower prices are available in Rothenburg and Nördlingen). Options include: **$$$ Hezelhof Hotel** (modern rooms in an old shell at Segringer Strasse 7, tel. 09851/555-420, www.hezelhof.com), **$$$ Weisses Ross** ("White Horse," attached to a historic restaurant at Steingasse 12, tel. 09851/579-890, www. hotel-weisses-ross.de), and Dinkelsbühl's unique **¢ youth hostel** (in a medieval granary at Koppengasse 10—steps from the Schweinemarkt, where Romantic Road buses stop once a day in each direction; tel. 09851/555-6417, www.dinkelsbuehl.jugendherberge.de).

▲Nördlingen

Though less cute than Dinkelsbühl, Nördlingen is a real workaday town that also has one of the best city walls in Germany, not to mention a surprising geological history. For centuries, Nördlingen's residents puzzled over the local terrain, a flattish plain called the Ries, which rises to a low circular ridge that surrounds the town in the distance. In the 1960s, geologists figured out that Nördlingen lies in the middle of an impact crater blasted out 15 million years

ago by a meteor, which hit earth with the force of 250,000 Hiroshima bombs.

Park in one of the big, free lots at the Delninger Tor and the Baldinger Tor, or in the free parking garage at the Berger Tor (parking inside the old town is time-limited).

After parking, head through one of the gates in the wall and into the center of town by zeroing in on the tower of **St. Georg's Church.** The inside is stripped-down austere—a far cry from the frilly Wieskirche two hours to the south. It's clear that Nördlingen and Wies straddle the Protestant-Catholic boundary.

Climb Nördlingen's **church tower** (which locals call "the Daniel") for sweeping views over the almost perfectly circular old town. The rickety 350-step climb up the tower rewards you with the very best view of the city walls and crater. You'll twist up a tight stone staircase, then tackle several flights of wooden ones—passing a giant wheel once used to winch materials up into the tower. Higher up is a modern winch used today. From the top, take a slow 360-degree spin; it's easy to visualize how the trees on the horizon sit on the rim of the meteorite crater.

The small square next to the church's main entrance is called Marktplatz, and just behind the step-gabled Rathaus (Town Hall) is the **TI** (tel. 09081/84116, www.noerdlingen.de).

Now walk out the bottom of Marktplatz and down Baldinger Strasse (past the Rathaus). At the traffic light, turn right and then left, past the skippable Stadtmuseum (town history, obscure local artists, and very little English), to the **Ries Crater Museum** (Rieskrater-Museum). Ask them to play the two 10-minute English films, which explain meteors. The exhibits are well presented but only described in German (tel. 09081/84710, www.noerdlingen.de).

With more time, walk all the way around on the top of the **town wall,** which is even better preserved than Rothenburg's or Dinkelsbühl's. Circle back to Baldinger Strasse and continue to the Baldinger Tor tower. This is one of five towers where you can climb the stairs to the walkway along the wall. From here, stroll atop the wall back to the lot where your car is parked. The city started building the wall in 1327 and financed it with a tax on wine and beer; it's more than a mile and a half long, has 16 towers and five gates, and offers great views of backyards and garden furniture. You could continue farther along the wall to the **City Wall Museum,** with a 108-step climb to the top—but the view from the church is better.

Sleeping in Nördlingen: Several small hotels surrounding St. Georg's Church offer mediocre but reasonably priced rooms. Try **$$ Hotel Altreuter** (over an inviting bakery/café at Marktplatz 11, tel. 09081/4319, www.hotel-altreuter.de).

Maypoles

Along the Romantic Road and throughout Bavaria, you'll see colorfully ornamented maypoles (*Maibaum*) decorating town squares. Many are painted in Bavaria's colors, white and blue. The decorations that line each side of the pole symbolize the craftspeople and businesses of that community (similar to the chamber of commerce billboards that greet visitors to small American towns today). Originally these allowed passing traders to quickly determine whether their services were needed in that town. The decorations are festively replaced each May Day (May 1). Traditionally, rival communities try to steal each other's maypole. Locals guard their new pole night and day as May Day approaches. Stolen poles are ransomed only with lots of beer for the clever thieves.

Harburg

You can't miss this town, thanks to the impressively intact, 900-year-old castle that looms high on a bluff over the river. Unusually well preserved from the Middle Ages (not a Romantic Age rebuild), it's still owned by the noble Wallerstein family. Locals enjoy repeating the story of how, years ago, Michael Jackson tried to buy this place—which he termed "the castle of my dreams."

Augsburg

Founded more than 2,000 years ago by Emperor Augustus, Augsburg enjoyed its heyday in the 15th and 16th centuries. Today, it's Bavaria's third-largest city (population 278,000). It lacks must-see sights, but the old town is pleasant, especially the small streets below the main square, where streams diverted from the River Lech run alongside pedestrians (www.augsburg.de).

FROM AUGSBURG TO FÜSSEN

From Augsburg, you can either continue south to Füssen on two-lane B-17, or you can hop on A-8, which brings you quickly into Munich (in about an hour).

Landsberg am Lech

Like many towns in this area, Landsberg (on the River Lech) has its roots in the salt trade. Every four years, the town hosts the Ruethenfest pageant, which brings Landsberg's medieval history to life. The town was shaped by the architect Dominikus Zimmerman (of Wieskirche fame). Adolf Hitler wrote *Mein Kampf* while serving his prison sentence here after the Beer Hall Putsch of 1923 (when Hitler and his followers unsuccessfully attempted to take over the government of Bavaria).

About 30 miles south of Landsberg, the nondescript village of **Rottenbuch,** near the Wieskirche, has an impressive church in a lovely setting.

▲▲Wieskirche

Germany's most glorious Baroque-Rococo church is beautifully restored and set in a sweet meadow. Romantic Road buses stop here for about 15-20 minutes—but depending on the day, the church may not be open during your visit; if not, you'll have to settle for an exterior-only photo op.

The Romantic Road Bus

From mid-April to mid-October, the Deutsche Touring company runs daily tour buses that roughly follow the Romantic Road. It's worthwhile mostly if you have no car but want to catch a fleeting glimpse of the towns along the Romantic Road, or if you're planning an overnight stay in a town that's poorly served by train (such as Dinkelsbühl). The bus also offers the convenience of a direct connection between towns where you'd have to transfer if traveling by train, such as between Rothenburg and the cities of Munich and Frankfurt.

The Frankfurt-Rothenburg leg passes through the small towns in the Tauber River valley (Bad Mergentheim, Weikersheim, and Creglingen) but only stops to pick up and drop off passengers. The Rothenburg-Munich leg includes short stops in both Dinkelsbühl and Augsburg—just enough for a glimpse of each. Between Munich and Füssen, the bus stops at the Wieskirche for just enough time to peek into the church. Be warned that in case of delays, these stops can be shortened.

Frankfurt to Rothenburg costs €45, Rothenburg to Munich is €43 (including train transfer), and from Augsburg to Füssen is €37 (each about the same as the train). The entire ride (Frankfurt to Füssen) costs €108. Students and seniors—without a rail pass—get a 10 percent discount. You can get a 20 percent discount if you have a German rail pass, Global Pass, or Select Pass (if Germany is one of your selected countries). You don't have to activate the use of a travel day of a flexipass to get this discount; if bus drivers say it takes a travel day, set them straight.

Romantic Road Bus Schedule

The Romantic Road bus runs daily from mid-April to mid-October.  Every day, one bus goes north to south (Frankfurt to Augsburg to Füssen), and another follows the reverse route south to north (Füssen to Munich to Frankfurt). You can begin or end your journey at any of these stops. The following times include only the main stops. The bus also stops elsewhere, including Bad Mergentheim, Weikersheim, Creglingen, Nördlingen, Harburg, Wieskirche, and Hohenschwangau. On the northbound route, the bus stops at Munich's central bus station (ZOB), not the train station. Check the full timetable at www.romantischestrasse.de (under "Romantic Road Coach").

The buses are fitted with Wi-Fi, and the free Romantic Road app provides details about the towns and villages you'll pass through. Free audioguides are available.

Southbound

Depart Frankfurt (platform A1-A3)	8:00
Arrive Würzburg (Residenz)	9:40
Depart Würzburg (Residenz)	10:10
Arrive Rothenburg (Schrannenplatz)	12:20
Depart Rothenburg (Schrannenplatz)	13:05
Arrive Dinkelsbühl	14:20
Depart Dinkelsbühl	14:50
Arrive Augsburg (Rathaus)	17:10
Depart Augsburg (Rathaus)	17:40
Arrive/Depart Augsburg (train station)	17:50
To Munich, train transfer required:	
Depart Augsburg	17:50
Arrive Munich	18:47
Arrive Wieskirche	19:35
Depart Wieskirche	19:50
Arrive Füssen	20:30

Northbound

Depart Füssen	8:00
Arrive/Depart Hohenschwangau (TI)	8:05
Arrive/Depart Schwangau Town (TI)	8:10
Arrive Wieskirche	8:35
Depart Wieskirche	8:55
Arrive/Depart Munich (central bus station)	10:40
Arrive Dinkelsbühl	14:35
Depart Dinkelsbühl	15:05
Arrive Rothenburg (Schrannenplatz)	16:05
Depart Rothenburg (Schrannenplatz)	16:50
Arrive Würzburg (Residenz)	18:35
Depart Würzburg (Residenz)	18:50
Arrive Frankfurt	20:30

Bus reservations are almost never necessary—you can pay by cash or credit card on the bus. But reservations are free and easy to make, and without one you could lose your seat to someone who has one (general information at www.romantic-road.com; reserve online at www.touring-travel.eu; info tel. 09851/551-387). The main ticket office is in Frankfurt; there's also a ticket office at the central bus station in Munich.

Bus stops are not well signed, but their location in each town is listed on the bus brochure and website. Look for a small *Touring* or *Romantische Strasse* sign.

WÜRZBURG

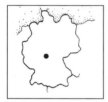

A historic midsized city, Würzburg (VE-WRTS-boorg) is worth a stop to see its stately prince-bishop's Residenz and the palace's sculpted gardens. Surrounded by vineyards and filled with atmospheric *Weinstuben* (wine bars), this tourist-friendly town is easy to navigate by foot or streetcar. Today, 25,000 of its 130,000 residents are students—making Würzburg feel young and very alive. It's also popular both with bike tourists (who enjoy the four-day pedal between Bamberg and here) and with river cruises.

While the town isn't all that charming (thanks to its unmistakable post-WWII-rebuild vibe), its quiet and appealing old center is scenically surrounded by vineyard-laced hills, with a stout fortress looming overhead. At one end of town is Würzburg's palace, among the most enjoyable to tour in Germany. On the other end is its atmospheric old bridge, lined by stone statues that make it reminiscent of Prague's famous Charles Bridge.

PLANNING YOUR TIME

Würzburg has a few hours' worth of sightseeing. Begin by touring the Residenz (prince-bishop's palace), then take my self-guided walk through town to the Old Main Bridge. With more time, cross the bridge and hike up to the hilltop Marienberg Fortress. If you're overnighting here, be sure to stroll the bridge at sunset, when you can join the friendly local crowd that gathers there in good weather for a glass of wine and mellow mingling.

Würzburg's Beginnings

The city was born centuries before Christ at an easy-to-ford part of the Main River under an easy-to-defend hill. A Celtic fort stood where the fortress stands today. Later, three Irish missionary monks came here to Christianize the local barbarians. In AD 686 they were beheaded, and their relics put Würzburg on the pilgrimage map. About 500 years later, when the town was the seat of a bishop, Holy Roman Emperor Frederick Barbarossa came here to get the bishop's OK to divorce his wife. The bishop said "No problem," and the emperor thanked him by giving him secular rule of the entire region of Franconia. From then on, the bishop was also a prince, and the prince-bishop of Würzburg answered only to the Holy Roman Emperor.

Orientation to Würzburg

Würzburg's old town core huddles along the bank of the Main (pronounced "mine") River. The tourists' Würzburg is bookended by the opulent Residenz (at the east end of downtown) and the hill-capping Marienberg Fortress (at the west end, across the river). You can walk from the Residenz to the river (below the fortress) in about 15 minutes; the train station is a 15-minute walk to the north.

TOURIST INFORMATION

Würzburg's helpful TI is in the yellow Rococo-style Falken Haus on Market Square (Mon-Fri 10:00-18:00, Sat and Sun until 14:00; shorter hours and closed Sun off-season; Market Square, tel. 0931/372-398, www. wuerzburg.de). If you're continuing on the Romantic Road (see previous chapter), the TI has information on routes and accommodations along the *Romantische Strasse*, including a very helpful route plan. The TI also has tips about biking along the Main River.

Sightseeing Passes: The **Würzburg Welcome Card** offers minimal discounts on a few sights and restaurants—you'll have to visit at least four sights to make it pay off (€3, valid 3 days, sold at TI). Würzburg's Residenz and Marienberg Fortress are covered by Bavaria's 14-day *Mehrtagesticket* (sold at participating sights).

ARRIVAL IN WÜRZBURG

By Train: Würzburg's train station is user-friendly and filled with services, including pay lockers and a handy *Reisezentrum* office that sells tickets (long hours daily). Walk out of the train station to the small square in front. Between the tram tracks and the small building with shops (ahead and on the right) is a good city map showing the easiest walking route between the station and the Residenz (and to other sights in town). Farther right are pay WCs, the post office, and the Romantic Road bus stop (look for *Touring* sign and schedule—usually platform 13).

From the tram cul-de-sac in front of the station, **tram** #1, #2, #3, or #5 will take you one stop to the Juliuspromenade stop, near most recommended hotels (easily walkable). Trams #1, #3, and #5 continue into town: The next stop (Dom) is close to Market Square, the TI, and the recommended Hotel zum Winzermännle. After that is the Rathaus stop, near the river and the recommended Hotel Alter Kranen.

To **walk** toward town (and some recommended hotels), cross over the busy Röntgenring and head up the shop-lined Kaiserstrasse. To reach the Residenz, it's simplest to walk (15 minutes), but you can get part of the way by taking tram #1, #3, or #5 to the Dom stop.

By Car: Drivers entering Würzburg can keep it simple by following signs to the *Residenz* and parking in the vast cobbled square that faces the palace. Cheaper parking is available in garages on the east bank of the river, just north of the old bridge.

HELPFUL HINTS

Festivals: Würzburg—always clever when it comes to trade—tightly schedules its biggest festivals in summer: Mozart (late May-June, with concerts in the Residenz, www.mozartfest-wuerzburg.de), wine (late May-early June, www.weindorf-wuerzburg.de), African music and dance (also late May-early June, www.africafestival.org), and the Kiliani Volksfest (first three weeks in July, www.wuerzburg.de/kiliani).

Supermarket: Kupsch, at Domstrasse 10, is just a few doors from City Hall (Mon-Sat 7:00-20:00, closed Sun). Another branch is on Kaiserstrasse, near the train station and recommended hotels.

Bike Rental: Ludwig Körner rents bikes right in the old town, a five-minute walk north of Market Square (€12/24 hours, Mon-Fri 9:00-18:00, Sat until 14:00, closed Sun, Bronnbachergasse 3, tel. 0931/52340).

Taxi: Call 0931/19410.

Local Guide: Julius Goldmann is a fine private guide in Würzburg (mobile 0175-873-2412, ju.goldmann@web.de). Rothen-

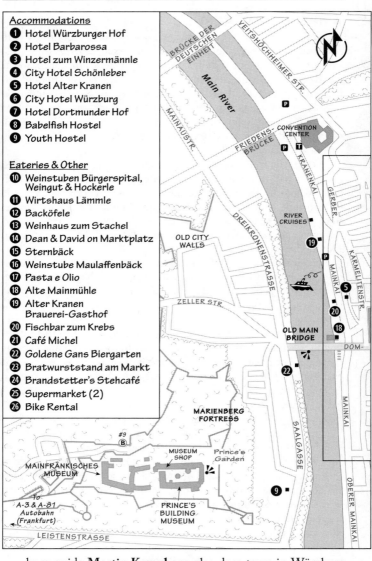

Accommodations
1. Hotel Würzburger Hof
2. Hotel Barbarossa
3. Hotel zum Winzermännle
4. City Hotel Schönleber
5. Hotel Alter Kranen
6. City Hotel Würzburg
7. Hotel Dortmunder Hof
8. Babelfish Hostel
9. Youth Hostel

Eateries & Other
10. Weinstuben Bürgerspital, Weingut & Hockerle
11. Wirtshaus Lämmle
12. Backöfele
13. Weinhaus zum Stachel
14. Dean & David on Marktplatz
15. Sternbäck
16. Weinstube Maulaffenbäck
17. Pasta e Olio
18. Alte Mainmühle
19. Alter Kranen Brauerei-Gasthof
20. Fischbar zum Krebs
21. Café Michel
22. Goldene Gans Biergarten
23. Bratwurststand am Markt
24. Brandstetter's Stehcafé
25. Supermarket (2)
26. Bike Rental

burg guide **Martin Kamphans** also does tours in Würzburg (tel. 09861/7941, www.stadtfuehrungen-rothenburg.de, kamphans@posteo.de).

Tourist Train: While most of the city is easily walkable, the tourist train is worth considering for a quick 40-minute town loop (€9, buy tickets on board, English headphone commentary, departs at the top of the hour from in front of the Residenz, daily June-Sept 10:00-17:00, May and Oct until 16:00, fewer

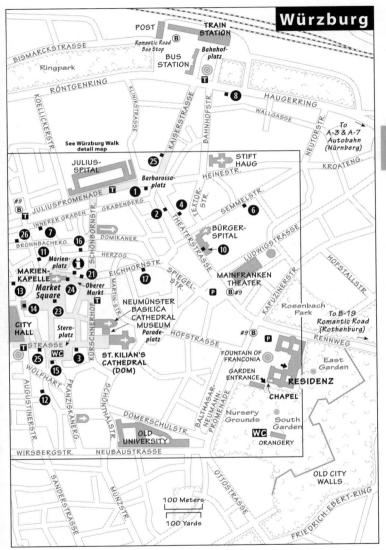

WÜRZBURG

departures and sometimes weekends only off-season, www.
city-tour.info).

GETTING AROUND WÜRZBURG

You can easily walk to everything except the hilltop Marienberg
Fortress (doable, but a steep hike). For public transit, the same tickets work on all city bus and tram lines (including the bus up to
the fortress). Your options include a short-trip ticket (*Kurzstrecke*

Eins +4-€1.35, good for up to four stops; this is all you need to get to my recommended hotels), a single ticket (*Einzelfahrschein*-€2.70, good for 1.5 hours in one direction with transfers), or a day pass (*Tageskarte Solo*-€5.10, also valid Sun if purchased on Sat). You can buy tickets from the bus driver or at streetside machines near tram stops (marked *Fahrausweise*). Most tickets come prestamped; if not, use the little box inside the tram or bus to validate it. Once on board, listen for the cute "next stop" transit announcements, recorded by local children. Transit info: Tel. 0931/362-320, www.vvm-info.de.

Residenz Tour

In the early 18th century, Würzburg's powerful prince-bishop decided to relocate from his hill-top residence at Marienberg, across the river, into new digs down in the city. His opulent, custom-built, 360-room palace (rated ▲▲) and its associated sights—the chapel (Hofkirche; also worth ▲▲) and garden— are the main tourist attractions of today's Würzburg. This Fran-

conian Versailles features grand rooms, 3-D art, and a massive fresco by Giovanni Battista Tiepolo. The palace has three sections: the central main rooms, the North Wing, and the South Wing (with the dazzling Mirror Cabinet; this wing is viewable only with a tour). The Residenz is impressive, yet quickly taken in; it's less overwhelming to visit than many other European royal palaces. Don't confuse the Residenz with Würzburg's Marienberg Fortress (on the hilltop across the river). The Residenz is the far more important sight to visit.

GETTING THERE

The Residenz is a 15-minute walk southeast of the train station. Easy parking is available in front of the Residenz (open daily 24 hours, get ticket as you enter, €1.50/hour for first 2 hours, €1/ each additional hour, pay at machine marked *Kasse* before leaving). Enter the palace through the main door at the middle of the sprawling complex (directly behind the big fountain).

ORIENTATION TO THE RESIDENZ

Cost and Hours: Palace-€7.50, includes guided tour, daily April-Oct 9:00-18:00, Nov-March 10:00-16:30; chapel-free, same hours as palace; gardens-free, daily until dusk (20:00 at the latest); tel. 0931/355-170 or 0931/355-1712, www.residenz-wuerzburg.de.

Sightseeing Strategies and Tours: A guided tour is included with your ticket and covers the main rooms (vestibule, Tiepolo fresco, White Hall, Imperial Hall), along with the otherwise inaccessible South Wing (tours last 45-60 minutes; English tours daily at 11:00 and 15:00, April-Oct also at 13:30 and 16:30; never full, just show up and wait in the vestibule—then be sure to request English; more tours in German: 2-3/hour). The English tour, while good, isn't worth planning your day around; you can see everything worthwhile in the Residenz on your own by following my self-guided tour (or consider the €5 English guidebook), and then, from the Imperial Hall, jump onto any German tour heading into the South Wing. You can do the history rooms behind the gift shop on your own.

Services: You'll find free WCs and self-service lockers (bags must be checked) on the right as you exit the ticket office. In the garden, WCs are to the right as you come in the main entrance, next to the orangery.

◯ SELF-GUIDED TOUR

This commentary gives you the basics to appreciate the palace (whether visiting on your own or with a tour), as well as an overview of the chapel and gardens.

Residenz Palace

• *Begin at the entrance.*

Vestibule and Garden Hall: This indoor area functioned as

a grand circular driveway, exclusively for special occasions—just right for six-horse carriages to drop off their guests at the base of the stairs. This area is relatively dark and serves as a good springboard for the dazzling palace that awaits.

Before climbing the formal staircase, pop into the adjacent Garden Hall (if open). This lovely, airy space is where the garden and the palace meet. The ceiling was painted by Johann Zick in 1750. Notice how he portrays his subjects without Greek-style idealism; they're shown realistically and in high contrast—quite edgy for the time.

• *Now picture yourself dressed up in your fanciest imaginary finery...and ascend the stairs.*

Grand Staircase: The elegant stairway comes with low steps, enabling high-class ladies to glide up gracefully, heads tilted back to enjoy Europe's largest and grandest fresco opening up above them. Hold your lady's hand high and get into the ascending rhythm. Enjoy the climb.

• *As you reach the top of the stairs, look up at the...*

Tiepolo Fresco: In 1752, the Venetian master Giovanni Battista Tiepolo was instructed to make a grand fresco illustrating the greatness of Europe, Würzburg, and the prince-bishop. And he did—completing the world's largest fresco (more than 7,000 square feet) in only 13 months. (The prince-bishop was in a rush to finish furnishing his new home in time for a visit from Habsburg Empress Maria Theresa.) Tiepolo was a master of three-dimensional illusion—and here, he employs one of his favorite tricks, with actual 3-D feet and other features breaking the frame of his faux 3-D frescoes.

The ceiling celebrates the esteemed prince-bishop, who smirks in the medallion with a red, ermine-trimmed cape. This guy had a healthy ego. The ceiling features Apollo (in the sunburst) and a host of Greek gods, all paying homage to the P-B. Ringing the room are the four continents, each symbolized by a woman on an animal and pointing to the prince-bishop. Walk the perimeter of the room to study and enjoy the symbolism of each continent one by one:

America—desperately uncivilized—sits naked with feathers in her hair on an alligator among severed heads. (Notice the cannibal BBQ going on just to the right. Eeew.)
She's being served hot chocolate, a favorite import and nearly a drug for Europeans back then. The black cloud hovering ominously above her head symbolizes (with great subtlety) how unenlightened Europeans of the time considered this savage continent to be.

Africa sits on a camel in a land of trade (notice the blue vase, the ivory tusk, and the kneeling servant with wafting frankincense) and fantasy animals (based on secondhand reports, and therefore inaccurate—the ostrich has human-horse-like legs). Father Nile, with his blue cloak, represents the river by pouring water from a jug.

Asia rides her elephant (with the backward ear) in the birthplace of Christianity (notice the crosses on the hill) and the alphabet (carved into the block beneath the obelisk).

Europe, who rides a bull, is shown as the center of high culture. And here, Lady Culture points her brush not at Rome, but at

Würzburg. A few portraits are hiding out in this area. The big dog is sniffing the purple-clad architect of the Residenz building. And Tiepolo includes a self-portrait as well: Find the burgundy-clad fellow in the corner just to the left, between the heads of the two white statues.

White Hall: This hall—with four big paintings portraying various prince-bishops—is actually gray (to provide better contrast) and was kept plain to punctuate the colorful rooms on either side. Also completed at a breakneck pace to meet the Maria Theresa deadline, it's a Rococo-stucco fantasy. (The word "Rococo" comes from the Portuguese word for the frilly rocaille shell.) The stucco decorations (particularly in the corners) have an armor-and-weapons theme, as this marked the entrance to the prince-bishop's private apartments—which had to be carefully guarded. Even the cloth-like yellow decorations above those weapons, draped high in the corners, are made of painted stucco. As you observe the stucco, dripping with symbolism that celebrates the prince-bishop, notice how the Rococo style is free from the strict symmetry of the Baroque. Also notice the stove, which heated the room. There's one in each room, all stoked from service hallways behind. The four gold cupids symbolize the seasons.

• *Straight ahead is the palace gift shop, which leads to a few other interesting rooms. Instead, from the White Hall, continue to your left, following signs for* Rundgang/Circuit.

Imperial Hall: Enjoy the artistic ensemble of this fine room in its entirety and feel its liveliness. This glorious hall—which was smartly restored—is the ultimate example of Baroque: harmony, symmetry, illusion, and the bizarre; lots of light and mirrors facing windows; and all with a foundation of absolutism (absolute power vested in one ruler, inspired by Louis XIV). Take a moment to marvel at all the 3-D tricks in the ceiling. Here's another trick: As you enter the room, look left and check out the dog in the fresco (at the top of the pillar). When you get to the window, have another look...notice that he has gotten older and fatter while you were crossing the hall.

The room features three scenes: On the ceiling, find Father Main (the local river—I call him "Dirty Old Man River") amusing himself with a nymph, whose blue shroud breaks the frame as it flows and flutters down the wall (subtly shifting from 3-D illusion to three actual dimensions). The two walls recount more history. On one (to the right as you enter), the bishop presides over the marriage (in 1156, but with more modern dress) of a happy Barbarossa (whose bride was actually 12 years old, unlike the woman in the painting, who looks considerably older; for more on Barbarossa, see the "Würzburg's Beginnings" sidebar, earlier). The bishop's power is demonstrated through his oversized fingers (giving the benediction) and through the details of his miter (tall hat), which—unlike his face—is not shown in profile, to allow you to see his coat of arms. Opposite that (left wall as you enter) is the payoff: Barbarossa, now the Holy Roman Emperor, gives the bishop Franconia and the secular title of prince. Notice the bishop touching Barbarossa's scepter with two fingers, performing an oath of fealty. From this point onward, the prince-bishop rules. Also in the Imperial Hall, the balcony offers a great vantage point for surveying the Italian section of the garden.

WÜRZBURG

• *If you're not already on a guided tour, keep a lookout for any group headed from here into the South Wing—if you see one, join it. Otherwise, continue with me into the...*

North Wing (Northern Imperial Apartments): This wing is a string of lavish rooms—evolving from fancy Baroque to fancier Rococo—used for the prince-bishop's VIP guests. It's a straight shot, with short descriptions in each room, to the **Green Lacquered Room** in the far corner. This room is named for its silver-leaf walls, painted green. The Escher-esque inlaid floor was painstakingly restored after WWII bombings. Have fun multiplying in the mirrors before leaving.

Keep going through a few more small rooms, which serve as a gallery for paintings, and then step out into the **hallway.** In this area, look for the little four-foot-tall doors that were used by tiny servants who kept the stoves burning, unseen from inside the walls. Also in the hallway are photos of the building's destruction in the 1945 firebombing of Würzburg, and its subsequent restoration. While about three-quarters of the Residenz was destroyed during World War II, the most precious parts—the first rooms on this tour, including the Tiepolo frescoes—were unscathed, partly because these important halls were located in a stout stone structure rather than a more fragile wooden one. A temporary roof saved the palace from total ruin, but it was not until the late 1970s that it was returned to more or less its original condition.

• *If you haven't yet joined a tour but want to see the South Wing, find your way back to the Imperial Hall and wait until a group comes along. Then tag along for about 15 minutes as you stroll the...*

South Wing (by Tour Only): The dark and woody South Wing feels more masculine than the North Wing. In this wing's string of rooms, you'll first come to the waiting room (antechamber), the audience chamber/throne room (with circa-1700 Belgian tapestries showing scenes from the life of Alexander the Great), and the Venetian Room (which was a bedroom; note the three tapestries, made around 1740 in Würzburg). The rooms become progressively more ornate until you reach the South Wing's climax: the Mirror Cabinet.

The 18th-century **Mirror Cabinet** was where the prince-bishop showed off his amazing wealth. It features six lavish pounds of gold leaf, lots of Asian influence, an allegory of one of the four continents in each corner, and painted figures on the reverse side of glass. Because it couldn't be removed, it was destroyed by WWII bombing raids in 1945. The doors in this room are original, but everything else was restored in the 1980s based on photos taken by the Nazis, who knew that regardless of how the war turned out, Germany would be rebuilding.

The **Art Gallery** room is next, with portraits of different prince-bishops who ruled until the early 1800s, when Napoleon said, "Enough of this nonsense" and secularized politics in places like Franconia.

You can leave the escorted tour at this point and explore the **history exhibit,** including Napoleonic-age furniture and a barbaric carousel where children competed to lop off papier-mâché heads and noses—illustrating child-oriented violent games long before videogames were known. This route eventually leads to the **gift shop.**

• *Finish your tour of the Residenz at the Court Chapel. To get there, head back down the stairs, past the ticket office and through the locker room. Follow signs to the southern wing of the big complex. An arch leads left into a courtyard, from which a humble door leads toward the ornate chapel. Follow signs to* Court Chapel/Hofkirche.

Court Chapel (Hofkirche)

This sumptuous chapel was for the exclusive use of the prince-bishop (private altar upstairs with direct entrance to his residence) and his court (ground floor).

The decor and design are textbook Baroque. Architect Johann Balthasar Neumann was stuck with the existing walls. His challenge was to bring in light and create symmetry—essential to any Baroque work. He did it with mirrors and hidden windows. All the gold is real—if paper-thin—gold leaf. The columns are "manufactured marble," which isn't marble at all but marbled plaster. This method was popular because it was uniform, and the color could be controlled. Pigment was mixed into plaster, which was then rolled onto the stone or timber core of the column. This half-inch veneer was then polished. You can tell if a "marble" column is real or fake by resting your hand on it. If it warms up, it's not marble.

The faded painting in the dome high above the altar shows

three guys in gold robes losing their heads (for more on these martyred Irish monks, see the "Würzburg's Beginnings" sidebar, earlier). The two side paintings are by the great fresco artist Tiepolo. Since the fresco plaster wouldn't dry in the winter, Tiepolo spent his downtime painting with oil.

• *To reach the garden, enter through the gate at the right of the Residenz building.*

Residenz Garden

One of Germany's finest Baroque gardens is a delightful park cradling the palace. It has three sections: the East Garden, the South Garden, and the nursery grounds. The South Garden, just inside the gate, features statues of Greek gods (with lots of kidnapping action); carefully trimmed, remarkably conical, 18th-century yew trees; and an orangery (at the far back). The nursery grounds (to the right) is like a rough park. The East Garden, directly behind

the palace around to the left, is grand—à la Versailles—but uses terraces to create the illusion of spaciousness (since it was originally hemmed in by the town wall). Behind the orangery is the replanted palace kitchen garden.

Würzburg Walk

This one-hour self-guided walk takes you from the Residenz (which you may want to tour first) to the Old Main Bridge (Alte Mainbrücke) via the key old-town sights. (If you're not touring the Residenz before taking this walk, you can start at St. Kilian's Cathedral.)

• *Begin at the fountain in front of the Residenz palace.*

Fountain of Franconia

In 1814, the prince-bishop got the boot, and the region of Franconia was secularized and given to the Bavarian Wittelsbach dynasty. Technically, Franconia is a part of Bavaria, but calling a Franconian a Bavarian is something like calling a Scot an Englishman. This statue—a gift from the townspeople to their then-new royal family—turns its back

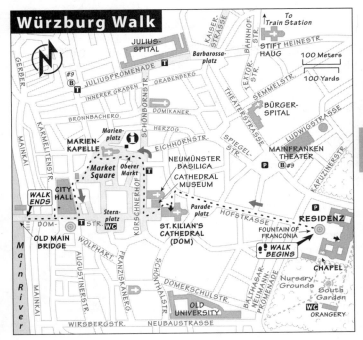

WÜRZBURG

to the palace and faces the town. It celebrates the artistic and intellectual genius of Franconia with statues of three great hometown boys (a medieval bard, the woodcarver Tilman Riemenschneider, and the Renaissance painter Matthias Grünewald).

• *If Franconia hopped down and ran 300 yards ahead on Hofstrasse, she'd hit the twin-spired cathedral. Meet her there. As you walk, think about how the city was essentially destroyed in 1945 and later rebuilt. At the cathedral, circle around the right, and enter the church through its heavy bronze side door (before the underground passage and across from the modern cathedral museum).*

St. Kilian's Cathedral (Dom)

This building's core is Romanesque (1040-1188), with Gothic spires and Baroque additions to the transepts. It was built as a Catholic church and stayed that way after the Reformation.

Cost and Hours: Free, Mon-Sat generally 10:00-19:00, Sun 13:00-18:00, daily Easter-Oct closes midday for brief services, tel. 0931/3866-2900, www.dom-wuerzburg.de.

Visiting the Church: The cathedral was destroyed in World War II and rebuilt in the 1960s with a passion for mixing historic and modern styles. Before 1945, the entire church was slathered in Baroque stucco decor, as the apse is today. The nave has a cohesive design, progressing from the menorah (representing the Old Testament) in the back, past tombstones of centuries of prince-bishops and a crucified Jesus (above the high altar), to the apse, where a resurrected Christ, riding a golden disc, welcomes you into a hopeful future. The skulls of Würzburg's three favorite saints—those Irish monks martyred in the seventh century—lie in a box within the altar (see "Würzburg's Beginnings" sidebar, earlier).

Halfway along the nave (on the left side, as you face the altar) is a fine memorial to the 15th-century Prince-Bishop Rudolf von Scherenberg, whose name means "scissors mountain" (see his coat of arms). Scherenberg ruled until he was 94 years old. Carved by Tilman Riemenschneider, this tombstone is an example of late-Gothic realism. Back then, it was outrageous to portray an old bishop as...an old bishop (looking at the tombstone, you can tell he needs dentures). The next prince-bishop, whose tomb is to the right of Scherenberg's, saw how realistic his predecessor's was and insisted on having an idealized portrait (also by Riemenschneider) done to his satisfaction before he died. (He's looking implausibly dashing.)

• *Leave the church the way you entered. Outside, look up at the three martyrs (before they were beheaded), high on the building opposite. Walk a few steps downhill (to the left) and notice, embedded in the cathedral wall, the tomb of the great local artist Riemenschneider, placed here after the church's cemetery was moved. If you're interested in a fresh take on religious art, go into the modern Cathedral Museum across the way. Otherwise, skip ahead and continue downhill through the tunnel on your way to the basilica.*

Cathedral Museum (Museum am Dom)

This museum features a refreshing, poignant juxtaposition of old and new religious art, managing to be provocative in a constructive way. It pairs 11th- to 18th-century works with modern interpretations, sprinkles it all with a Christian theme, and wraps it in a shiny modern building. With an emphasis on more cutting-edge contemporary works, it does an impressive job of respecting "religious art" for both its artistic and spiritual qualities.

Cost and Hours: €4, €5 combo-ticket includes Cathedral

Treasury, Tue-Sun 10:00-17:00, closed Mon, tel. 0931/3866-5600, www.museum-am-dom.de.

• *Upon leaving the museum, hook right through a tunnel, which emerges on a delightful urban scene. Straight ahead, Domstrasse leads down to the spire of the City Hall and the Old Main Bridge (where this walk ends). But we're looping right. Go a block up Kürschnerhof, where a staircase leads into the...*

Neumünster Basilica

Like the cathedral, this church has a Romanesque body with a Baroque face. Climb the stairs to take a look inside, appreciating the church's rounded Romanesque nave decorated (like the outside) with bubbly Baroque stucco.

Return to Kürschnerhof and continue up the street, noticing the vineyards in the distance. Appreciate the relative quiet here in the heart of town. Locals wouldn't have it any other way—electric trolleys, bikes, and pedestrians in a thriving and car-free commercial zone.

• *Enter the square on the left with the lacy, two-tone church.*

Upper Market Square (Oberer Markt)

Imagine this square during the wine fest in June—with 75 vintners showing off their best wines—or during the Christmas market, when the square is full of quaint stalls selling holiday goodies. The fancy yellow-and-white, Rococo-designed Falken Haus (House of the Falcon) dates from 1751, when the landlady gave a wandering band of stucco artists a chance to show their stuff (inside are the TI and library).

• *Continue past the Falken Haus, passing the church on your right, into...*

Market Square (Marktplatz)

Würzburg's Marktplatz is a great scene. The obelisk at its center, built in 1805, has a relief showing romantic maidens selling fruits, a hare, and other wares. To this day, the square is host to a bustling produce and flower market four days a week. Under the covered walkway, find a fountain with the modern statue nicknamed "Market Barbara" *(Markt Barbel)*, which recalls a traditional merchant woman. From there, a line often leads to the **Bratwurststand am Markt** (under the yellow-and-white awning, near the covered walkway), where cheap sausage sandwiches are made and sold to eager locals. Watch the wiener-folding action through the side window, or grab a wurst yourself (let them know whether you want yours *"mit"*—with mustard—or *"ohne"*—without). Beyond that, anchored like a Hansel-and-Gretel barnacle to the foot of the church, is **Brandstetter's Stehcafé,** a venerable choice for a coffee-and-cake break while you stand and watch the crowds.

Marienkapelle

The two-tone late-Gothic church was the merchants' answer to the prince-bishop's cathedral. Since Rome didn't bankroll the place, it's ringed with "swallow shops" (like swallows' nests cuddled up against a house)—enabling the church to run little businesses. The sandstone statues (in the small alcoves partway up the columns; they're replicas of Riemenschneider originals) depict the 12 apostles and Jesus. The famous Adam and Eve statues (flanking the side entrance to the church) show off Riemenschneider's mastery of the human body. Continue around the church to the west portal, where the carved Last Judgment (above the main doors) shows kings, ladies, and bishops—some going to heaven, others making up the chain gang bound for hell, via the monster's mouth. (This was commissioned by those feisty town merchants tired of snooty bluebloods.) Continue around to the next entry (which faces a *Biergarten* under chestnut trees) to see the Annunciation, with a cute angel Gabriel telling Mary (the lilies symbolize her virginity) the good news. Notice how God whispers through a speaking tube as Baby Jesus slips down and into her ear.

• *Go back around to the market (Adam-and-Eve side) and leave—passing the obelisk—in the direction of the yellow building. Follow Schustergasse, a pedestrian lane lined with shops that leads back to Domstrasse (with tram tracks). The cathedral is on your left, while the City Hall and Old Main Bridge are to the right. Head right to the City Hall's tower.*

City Hall (Rathaus)

Würzburg's City Hall is relatively humble because of the power of the prince-bishop. As you face the building, go around the left side to find the *Gedenkraum 16 März 1945* memorial (free, always open). This commemorates the 20-minute Allied bombing raid on March 16, 1945, and the resulting firestorm that destroyed—and demoralized—Würzburg six weeks before the end of World War II. The damage was almost as bad as in Dresden: Nearly every downtown building was reduced to a shell, with roofs, floors, and windows gone. Most residents survived in bomb shelters, but 5,000 died—largely women and children. Check out the model of the devastated town, and read the interesting panels about the rise of Nazism and the brutality of war, and the hope brought by a spirit of reconciliation.

• *As you leave City Hall, notice the horizontal lines cut into the archway on your right. These mark the floodwaters* (Hochstand des Maines) *of the years 1342, 1682, and 1784. Now, find the bridge.*

Old Main Bridge (Alte Mainbrücke)

This isn't the town's "main" (as in primary) bridge; rather, it spans the Main (pronounced "mine") River, which flows through Frankfurt and into the Rhine.

The bridge, from 1133, is the second-oldest in Germany. The 12 statues lining the bridge are Würzburg saints and prince-bishops. Walk to the St. Kilian statue (with the golden sword)—one of the three monks who are shown being beheaded in the Residenz Palace's chapel. Squint up at Kilian, still with his head on, pointing to God. This is a great spot to linger with the locals as

you drink in the view and perhaps a glass of the local wine.

Beyond Kilian you may see river cruise ships moored by the next bridge. The rising popularity of river cruising (from Amsterdam to Budapest) is bringing lots of crowds and business to towns like Würzburg.

High above the city, capping the hill beyond the bridge, is the Marienberg Fortress (described at the end of this walk). And downstream are three stacks marking a power plant. Between here and there find the old crane, built in 1770 to further the city's desirability as a river trading port. Along the embankment near the crane are a recommended beer garden (named for the crane) and a fish-and-chips boat—and lots of people picnicking (all described later, under "Eating in Würzburg").

The hillside (beyond the crane) is blanketed with grapevines destined to become the fine Stein Franconian wine. Goethe, the

great German author, ordered 900 liters of this vintage annually. A friend once asked Goethe what he thought were the three most important things in life. He said, "Wine, women, and song." The friend then asked, "If you had to give one up, which would it be?" Without hesitating, Goethe answered "Song." Then, when asked what he would choose if he had to give up a second item, Goethe paused and said, "It depends on the vintage."

• *Consider stopping here and having lunch at the recommended Alte Mainmühle restaurant, with a terrace overlooking the bridge (at the near end). On warm summer evenings, the restaurant sets up a little wine stand at the start of the bridge—worth returning to at sunset to buy a glass of wine to sip while you do laps around the bridge. Or you can continue on to the fortress on the hill above you.*

Marienberg Fortress (Festung Marienberg)

This 13th-century fortified retreat was the original residence of Würzburg's prince-bishops (before the opulent Residenz across the river was built). After being stormed by the Swedish army during the 17th-century Thirty Years' War, the fortress was expanded in Baroque style.

Cost and Hours: Grounds-free; Prince's Garden-free, daily 9:00-17:30 except Mon until 16:00, closed Nov-March; Prince's Building Museum-€4.50, €6.50 combo-ticket includes Mainfränkisches Museum, different €6 combo-ticket includes tour—described next, Tue-Sun 9:00-18:00, closed Mon and Nov-March, tel. 0931/355-1750, www.schloesser.bayern.de; Mainfränkisches Museum-€4, €6.50 combo-ticket includes Prince's Building Museum, Tue-Sun 10:00-17:00, Nov-March until 16:00, closed Mon year-round, tel. 0931/205-940, www.mainfraenkisches-museum.de.

Tours and Information: On weekends from April to October, a 45-minute English-language tour brings the fortress to life (€3.50 or €6 combo-ticket that includes Prince's Building Museum, Sat-Sun at 15:00, none off-season, buy tickets at museum shop in the inner courtyard). The inexpensive *Marienberg Castle* booklet, sold throughout the fortress, is well-written and has basic information on both museums.

Getting There: To walk there, cross the Old Main Bridge and follow small *Festung Marienberg* signs to the right uphill for a heart-thumping 20 minutes. Or take infrequent bus #9 (direction: Festung) from the middle of town—not the bridge—to the last stop (Schönborntor) and walk through the tunnel to enter the fortress (runs every 30 minutes daily 9:30-18:00, times listed at stops, departs from Residenzplatz and Juliuspromenade). Consider taking the bus up and walking down (follow *Fussweg zur Altstadt* signs). Taxis wait near the Old Main Bridge (€10 to fortress).

Visiting the Fortress: The **fortress grounds** provide fine city views and a good place for a picnic. You can wander freely through the fortress courtyards and peek into the bottom of the original keep (tower stronghold at the center of the complex) and the round church, where carved relief monuments to former bishops decorate the stone floor. For the best views of the town, go through the archway off the inner courtyard (next to church entrance) into the **Prince's Garden**—look for the *Fürstengarten* sign.

The fortress houses two museums: The **Mainfränkisches Museum,** which highlights the work of Tilman Riemenschneider, Germany's top woodcarver and onetime mayor of Würzburg, is in the red-and-white building at the back of the fortress, near the bus stop. Riemenschneider fans will also find his work throughout Würzburg's many churches (such as in the cathedral, described on page 65). A visitor's guide (in English) directs the way, but it provides little real information.

The **Prince's Building Museum** (Fürstenbaumuseum) is in the inner courtyard. The first floor shows off relics of the prince-bishops (some signs in English), and the second floor focuses on the history of Würzburg (German only). You'll wander through big, mostly empty rooms with a few sparse exhibits and Würzburg views through hazy windows.

Sleeping in Würzburg

Würzburg's hotels and hostels are a stress-free option for a first or last night when flying into or out of Frankfurt. Trains run at least hourly between Würzburg and Frankfurt's airport; the journey takes 1.5 hours. Hotels tend to discount the prices listed during slow months—November to April, and sometimes in August as well.

As Würzburg is a convention town, it has ample chain hotels that can be a great value in slow times—consider searching online for the dates you're in town. My listings are smaller places with more personality and rates that are less likely to fluctuate. In these hotels, quieter rooms are in back, front rooms have street noise, and all rooms are entertained by church bells.

Most of these listings are less than a 10-minute walk from the train station and perfectly situated for sightseeing. To reach nearly all of them, head up Kaiserstrasse from the station to Barbarossaplatz (with the circular awning) or take the tram one stop to Juliuspromenade. Hotel zum Winzermännle and Hotel Alter Kranen are closer to the river; consider riding a tram to the Dom or the Rathaus stops, respectively. If you're driving, you'll likely have to park in a garage near your hotel (about €8/day) as street parking is scarce.

$$$ Hotel Würzburger Hof has an elegant lobby and 34 large, Baroque rooms right at the Juliuspromenade tram stop. They have two types of rooms: smaller but perfectly fine "comfort" rooms and larger "superior" rooms (elevator, good windows that dampen street noise, Barbarossaplatz 2, tel. 0931/53814, www.hotel-wuerzburgerhof.de, info@hotel-wuerzburgerhof.de).

$$ Hotel Barbarossa, tucked away on top of a tall medical-office building above the busy Barbarossaplatz intersection, has a more modern, youthful sensibility than the others listed here and is a good value. Its 18 rooms combine sleek minimalism and a respect for traditional design (RS%, rooftop terrace, elevator, Theaterstrasse 2, fourth floor, tel. 0931/3291-9091, www.hotelbarbarossa-wuerzburg.de, info@hotelbarbarossa-wuerzburg.de, run by hardworking Christine).

$$ Hotel zum Winzermännle has 20 bright rooms along a busy pedestrian street in the city center, but its double-paned windows keep things quiet. The atmosphere is simple but tastefully done, in a hotel the Fick family has run for three generations (elevator, reception up one floor from street, Domstrasse 32, tel. 0931/54156, www.winzermaennle.de, info@winzermaennle.de, friendly Alexandra and her parents).

$$ City Hotel Schönleber has 33 simple, up-to-date rooms fronting a busy street—in open-window weather, it's worth requesting a room on the courtyard (cheaper rooms with shared bath, elevator, from Barbarossaplatz angle left down Theaterstrasse to #5, tel. 0931/304-8900, www.cityhotel-schoenleber.de, reservierung@cityhotel-schoenleber.de, Ulrich Kölbel).

$$ Hotel Alter Kranen has 16 standard rooms with a tidy, business-class vibe right along the river (but only three rooms have views—try requesting one when you reserve). This hotel is farther from the train station than the others listed here, but a bit handier to the Market Square/Old Main Bridge action (air-con in top-floor rooms only, elevator, Kärrnergasse 11, tel. 0931/35180, www.hotel-alter-kranen.de, mail@hotel-alter-kranen.de).

$$ City Hotel Würzburg has 33 comfortable rooms on a street with a pleasant neighborhood feel (no elevator, from Barbarossaplatz follow Theaterstrasse and take your first left onto Semmelstrasse, Semmelstrasse 28, tel. 0931/780-0990, www.cityhotel-wuerzburg.de, info@cityhotel-wuerzburg.de, Ulrich Kölbel).

$ Hotel Dortmunder Hof offers 13 simple, bright, slightly musty rooms on a quiet back street. Mellow jazz tunes sometimes play in the cozy restaurant and wine bar, where you'll check in and enjoy a warm welcome (wonderful breakfast, elevator, reception in wine bar to right of entrance; from train station, turn right onto Juliuspromenade, then jog left a block onto Innerer Graben, Innerer Graben 22, tel. 0931/56163, www.dortmunder-hof.de, info@dortmunder-hof.de, Hennig-Rink family).

¢ Babelfish Hostel, across the street from the station, welcomes travelers of all ages to its 18 colorful rooms. This laid-back place is eco-friendly, modern, and feels safe (private rooms available—some with kitchenettes, breakfast extra, roof deck, wheelchair-accessible, reception on second floor, Haugering 2, tel.

0931/304-0430, www.babelfish-hostel.de, info@babelfish-hostel.de).

¢ Würzburg's official **youth hostel** *(Jugendherberge)* is across the river in a former women's prison (private and family rooms; 20-minute walk from station: cross Old Main Bridge and turn left on Saalgasse to Fred-Joseph-Platz 2; or take tram #3 or #5 to Löwenbrücke stop, then follow *Jugendherberge* signs; tel.0931/4677-860, www.wuerzburg.jugendherberge.de, wuerzburg@jugendherberge.de).

Eating in Würzburg

IN THE CENTER

The **Bürgerspital** is a grand Baroque complex that once housed one of the city's medieval charity hospices. Back then, rich Würzburgers created charitable foundations to support the city's elderly and poor. They began making and selling wine to fund their charity work, and this tradition continues today. Still occupying grand Baroque complexes, the foundations have restaurants, wine shops, and extensive wine cellars. These are no longer basic soup kitchens but well-respected, quite elegant eateries that also happen to support a good cause. The Bürgerspital—the oldest and best-known of these foundations—now cares for about a hundred local seniors and also provides two eating options:

$$ Weinstuben Bürgerspital is a candlelit but informal restaurant that serves beautifully presented Franconian specialties. Depending on the weather, you can dine outside in a fine old courtyard or indoors in traditional or modern rooms (daily 10:00-24:00, enter at Theaterstrasse 19, tel. 0931/352-880).

$$ Weingut Bürgerspital, an unintimidating wine shop/tasting room on a busy corner, serves up small dishes in a contemporary setting. The staff is happy to educate you on the basics of Franconian wine (flights available, Tue-Sat 9:00-24:00, Sun-Mon 11:00-18:00, Theaterstrasse 19, tel. 0931/350-3441).

The Bürgerspital's fun, drinks-only place, **Hockerle,** is described later, under "Places for a Memorable Snack or Drink."

Other Central Options

$$ Wirtshaus Lämmle is just right for a wine garden serving traditional Franconian dishes under chestnut trees with a view of the back side of the Marienkapelle (Mon-Sat 11:00-22:00, Sun until 16:00, Marienplatz 5, tel. 0931/54748).

$$$ Backöfele is a fun hole-in-the-wall (literally, though it's quite big once you enter). Named "The Oven" for its entryway, this place is a hit with Germans, offering a rustic menu full of traditional meat and fish dishes. You can sit inside or in the delightful, glassed-in, cobbled courtyard (daily 12:00-23:00, reservations smart; a couple of blocks beyond City Hall, Ursulinergasse 2; tel. 0931/59059, www.backoefele.de).

$$$ Weinhaus zum Stachel, Würzburg's oldest *Weinhaus,* originated as the town's tithe barn—where people deposited 10 percent of their produce as tax. In 1413, it began preparing that produce and selling wine. Today, its stone-and-ivy courtyard is one of the city's most elegant settings for enjoying fresh fish and gourmet Franconian meals. In bad weather, you'll eat in the woody medieval dining room, where the ceiling depicts a *Stachel* (mace) in deadly action (Tue-Sat 11:30-22:00, Sun until 16:00, closed Mon, reservations smart, Gressengasse 1, tel. 0931/52770, www. weinhaus-stachel.de).

$ Dean & David on Marktplatz, part of a national chain, is deservedly a favorite for a fast, inexpensive, and healthy meal with views of the market action. They have a pleasant modern interior and tables on the square (super-fresh salads, veggie dishes, curries, soups, wok plates, sandwiches, smoothies, Mon-Sat 10:00-21:00, Sun 11:00-19:00, look for modern building kitty-corner from church, Marktplatz 4, tel. 0931/4522-8303).

$$ Sternbäck is an inviting *Kneipe* (pub) with rickety tables spilling onto a busy square. This is where locals from all walks of life gather for a drink and cheap eats. The hip, friendly staff can recommend something that will satisfy you, including Franconian classics and curries (daily 9:00-late, breakfast served until 13:00, Sternplatz 4, tel. 0931/54056).

$ Weinstube Maulaffenbäck, hidden in an alley near Market Square with a few outdoor tables, is a characteristic place for cheap Franconian meals and good wine. In accordance with a unique Würzburger tradition, if you order wine at lunch between 10:00 and 12:00, you're welcome to bring your own cold cuts and bread (the butcher next door is open until 18:00)—they'll provide the plate and fork (Mon-Thu 10:00-22:00, Fri-Sat until 23:00, closed Sun in summer, otherwise 10:00-16:00, Maulhardgasse 9, tel. 0931/4677-8700).

Lunch: A couple of blocks east of Market Square, **$ Pasta e Olio** may look like an anonymous fast-food stand, but here the pasta is made fresh daily by the same family that's been running the place for three generations. The limited menu usually includes a pasta dish, lasagna, a vegetarian option, and mixed *antipasti.* Place your order cafeteria style, then eat standing at one of the tables (Mon-Fri 8:00-17:00, Sat until 16:00, closed Sun, no WC, Eichhornstrasse 6, tel. 0931/16699). Lots of other cheap, fast, stand-up lunch places—serving various cuisines—are nearby, between here and Market Square.

ON THE RIVERFRONT

$$$ Alte Mainmühle, on the bridge in a converted mill, is a great place to end your walking tour or enjoy a sunset. On a warm day,

nothing beats a cold beer on their deck, which overlooks the river and the fortress—choose from their sunny top-floor terrace or the shade below. (They also run a wine stand on the Old Main Bridge on summer evenings.) If dining inside, I'd sit upstairs rather than on the lower level. They have fresh fish specials and traditional fare with a Franconian twist. Their homemade sourdough bread *(Natursauerteigbrot)* is a delicious nod to their milling history (daily 11:00-22:00, Mainkai 1, tel. 0931/16777).

$$ Alter Kranen Brauerei-Gasthof is a youthful eatery with a big beer hall interior and outdoor tables around the old crane overlooking the river (try the local brew—Würzburger Hofbräu, table service only, daily 11:00-24:00, a couple of blocks down from the Old Main Bridge at Kranenkai 1, tel. 0931/9913-1546). They kick off evenings with a popular happy hour (cheap beer and cocktails, 17:00-19:00).

$ Fischbar zum Krebs, a fun-loving little fish-and-chips boat, is permanently tied up a bit downstream from the Old Main Bridge. With a commotion of funky tables and lots of riverside park benches nearby, it caters to a youthful crowd and is the cheapest meal on the water. They serve local fish—trout, pike-perch, and carp—with English-style malt vinegar and sea salt. Place your order at the counter onboard. You'll have to fetch your own beer, and if ordering beer or wine you have to stay on the boat (likely daily 14:00-23:00 in summer, closed in bad weather and Nov-April).

Riverfront Picnic: A parklike stretch of riverbank from the Old Main Bridge to the crane is made-to-order for picnicking. There are plenty of benches and a long, inviting concrete embankment to spread out your meal. It comes with beer-drinking students, the down-and-out collecting their bottles, and great views of the river, bridge, and castle.

PLACES FOR A MEMORABLE SNACK OR DRINK

$ Café Michel, right on Upper Market Square and next to the TI, is a family-oriented bakery and teahouse with quiet indoor seating and tables on the square. They offer soups, sandwiches, and an impressive selection of cakes and strudels (daily until 18:00, Marktplatz 11).

WÜRZBURG

$ Goldene Gans Biergarten is a sloppy riverside beer garden on the west side of the river, with wooden benches, shaded views of the Old Main Bridge, forgettable food, and good beer (daily 11:00-23:00—weather permitting, closed off-season; to the left about a block after you cross the Old Main Bridge).

Hockerle, a funky little time warp, is a pub tucked away right next to Weingut Bürgerspital (listed earlier). It serves wine on tap to locals and outgoing tourists who bring in their own food. The regulars start drinking early (no food, wines listed on blackboard, Mon-Fri 9:00-18:00, Sat until 15:00, closed Sun).

Würzburg Connections

From Würzburg by Train to: Rothenburg (hourly, 70 minutes, transfer in Steinach; 45 minutes to Steinach, then 15 minutes to Rothenburg; tiny Steinach-Rothenburg train leaves usually from track 5 shortly after the Würzburg train arrives), **Frankfurt Airport** (1-2/hour, 1.5 hours), **Frankfurt** (1-2/hour, 70 minutes, or 2 hours on cheaper RE trains), **Nürnberg** (2-3/hour, 1 hour), **Munich** (1-2/hour, 2 hours), **Cologne** (hourly, 2.5 hours by ICE; also 3/day by IC, 4 hours), **Leipzig** (hourly, 3 hours, some transfer in Fulda or Bamburg), **Berlin** (hourly, 4 hours, change points vary). Train info: www.bahn.com.

FRANKFURT

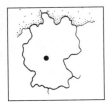

Frankfurt, while low on Old World charm, offers a good look at today's no-nonsense, modern Germany. There's so much more to this country than castles and old cobbled squares. Ever since the early Middle Ages, when—as the city's name hints—this was a good place to ford the river, people have gathered here to trade. Frankfurt is a pragmatic city, and its decisions are famously based on what's good for business. Destroyed in World War II? Make that an opportunity to rebuild for trade better than ever. And that's what they did.

With trade came people from around the world. Cosmopolitan Frankfurt—nicknamed "Bankfurt"—is a business hub of the united Europe and home to the European Central Bank. Especially in the area around the train station, you'll notice the fascinating multiethnic flavor of the city. A quarter of its 700,000 residents carry foreign passports, representing 200 different nationalities. Though Frankfurt is often avoided by tourists who consider it just a sterile business and transportation hub, the city's modern energy, fueled in part by the entrepreneurial spirit of its immigrant communities, makes it a unique and entertaining city. And if you visit on a Sunday, when Frankfurt takes the day off from its usual hustle and bustle, you'll find a city cloaked in a village-like charm.

PLANNING YOUR TIME

You might fly into or out of Frankfurt am Main, or at least pass through, as this glossy city links the best wine-and-castles stretch of the Rhine to the north with the fairy-tale Romantic Road to the south. Even two or three hours in Frankfurt leaves you with some powerful impressions: The city's main sights can be enjoyed in a half-day by using its train station (a 12-minute ride from the airport) as a springboard. At a minimum, ride up to the top of the Main Tower for commanding city views and wander through the pedestrian zone to the Old Town area (Römerberg). My self-guided walk provides a framework for your explorations. With more time or an overnight, Frankfurt has plenty of museums and other attractions to choose from.

Orientation to Frankfurt

Frankfurt, with its forest of skyscrapers perched on the banks of the Main (pronounced "mine") River, has been dubbed Germany's "Mainhattan." The city is Germany's trade and banking capital, leading the country in high-rises (mostly bank headquarters)...and yet, a third of Frankfurt is green space.

The convention center *(Messe)* and the red light district are near the train station. Just to the east is the skyscraper banking district and the shopping and pedestrian area around the distinctive Hauptwache building. Beyond that is what remains of Frankfurt's Old Town, around Römerberg, the city's central market square. A short walk across the river takes you to a different part of town: Frankfurt's top museums line the south bank of the Main, and nearby is Sachsenhausen, a charming residential neighborhood and schmaltzy restaurant zone.

TOURIST INFORMATION

Frankfurt has several TIs. The handiest is just inside the **train station**'s main entrance (Mon-Fri 8:00-21:00, Sat-Sun 9:00-18:00, tel. 069/212-38800, www.frankfurt-tourismus.de). Another TI is on **Römerberg square** (Mon-Fri 9:30-17:30, Sat-Sun 10:00-16:00); there's also one at the **airport**. At any TI, buy the city/subway map (the inexpensive basic version is fine). The TI also offers city bus tours and walking tours (see "Tours in Frankfurt," later).

Discount Deals: Two passes sold at TIs are good deals and worth considering if you'll be taking public transportation and visiting several sights. The **Museumsufer Ticket** covers 34 museums (€18, €28 family ticket; valid 2 consecutive days but can be used Sun and Tue since many are closed Mon). The **Frankfurt Card** gives you a transit pass (including connections to and from the airport), up to 50 percent off major museums, and 20 percent off the TI's walking tours, which virtually pays for the pass (€10.50/1 day,

€15.50/2 days; group rate for 2-5 people-€22/1 day, €32/2 days). A third pass, the **RheinMainCard,** is worthwhile only for travelers with time and interest for farther-flung destinations (€22, €46 group rate for 2-5 people valid 2 days).

ARRIVAL IN FRANKFURT

By Train: Frankfurt's main train station (Hauptbahnhof) bustles with travelers. The TI is in the main hall just inside the front door on the left and lockers are along track 24. Pay WCs and showers are down the stairway by tracks 9 and 10. Inquire about train tickets in the *Reisezentrum,* off the main hall (long hours daily).

Getting out of the station can be a bit tricky. Use the underground passageway *(Bahnhofspassage)* and follow the signs, or better yet, exit straight out the main door located in the middle of the terminal to reach a crosswalk. The station is a 20-minute walk from the convention center *(Messe),* a three-minute subway ride or 20-minute walk from Römerberg, and a 12-minute train ride from the airport. A taxi stand is just outside the main entrance of the train station to your left.

By Car: Follow signs for *Frankfurt,* then *Messe,* and finally *Hauptbahnhof* (train station). The Hauptbahnhof garage (€35/day) is under the station, near most recommended hotels. For information on parking elsewhere in Frankfurt, visit www.parkhausfrankfurt. de.

By Plane: See "Frankfurt Connections," at the end of this chapter.

HELPFUL HINTS

Museum Hours: Most museums are closed Monday. Many stay open until 20:00 on Wednesday.

Festivals and Events: Frankfurt keeps a busy and fun-loving calendar of events. When you're here, be sure to check out what's happening.

Laundry: Located near the train station, **Miele Wash World** is small and often crowded, with loud music from the next-door kiosk likely at night (Moselstrasse 17, by the corner of Münchener Strasse, signs in English). In Sachsenhausen, by the recommended Fichtekränzi restaurant, is a **Wasch Treff** (Wallstrasse 8, instructions in German only). Both are open Monday-Saturday 6:00-23:00 (closed Sun).

Theater: The most active English-language theater on the Continent, **English Theatre Frankfurt** hosts companies from the UK and the US. The quality is good and the delightful theater is small, so it books up well in advance (Gallusanlage 7, closed July-Aug, tel. 069/242-31620, www.english-theatre.de).

Helpful Website: For highlights of the best Frankfurt events

FRANKFURT

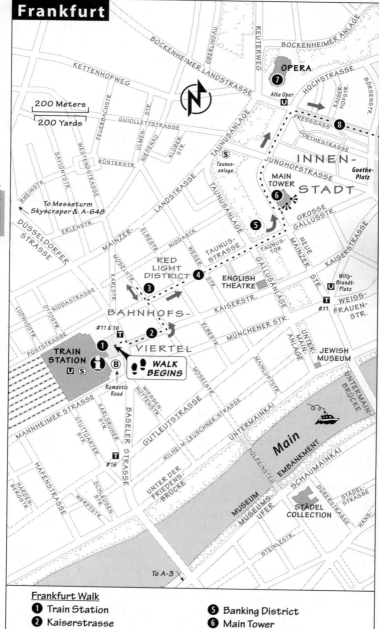

Frankfurt

200 Meters
200 Yards

To Messeturm
Skyscraper & A-648

To A-3

Frankfurt Walk
1. Train Station
2. Kaiserstrasse
3. Junkies
4. Brothels
5. Banking District
6. Main Tower
7. Opera House
8. Fressgass'

FRANKFURT

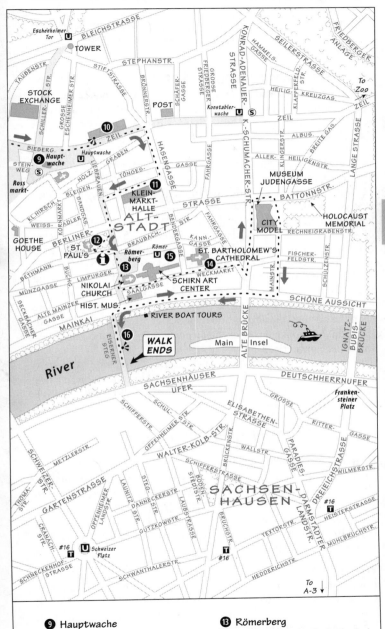

9 Hauptwache

10 Zeil

11 Kleinmarkthalle

12 St. Paul's Church

13 Römerberg

14 St. Bartholomew's Cathedral

15 Altstadt

16 Eiserner Steg Bridge

and sights, get the inside scoop from veteran tour guides Jodean and David Ator at http://frankfurt-on-foot-cityguide.blogspot.com.

GETTING AROUND FRANKFURT

By Public Transportation: Frankfurt's subway (U-Bahn) and suburban train (S-Bahn) network is easy to use, but trams are more convenient and give you a better look at the city. For transit information in English, see www.rmv.de.

For all forms of public transit, buy your tickets *(Fahrkarten)* from an RMV machine (carry cash, some machines don't accept US credit cards). Tickets are issued with a validating stamp already on them, and are valid only immediately after they're bought. Choose the British flag to see the menu in English. If you don't see your destination listed, type "Frankfurt" first, along with the name of your stop. Choose a regular single ticket (€2.75), short ride ticket (€1.85—valid destinations listed on machines), all-day pass (€5.35 without the airport, €9.55 with), or all-day group ticket (up to 5 adults, €11.30 without the airport, €16.80 with). If you'll be going to or from the airport, note that the one-day Frankfurt Card (described earlier, under "Tourist Information") costs just a bit more than the all-day transit pass and includes sightseeing discounts. An individual one-way ticket to the airport costs €4.90 (no group rate for airport-only trips).

By Taxi: A typical ride, such as from the train station to Römerberg square, costs about €7 (up to €10 in slow traffic). A ride to the airport from my recommended hotels is about €30. There is no Uber in Frankfurt.

Tours in Frankfurt

Hop-On, Hop-Off Bus Tours

Double-decker hop-on, hop-off buses give you an easy orientation to Frankfurt. Two bus companies offer one-hour tours, each with about 14 stops. There's also a "Skyline Tour" that focuses on city architecture. For information and tickets, visit the TI (departures daily 10:00-17:00, about every 30 minutes from train station or near St. Paul's Church).

Walking Tours

Frankfurt on Foot's 3.5-hour walks, led by longtime Frankfurt residents (and Ohio natives) Jodean Ator and her husband David, hit the major sights and make Frankfurt's history meaningful (€14, RS%—€1 off with this book, basic walk leaves daily at 10:30 from Römer/Paulskirche tram stop—just show up, private walking tours-€55/hour, mobile 01520-846-4200, www.frankfurtonfoot.

com, info@frankfurtonfoot.com). Their flexible **"Frankfurt Lay-over Tour"** is ideal for those with long Frankfurt Airport layovers and includes pickup and drop-off at the airport.

The **TI** offers one-hour walking tours of the historic center (€10.90, daily at 10:30 and sometimes at 14:30, less frequent off-season). They also give 1.5-hour tours of the reconstructed Dom-Römer Quarter at 14:30 (€12.90, daily June-Oct). Reserve ahead by phone, online, or via email (20 percent discount with Frankfurt Card, tours depart from the Römerberg TI; tel. 069/2123-8800, www.frankfurt-tourismus.de, info@infofrankfurt.de).

Local Guide

Elisabeth Lücke loves her city and shares it very well (€70/hour, cash only, reserve in advance, tel. 06196/45787, mobile 0173-913-3157, www.elisabeth-luecke.de, elisabeth.luecke@t-online.de). She enjoys tailoring tours (for example, to the IG Farben building, a.k.a. the "Pentagon of Europe") for military personnel once based around here.

River Boat Tours

These tours are relaxing but pretty boring (with no medieval castles in sight). You can go an hour in either direction or take a grand two-hour ride (departures from near the Eiserner Steg pedestrian bridge). You'll see the impressive skyline, but a river ride in the Romantic Rhine gorge is far more interesting.

Frankfurt Walk

This self-guided sightseeing walk, worth ▲▲, shows you the new Frankfurt and the old, as well as its hard edges and softer side. Starting at the main train station (Hauptbahnhof), it takes you past junkies and brothels, up the Main Tower, through the mod-ern shopping and eating districts, and into the lively square at the center of the Old Town (where you could continue on to the Jew-ish Holocaust Memorial), before finishing on a bridge overlooking the city and its river. Allow three leisurely hours to complete the full walk. Ideally, do the walk in the morning when the streets are relatively quiet, and you'll finish near lots of great lunch options. To trace the route, see the "Frankfurt" map earlier in this chapter.

Train Station

Frankfurt has Germany's busiest train station: 350,000 travelers make their way to 24 platforms to catch 1,800 trains every day. Hop a train and you can be in either Paris or Berlin in around four hours. While it was big news when it opened in the 1890s, it's a dead-end terminus station, which, with today's high-speed trains, makes it outdated. Complaining that it takes an extra 20 minutes to stop here, railway officials threatened to have the speedy ICE trains bypass Frankfurt altogether unless it dug a tunnel to allow for a faster pass-through stop. But this proved too expensive, and—while some trains stop only at the pass-through airport station—most fast trains begrudgingly serve downtown Frankfurt.

Leaving through the front door, walk directly away from the station to the traffic island facing the pedestrian Kaiserstrasse, and turn to look back at the building's Neo-Renaissance facade—a style popular with Industrial Revolution-era architects. This classic late-19th-century glass-and-iron construction survived World War II. High above, a statue of Atlas carries the world—but only with some heavy-duty help: Green copper figures representing steam power and electricity pitch in. The 1890s were a confident age, when people believed that technology would solve the world's problems.

• With your back to the station, look down...

Kaiserstrasse

This grand 19th-century boulevard features appropriately elegant facades that were designed to dress up the approach to what was a fine new station. Towering above and beyond the 100-year-old buildings are the skyscrapers of Frankfurt's banking district. Until a few years ago, the street was rife with local riffraff. But city officials have directed that crowd a couple of blocks to the left, and Kaiserstrasse is fast becoming a people-friendly eating zone.

Warning and Alternate Route: This walk now goes into a neighborhood of hard-drug users and sex workers. If you use common sense, it's not dangerous, but it can be unnerving and creepy at any time of day.

If you'd rather **go directly to the Banking District** and the Main Tower, simply walk straight down Kaiserstrasse four blocks to the park and skip ahead to the "Banking District" section, later in this walk.

• Walk down Kaiserstrasse, one block away from the station. If you're *game, jog left on Moselstrasse and walk a block to the corner of Tau-nusstrasse. This is where the city contains and controls its sex-and-drug scene. To the right, Taunusstrasse is lined half with brothels and half with bank towers. And across Taunusstrasse and farther down Mosel-strasse is a heroin-maintenance clinic, known here as a "drug-consump-tion room."*

▲Junkies

A half-block down Moselstrasse, you'll probably see a gang con-gregating near one of several **"junkie cafés"** in Frankfurt (no pho-tos allowed). In the 1980s Frankfurt was plagued by one of the largest open drug markets in Europe. Its parks (and police) were overwhelmed with needle addicts. Then Frankfurt decided to get creative, take the crime out of the equation, and go for a pragmatic harm-reduction approach.

In 1992, Frankfurt began offering "pump rooms" to its hard-drug users. The idea: Provide a safe haven for addicts (mostly her-oin, but also crack and methadone) to hygienically maintain their habit. Heroin addicts still buy their stuff on the street, but inject it here with clean needles, with medical help standing by, and a place to stay if needed. It's strictly not for first-time users and no dealing or sharing of drugs is allowed. These centers provide a safe and caring place for addicts to go to maintain their habit and get counseling and medical help.

These days, overdose deaths are down 75 percent in general, and there's never been a death in a drug-consumption room. Lo-cals consider the program a success and are accustomed to wasted people congregating in neighborhoods like this one. While un-sightly, the compassionate harm-reduction approach that much of Europe uses to deal with this problem saves lives. Meanwhile, the US continues to suffer about double the heroin-related deaths per capita as Europe.

• *Now for the sex. Take a right on Tau-nusstrasse and walk to Elbestrasse.*

▲▲Brothels

From Taunusstrasse, look (or detour) left down Elbestrasse, to see a row of high-rise brothels, or **"eros towers."** With all the businessmen coming into town, Frankfurt found there was no ef-fective way to outlaw prostitution. So the city (like any German city over a certain population threshold) decided to funnel sex workers into what it calls a "tolerance area."

FRANKFURT

About 20 five-story brothels fill original, late-19th-century apartment flats within a block of this spot. Legal since 2002, prostitution is big business here. The women, who are mostly from Eastern Europe, Latin America, and Thailand (only about 2 percent are from Germany), essentially run their own little businesses. They charge around €20 for services and rent their rooms for about €130 a day. It's said that they cover their rent by the end of the businessmen's lunch break (look at the bank towers nearby). German sex workers get health care just like any other workers and pay taxes (on €14 billion of declared income each year).

Crazy Sexy, at Elbestrasse 51, is the biggest of these brothels, with 180 rooms. The first three floors are for women. The fourth floor is for transsexuals. (I was told, "A sex change is expensive, and many workers are making money to pay for their operation.") While it's safe to discreetly climb through these towers, the experience isn't for everyone. And the aggressive women at the neighboring strip shows can be unsettling.

Ever since the Middle Ages, Frankfurt's prostitution industry has gone hand-in-hand with its trade fairs. Today, prostitution thrives with the *Messe* (convention center). Both hotels and sex workers double their prices during big trade fairs, and business varies with the theme of the trade show—the auto show is boom time and the butchers' convention is famously hungry, but Frankfurt's massive book fair is a bust.

To the right of Taunusstrasse, at Elbestrasse 31, is a strip joint called **Pik-Dame.** Old-timers are nostalgic about this lone remnant from "the good old days" in the years after World War II, when 30,000 US soldiers stationed in Frankfurt provided a stimulus for this neighborhood's economy. When the troops left, the Russian mob moved in, replacing any old-time gentility with a criminal and thuggish edge. (Note that there's another drug-consumption center across the street from Pik-Dame.)

Also across the street (at Elbestrasse 34), look for an inconspicuous, dark door, which leads to a cocktail bar, **The Kinly.** Like a Prohibition-era speakeasy, it has no signs, just a call button by the door. Press it, wait for the door to open, then descend the stairs into a cozy, softly lit salon right out of the 1920s (Mon-Sat 19:00-late, closed Sun).

• *Enough sex and drugs. Back on Taunusstrasse, continue out of the red light district and into the banking district. Look up and see why this city (on the Main River) is nicknamed "Mainhattan." Cross the street to the park.*

▲Banking District

Find the statue of the poet Schiller (a Romantic and friend of Goethe), on your left. This park is part of a greenbelt that encircles

FRANKFURT

the old center and marks the site of Frankfurt's medieval moat and fortifications. These walls (along with many castles on the Rhine) were destroyed by the French in 1806. Napoleon had just beaten the Austrians and Russians at Austerlitz, and, since he had the upper hand, he figured it was wise to preemptively obliterate any German fortifications that might haunt him if the Germans turned against France in the future.

The park is the center of Frankfurt's banking district. The post-WWII Marshall Plan was administered from here—requiring fancy money-handling. And the mighty deutsche mark was born in a 1930s-era building facing the park (in the third building, a low Art Deco mansion, now a Deutsche Bundesbank headquarters, on the left of the square as you entered). After World War II, Germany's economy was in chaos. In 1948, the US gave it a complete currency transfer—like a blood transfusion—literally printing up the new deutsche marks and shipping them across the Atlantic to inject them from here directly into the German economy. As if catching water from a fountain, banks naturally grew up around this square.

But Frankfurt was "Bankfurt" long before World War II. This was the Rothschilds' hometown. Born in Frankfurt's Jewish ghetto in 1744, Mayer Rothschild went from being a pauper to the richest banker in the world. His five sons set up businesses in Rome, London, Paris, and Vienna, and in two generations the Rothschild banking dynasty was established. (Their former palace now houses Frankfurt's Jewish Museum, described later, under "Sights in Frankfurt"). Today, locals call Frankfurt's legion of bankers "penguins," as they all dress the same. Tour guides here talk of banks as part of the cultural soil (the way French Riviera guides talk of the big yachts).

Beyond the statue of Schiller stand the twin towers of the Deutsche Bank (not to be confused with the DB—Deutsche Bahn—tower to your left). This country's #1 bank, its assets are greater than the annual budget of the German government. If money makes the world go round, the decisions that spin Germany are made in Frankfurt.

Make a 360-degree spin and survey all the bank towers. Notice the striking architecture. By law, no German worker can be kept out of natural light for more than four hours, so work environments are filled with windows. And, as you can see, Germans like their skyscrapers with windows that open.

• *Find the skyscraper with the red-and-white candy cane on top. That's your destination—the Main Tower. To reach it, continue straight along Taunustor a block, then turn left on Neue Mainzer Strasse and look for the tower symbol on the doors on the right.*

▲▲Main Tower

Finished in 2000, this tower houses the Helaba Bank and offers the best (and only public) open-air viewpoint from the top of a Frankfurt skyscraper. A 55-second, ear-popping elevator ride to the 54th floor (watch the meter on the wall as you ascend) and then 50 stairs take you to the rooftop, 650 feet above the city.

Cost and Hours: €7.50, 20 percent discount with Frankfurt Card; Sun-Thu 10:00-21:00, Fri-Sat until 23:00; closes earlier off-season and during bad weather; enter at Neue Mainzer Strasse 52, between Taunustor and Junghofstrasse, tel. 069/3650-4878, www.maintower.de.

◐ Self-Guided Spin-Tour: Here, from Frankfurt's ultimate viewpoint, survey the city by circling clockwise, starting with the biggest skyscraper (with the yellow emblem).

Designed by Norman Foster (of Berlin Reichstag and London City Hall fame), the **Commerzbank building** was finished in 1997. It's 985 feet high, with nine winter gardens spiraling up its core and windows that open. It's considered the first ecological skyscraper...radically "green" in its day. Just to the left is Römerberg—the Old Town center (the half-timbered houses huddled around the red-and-white church with a green spire; we'll visit there soon).

The **Museum Embankment** (see "Sights in Frankfurt," later) lines Schaumainkai on the far side of the Main River, just beyond the Taunus Tower.

The Rhine-Main **airport,** off in the distance (like a city in the forest), is the largest employment complex in Germany, with 70,000 workers. Frankfurt's massive train station dominates the foreground. From the station, the grand Kaiserstrasse cuts through the city to Römerberg.

The **Frankfurt fair** *(Messe),* marked by the brown skyscraper with the pointy top, is a huge convention center—the size of 40 soccer fields. It sprawls behind the skyscraper that looks like a classical column sporting a visor-like capital. (The protruding lip of the capital is heated so that icicles don't form, break off, and impale people on the street below.) Frankfurt's fair originated in 1240, when the emperor promised all participating merchants safe passage. The glassy black twin towers of the Deutsche Bank in the foreground (nicknamed "Debit and Credit") are typical of mid-1980s mirrored architecture.

The **West End,** with vast green spaces and the telecommunications tower, is Frankfurt's priciest residential quarter. The city's most enjoyable zone cuts from the West End to the right. Stretching from the classic-looking Opera House below are broad and people-filled boulevards made to order for eating and shopping. Find the "Beach Club" filling the rooftop of a parking garage with white tents, two pools, and colorful lounge chairs. This is a popular family zone by day and a chic club after dark.

From here, you can see how the city walls, demolished in 1806, left a string of green zones arcing out from the river. This defined the city limits in the 19th century.

Take a moment from this vantage point to trace the rest of this walk: from the Opera House, along the tree-lined eating and shopping boulevards to St. Paul's Church and Römerberg. After side-tripping from Römerberg out to the cathedral, we'll finish on Eiserner Steg, the iron pedestrian bridge over the Main River.

Now look east, farther out along the river, to the glistening twin towers (standing all alone). At 600 feet tall, these are the striking headquarters of the **European Central Bank.**

As you leave the Main Tower, step into the **Helaba Bank** lobby (next door over from base of elevator). A black-and-white mosaic filling the wall shows cultural superstars of 20th-century Frankfurt, from composer Paul Hindemith to industrialist and humanitarian Oskar Schindler to Anne Frank (see the key on the post nearby for a who's who).

• *Exit right from the Main Tower and continue walking along Neue Mainzer Strasse (crossing Junghofstrasse) for a couple of blocks, to where you see a large square open to your left. Across the square is the Opera House.*

Frankfurt's Good-Living People Zone

Opera House (Alte Oper): Finished in 1880, Frankfurt's opera house celebrated German high culture and the newly created nation. Mozart and Goethe flank the entrance, reminders that this is a house of both music and theater. On a hot day, people of all ages cool their heels in the refreshing fountain in the plaza out front. The original opera house was gutted in World War II. Over the objections of a mayor nicknamed "Dynamite Rudi," the city rebuilt it in the original style, and it opened in 1981. Underneath is a U-Bahn station (Alte Oper).

• *Facing the Opera, turn right down Frankfurt's famous...*

Fressgass': The official names for this pedestrian street are Grosse Bockenheimer Strasse and Kalbächer Gasse...but everyone in Frankfurt calls it the Fressgass', roughly "Feeding Street." Herds of bank employees come here on their lunch breaks to fill their bellies before returning for another few hours of cud-chewing at their computers. It's packed gable-to-gable with eateries and shoulder-to-shoulder with workers wolfing cheap sandwiches, plates of

Asian food, and more. It also offers great people-watching. Join in if you're hungry—or wait for more eating options in a couple of blocks.

• *Fressgass' leads to a square called Rathenauplatz, but it's known as Goethe Platz for its central statue. Cross the square and continue straight—the pedestrian street is now called Biebergasse—another block to the...*

Hauptwache: The small, red-and-white building—which has given its name to the square (and the subway station below it)—was built in 1730 to house the Frankfurt city militia. Now it's a café. The square, entirely closed to traffic, is one of the city's hubs.

• *To the right, at the south side of the square, is the Protestant Katharinenkirche, which was destroyed in the bombing raids of March 1944 and rebuilt after the war. Straight ahead of you is a boulevard called the...*

Zeil: This tree-lined pedestrian drag is Frankfurt's main shopping street. Crowds swirl through the Galeria Kaufhof department store, the Zeil Galerie, and the MyZeil shopping center (the one with the glassy hole in its wall) along the left side of the street. MyZeil has a huge glass atrium shaped like two massive funnels—and can be a mesmerizing sight on a rainy day. A really long escalator, claiming to be the longest in Germany (behind the much shorter twin set by the door) leads straight to the top-floor food court (with good, free WC). On your way, stop on the fourth floor and head toward the streetside windows to see a huge aerial photo of Frankfurt on the floor.

This top-down view shows the surprising amount of green space there is in this city.

Lunch and Views at Department Stores: The Galeria Kaufhof has a recommended rooftop cafeteria, Leonhard's (good for lunch or just the views). There's a supermarket with a snack stand and seating in the basement of the MyZeil shopping center (Mon-Sat 7:00-24:00, closed Sun).

• *Continue down Zeil a block to the fountain at the next intersection. Turn right on Hasengasse. In the distance is the lacy red-brick spire of the cathedral. Halfway there, after about two blocks, find the low-key green entrance to Kleinmarkthalle on the right. Enter the market (pay WC downstairs at entry).*

Kleinmarkthalle: This delightful, old-school market was saved from developers by local outcry, and to this day it's a neighborhood favorite. Explore and sample your way through the ground floor. It's an adventure in fine eating (with a line of simple eateries upstairs, too; see "Eating in Frankfurt," later) and a delight for photographers. The far wall is filled with a fun piece of art offering a bird's-eye view of Frankfurt over a charming montage of the many ways locals love their hometown.

• *Exit the Kleinmarkthalle opposite where you entered. Angle right, and climb five steps into a square (Leibfrauenberg) with a red-brick fountain and the 14th-century Church of Our Lady (rebuilt after World War II). On the far side is Lebkuchen-Schmidt, a fun shop selling traditional gingerbread, a local favorite. Turn left and head downhill on Neue Kräme, then cross Berliner Strasse to Paulsplatz.*

FRANKFURT

▲St. Paul's Church (Paulskirche)

To your right, the former church dominating the square is known as the "cradle of German democracy." It was here, during the political upheaval of 1848, that the first freely elected National Assembly met and the first German Constitution was drafted, paving the way for a united Germany in 1871. Following its destruction by Allied bombs in 1944, the church became the first historic building in the city to be rebuilt. This was a symbolic statement from the German people that they wanted to be free (as they had demonstrated here in 1848), democratic...and no longer fascist. Around the outside of the building, you'll see reliefs honoring people who  contributed to the German nation, including Theodor Heuss, the first president, and John F. Kennedy, who spoke here on June 25, 1963.

Step inside; the entrance is around to the left (free, daily 10:00-17:00). Displays described in English tell the story of 1848. Check out the circular mural from the 1980s. Called *The March of Members of Parliament,* it was controversial when unveiled. Commissioned to honor the political heroes of 1848, the portraits are cartoonish figures, with faces hinting of contemporary politicians. Political leaders seem to sneer at the working class, and two naked men who look like they're having sex represent the forces of democracy and monarchy fighting within Germany. Upstairs is a 900-seat assembly hall with no decor except the flags of the 16 states of the Federal Republic of Germany.

FRANKFURT

• *Walk across the square. If you need a break, a variety of eateries offer inviting seating that's perfect for some fun people-watching. Then, cross the next street and tram tracks and you'll enter what's left of Frankfurt's Old Town.*

▲Römerberg

Frankfurt's market square was the birthplace of the city. This is the site of the first trade fairs (12th century), bank (1405), and stock exchange (1585). Now, crowds of tourists convene here. Römerberg's central statue is the goddess of justice without her customary blindfold. She oversees the Town Hall, which itself oversees trade. The Town Hall *(Römer)* houses the *Kaisersaal,* or Imperial Hall, where Holy Roman Emperors celebrated

their coronations. Today, the *Römer* houses the city council and mayor's office. Marriages must be performed in a civil ceremony here to be legal, so you'll see lots of brides and grooms celebrating outside. The cute row of half-timbered homes (rebuilt in 1983) opposite the *Römer* is typical of Frankfurt's quaint old center before the square was completely destroyed in World War II.

The Gothic red-and-white Old Nikolai Church (Alte Nikolaikirche, with fine stained glass from the 1920s by a local artist) dates from the 13th century and was restored after the war. Behind it, closer to the river, is the new **Frankfurt Historical Museum** (€8, Tue-Fri 10:00-18:00, Wed until 21:00, Sat-Sun 11:00-19:00, closed Mon).

Hosting everything from Christmas markets to violent demonstrations, this square is the beating heart of Frankfurt. In its center, the metal plaque that looks like a large manhole cover reminds us that a Nazi book-burning took place in the square on May 10, 1933. Around the edge of the plaque is a quote from the German poet Heinrich Heine, who presciently pointed out that it's a short step from burning books to burning people.

• *Facing the Town Hall, the river and the bridge where this walk ends are just two blocks to the left. But first, we'll take a short detour. Turn left past the Old Nikolai Church and walk through the courtyard of the Schirn Art Center to the big red...*

St. Bartholomew's Cathedral (Kaiserdom)

Holy Roman Emperors were elected at this Catholic church starting in 1152 and crowned here between 1562 and 1792. The cathedral was gutted by fire in 1867 and had to be rebuilt. It was seriously damaged in World War II, but repaired and reopened in 1953. Though the cathedral is free, you must pay to access two sights within the church: a museum (not particularly interesting) and a 328-step tower climb with city views at the top.

Cost and Hours: Cathedral-free, Mon-Thu and Sat 9:00-20:00, Fri and Sun from 13:30, www.dom-frankfurt.de; museum-€4, Tue-Fri 10:00-17:00, Sat-Sun from 11:00, closed Mon, enter from church vestibule, www.dommuseum-frankfurt.de; tower-€5, daily 9:00-18:00, weather permitting, shorter hours Nov-March; tel. 069/7808-9255, www.domturm-frankfurt.de.

Visiting the Cathedral: Enter on the side opposite the river. Note the painted white lines that imitate mortar between stones.

This illusionist architecture was a popular technique for churches. Frescoes from the 15th century survive (flanking the high altar and ringing the choir). They show 27 scenes from the life of St. Bartholomew. The Electors Chapel (to the right of the altar) is where the electors convened to choose the Holy Roman Emperor in the Middle Ages. Everything of value that could be moved was taken out of the church before the WWII bombs came. The delightful sandstone Chapel of Sleeping Mary (to the left of the high altar), carved and painted in the 15th century, was too big to move—so it was fortified with sandbags. The altarpiece and stained glass next to it survived the bombing. As you wander, appreciate the colorful and extravagant tombstones embedded in the walls when the church's cemetery was emptied.

• *Exit the cathedral where you entered and turn left, passing the red-and-white half-timbered, gold-trimmed house that marks the start of the...*

Altstadt ("New Old Town")

This "new" development (officially called the DomRömer Quarter)—70 years in the making—is a reconstruction of the half-timbered Old Town destroyed during World War II. Following the war, some locals wanted to rebuild the original buildings, while others wanted to modernize. The compromise was an ugly concrete building in typical 1970s style that remained until 2010, when reconstruction of this more modern version of the Old Town began.

Pause at the fountain in the center of the main square (a former poultry market), featuring a statue of Friedrich Stoltze, a writer and poet who was born in the former Old Town. Notice the buildings' eclectic mix of colors and styles, some with slate roofs, others with red sandstone facades, and others with doors made from

300-year-old oak. This mix of new and old architecture is a micro-cosm of today's Frankfurt.

Before the war, this was a lively center of pubs, small business-es, and workshops. While today's Altstadt feels a bit saccharin, the city hopes this mix of reconstructed and new buildings will return the square to something close to its former character.

As you pass Stoltze, turn left to do a loop around the develop-ment, checking out the red sandstone columns at #9. Keep turn-ing left until you're parallel with the Schirn Art Center. Look for an opening behind the last set of new buildings on the right: The Stadthaus am Markt is a public area and event space floating above the "Franconofurd"—Roman ruins that were revealed by the Old Town's destruction.

• *Returning to the cathedral, you can turn left on Weckmarkt and con-tinue a couple of blocks to visit the Jewish Holocaust Memorial, and/or the Frankfurt City Model (both free and described later, under "Sights in Frankfurt"). Or head down to the river, turn right, and walk along the pleasant riverfront park to the next bridge. Head out to its center.*

Eiserner Steg Bridge
This iron bridge, the city's second oldest, dates to 1869. (The oldest is just upstream: the Alte Brücke, site of the first "Frank ford"—a fifth-century crossing.) From the middle of the bridge, survey the skyline and enjoy the lively scene along the riverbanks of Frankfurt. These grassy areas are some of the most pleasant parts of the city.

• *For a quick return to your starting point at the main train station (Hauptbahnhof), walk back to Römerberg and take the U-Bahn or board tram #11 or #12.*

Sights in Frankfurt

NEAR RÖMERBERG
▲Goethe House (Goethehaus)
Johann Wolfgang von Goethe (GUH-teh; 1749-1832), a scientist, minister, poet, lawyer, politician, and playwright, was a towering figure in the early Romantic Age; his two-part tragedy, *Faust,* is a masterpiece of world literature. His birthplace, now a fine museum, is furnished as it was in the mid-18th century, when the boy des-tined to become the "German Shakespeare" grew up here.

Borrow a laminated card at the bottom of the stairs for a re-freshingly brief commentary on each of the 16 rooms. Since noth-ing's roped off and there are no posted signs, it's easy to picture real people living here. Goethe's father dedicated his life and wealth to cultural pursuits, and his mother told young Johann Wolfgang fairy tales every night, stopping just before the ending so that the boy could exercise his own creativity. Goethe's family gave him all the money he needed to travel and learn. His collection of 2,000 books was sold off in 1795. In recent decades, more than half of these have been located and repurchased by the museum (you'll see them in the library). This building honors the man who inspired the Goethe-Institut, which is dedicated to keeping the German language strong.

Cost and Hours: €7, Mon-Sat 10:00-18:00, Sun until 17:30, €3 high-tech but easy-to-use and informative audioguide, English booklet has same info as free laminated cards—worthwhile only as a souvenir; 15-minute walk from Hauptbahnhof up Kaiserstrasse, turn right on Am Salzhaus to Grosser Hirschgraben 23; tel. 069/138-800, www.goethehaus-frankfurt.de.

Schirn Art Center (Schirn Kunsthalle)

This facility is one of Europe's most respected homes of modern and contemporary art. Rotating exhibits pay homage to everything and everyone from Kandinsky and Kahlo to contemporary artists, movements, and topics.

Cost and Hours: €7-10 depending on exhibits, Tue-Sun 10:00-19:00, Wed-Thu until 22:00, closed Mon, Römerberg, tel. 069/299-882-112, www.schirn.de.

IN THE FORMER JEWISH GHETTO

During the early Middle Ages, the most important Jewish communities north of the Alps were along the Rhine, in towns like Cologne, Speyer, Worms, and Frankfurt. Even after the center of Jewish life moved east to Poland and Lithuania, Frankfurt had a large and prominent Jewish community, which included the Rothschilds (the famous banking family).

You can get a feel for Frankfurt's Jewish history with a visit to the Museum Judengasse and the nearby Jewish Holocaust Memorial (at the old Jewish cemetery, just down Battonnstrasse). These sights are a short walk (or one tram stop) east of Römerberg and St. Bartholomew's Cathedral.

▲Jewish Holocaust Memorial, Jewish Cemetery, and Museum Judengasse

This memorial to Frankfurt's Jewish community—devastated by the Holocaust—marks the site of the old Jewish ghetto and where the city's main Börneplatz Synagogue once stood. Commemorating 12,000 murdered Jews, it's a powerful and evocative collection of images.

Museum Judengasse's permanent exhibit focuses on Jewish life in Frankfurt, covering everything from work and school to the arts to relations between the community and Frankfurt's government. The exhibit is built around and within a section of excavated ruins of Europe's oldest Jewish ghetto, where 4,000 people once lived

FRANKFURT

on a quarter-mile stretch of street. You'll see artifacts found in the ruins. Interactive exhibits let you listen to evocative music and Jewish hymns.

Back outside, around the old Jewish cemetery is the Wall of Names, with a tiny tombstone for each Frankfurt Jew deported and murdered by the Nazis (with location and date of death, if known). Pebbles atop each tomb represent Jewish prayers. The memorial gives each victim the dignity of a tombstone and of being named, while a databank inside the adjacent Museum Judengasse keeps their memory alive with a record of everything

known about each person. The markers are alphabetical by last name: Look for Anne Frank (Annelies Marie Frank) about halfway between the cemetery entrance and the end of the wall. The Frank family left Frankfurt for Amsterdam in 1933 and eventually went into hiding. Upon discovery by the Nazis, Anne and her sister were sent to Bergen-Belsen, where she died of typhus.

By peeking through the locked black-metal gate into the cemetery, you can see a few original tombstones that survived the Nazi rampage. In the tree-filled square is a stone tower, built with foundation stones from homes excavated from the Jewish ghetto. The gravel is designed to evoke train tracks and the deportation of so many people to concentration camps.

The paved section marks the footprint of the Börneplatz Synagogue, destroyed on November 9, 1938—a night traditionally known as Kristallnacht. (Because people's lives were also destroyed on that night along with lots of windows and glass, the preferred name is "Pogrom Night.") A plaque on the wall opposite recalls this terrible event. In the wake of World War II, American troops made Frankfurters memorialize each synagogue they destroyed with a plaque like this.

Cost and Hours: Wall of Names and cemetery-always free and viewable (key for cemetery available when museum is open); museum-€6, Tue 10:00-20:00, Wed-Sun until 18:00, closed Mon; Battonnstrasse 47, tel. 069/212-70790, www.museumjudengasse.de.

▲Frankfurt City Model

This ever-evolving model, unrelated to the Jewish story, is next to the Jewish Holocaust Memorial in the City Planning Office (Stadtplanungsamt), located in the same building as the Museum Judengasse. Enter through the frosted sliding doors and step left past the receptionist into an atrium to view a 30-by-20-foot layout on a 1:500 scale. Frankfurt's inner-city skyscrapers are marked *Planungsdezernat*. Since 1960 this model has helped planners envision and track the development of the city and its many massive building projects—even seeing where shadows of new buildings  will fall. Red buildings are those under construction (the city has plans for 20 more skyscrapers in the next decade).

Cost and Hours: Free, Mon-Fri 8:30-18:00, closed Sat-Sun, Kurt-Schumacher-Strasse 10.

NEAR THE RIVER, ON THE NORTH BANK
Jewish Museum (Jüdisches Museum)
This museum, which may be open after a lengthy renovation when you visit, is housed in the former Rothschild family palace, along the river between Römerberg and the train station (Untermainkai 14, tel. 069/2123-5000, www.juedischesmuseum.de).

Riverside Promenade
Just across the road from the Jewish Museum is a lovely riverside promenade—a perfect place to rest your feet and watch people and planes go by.

ACROSS THE RIVER, ON THE SOUTH BANK
▲Schaumainkai and Frankfurt's Museum Embankment (Museumsufer)
The Schaumainkai riverside promenade (across the river from Römerberg over the Eiserner Steg pedestrian bridge, and then to the right) is great for an evening stroll or people-watching on any sunny day. Keep your eyes peeled for nude sunbathers. Every other Saturday, the museum strip street is closed off for a sprawling flea market, and in late August a weekend cultural festival brings food, art, and music to "museum row."

Nine museums in striking buildings line the Main River along Schaumainkai. In the 1980s, Frankfurt decided that it wanted to buck its "Bankfurt" and "Krankfurt" (*krank* means "sick") image. It went on a culture kick and devoted 11 percent of the city budget to arts and culture. The result: Frankfurt has become a city of art. These nine museums (covering topics such as architecture, film, world cultures, and great European masters—the Städel Collection) and a dozen others are all well-described in the TI's *Museum-*

sufer brochure. Of these, a visit to the Städel (listed next) is most worthwhile.

Cost and Hours: All museums here are covered by the Museumsufer Ticket (for details see "Tourist Information," earlier in this chapter); most museums open Tue-Sun 10:00-17:00, Wed until 20:00, closed Mon; www.kultur-frankfurt.de.

Getting There: Take tram #15 or #16 to the Otto-Hahn-Platz stop; bus #46 to the Städel stop; or U-1, U-2, U-3, or U-8 to the Schweizer Platz stop. Or, walk: It's 15 minutes from the Hauptbahnhof via Holbeinsteg Bridge, or just a few minutes' walk over the Eiserner Steg pedestrian bridge from the center of Frankfurt.

▲Städel Museum

With an enormous yet approachable collection spanning Old Masters to modern day, this museum offers up a one-stop European art retrospective.

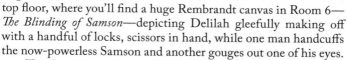

Cost and Hours: €14, open Tue-Sun 10:00-18:00, Thu-Fri until 21:00, closed Mon; audioguide-€4, on-site restaurant; Schaumainkai 63, tel. 069/605-098-0299, www.staedelmuseum.de.

Visiting the Museum: Begin with Old Masters on the top floor, where you'll find a huge Rembrandt canvas in Room 6— *The Blinding of Samson*—depicting Delilah gleefully making off with a handful of locks, scissors in hand, while one man handcuffs the now-powerless Samson and another gouges out one of his eyes.

The floor below has works by Renoir, Paul Klee, and Marc Chagall, as well as a female head sculpture by Picasso and his 1909 Cubist portrait of Fernande Olivier. Don't miss the canvases by Max Beckmann, who lived in Frankfurt for nearly 20 years before the Nazis banned his work, classifying his art as "degenerate." *Frankfurt Main Station*—looking not at all seedy—was done from memory while Beckmann lived in exile in Amsterdam. In Room 11, *Dog Lying in the Snow* by Franz Marc (who founded the Blue Rider group with Kandinsky) is one of the museum's most popular paintings.

On the museum's lower level, you'll find contemporary work—including more by Picasso, a skinny Giacometti sculpture, and avant-garde installations.

Sleeping in Frankfurt

Sleeping in Frankfurt is a gamble: The city's numerous trade fairs *(Messe)* send hotel prices skyrocketing—a €70 double can suddenly shoot up to €300. For an exact schedule, visit www.messefrankfurt. com (scroll down to "Messe Frankfurt Calendar"). During trade fairs, it's best to skip Frankfurt altogether and stay in Würzburg, Bacharach, or St. Goar.

When trade fairs aren't in town, room prices in most Frankfurt hotels fluctuate €10-50 with the day of the week. If you'll be staying overnight in Frankfurt during a nonconvention summer weekend, you can land a great place relatively cheaply. Frankfurt hotels are business-oriented, so many are empty and desperate for guests from Friday night to Monday morning. Although the price categories listed are typical, varying demand may skew them higher or lower.

Keep overnights in Frankfurt to a minimum: Pleasant Rhine and Romantic Road towns are just a quick drive or train ride away, offering a mom-and-pop welcome that you won't find here in the big city.

NEAR THE TRAIN STATION

The following places are within a few blocks of the train station and its fast and handy train to the airport (to sleep even closer to the airport, see "Sleeping at or near Frankfurt Airport," later in this chapter). The Hamburger Hof, Bristol, and Topas hotels are on the north (and most sedate) side of the station. The Manhattan, Concorde, and EasyHotel are along the busy streets just to the northeast of the station. The Victoria, Holiday Inn Express, Ibis Styles, and Five Elements hostel are in the multiethnic neighborhood east of the station. The Ibis Hotel Frankfurt Centrum is south of the station, close to the Main River and within walking distance of the Museum Embankment (Museumsufer). For locations, see the "Frankfurt Hotels & Restaurants" map.

All these listings are well-run and feel safe and respectable. I like staying in this colorful and convenient neighborhood (which gets more gentrified every year). But the red light district is close by, with gritty clubs and hard-drug users. Don't wander into seedy-feeling streets, and use care and common sense after dark.

$$ Hotel Concorde, across the street from the station and then a few doors down Karlstrasse in a restored 1890s building, offers 45 air-conditioned rooms and four-star comfort and professionalism, all at a reasonable price (breakfast extra, elevator, Karlstrasse 9, tel. 069/242-4220, www.hotelconcorde.com, info@ hotelconcorde.de, Marc is manager). Exit the station by track 24, cross the street and head right, walking past the Manhattan Hotel and around the corner to the Concorde. A REWE supermarket is across the street.

$$ Hotel Hamburger Hof, right next to the train station but in a quiet and safe-feeling location, has a classy, shiny lobby and 62 modern rooms. The side facing the station is cheerfully sunny, while rooms on the other side are quieter (air-con, elevator, Poststrasse 10, tel. 069/2713-9690, www.hamburgerhof.com, info@hamburgerhof.com). Exit the station by track 24, cross the street, turn left, and walk to the end of the block.

$$ Bristol Hotel is a swanky 145-room place that serves up style and flair, from its nod to Pacific Rim architecture to its spacious breakfast room and relaxing patio bar. It's just two blocks from the station and enjoys quiet and respectable surroundings (air-con, elevator, huge breakfast buffet, Ludwigstrasse 15, tel. 069/242-390, www.bristol-hotel.de, info@bristol-hotel.de). Exit the station by track 24, cross the street, turn left, then right on Ottostrasse, then left on Niddastrasse to Ludwigstrasse.

$$ Victoria Hotel, two blocks from the station along the grand Kaiserstrasse, has 73 rooms and feels a world apart from the red light district a block away (air-con, elevator, Kaiserstrasse 59, entrance on Elbestrasse, tel. 069/273-060, www.victoriahotel.de, info@victoriahotel.de). From the station, go down the escalators to the underground passageway below the station and follow the *Kaiserstrasse* signs.

$$ Manhattan Hotel, with 55 rooms and an energetic vibe, is a few doors from the station on a busy street. Friendly manager Robert tries to greet all of his guests personally (RS%, air-con, elevator, Düsseldorfer Strasse 10, tel. 069/269-5970, www.manhattan-hotel.com, info@manhattan-hotel.com). Exit the station by track 24, cross the street, and go right until you see the hotel; to cross Düsseldorfer Strasse safely, walk up to the tram stop.

$$ Holiday Inn Express Hauptbahnhof has 116 fresh rooms two blocks from the station, in a quiet location just off Münchener Strasse in the Turkish district (air-con, elevator, Elbestrasse 7, tel. 069/8700-3883, www.fmhos.com, frankfurt@fmhos.com). From the front of the station, use the crosswalk by the tram stop and follow the tracks down Münchener Strasse two blocks to Elbestrasse and turn right.

$$ Ibis Styles Frankfurt City is a small step up from the Ibis Hotel (next listing) and is centrally located just a few blocks from the station. Its 96 funky, colorful rooms help you forget that this is a popular chain hotel (air-con, elevator, Moselstrasse 12, tel. 069/6925-6110, https://ibis.accorhotels.com, H7561@accor.com). From the front of the station, use the crosswalk by the tram stop and follow the tracks down Münchener Strasse one block to Moselstrasse and turn right.

$$ Ibis Hotel Frankfurt Centrum is a good value, with 233 rooms on a quiet riverside street away from the station (breakfast extra, elevator, pay parking, Speicherstrasse 4, tel. 069/273-030, https://ibis.accorhotels.com, h1445@accor.com). Exit the station by track 1 and follow busy Baseler Strasse three blocks, then turn right before the river; it's across the street from the green office tower and park.

$ Hotel Topas, a decent budget choice with 33 rooms, is a block north of the train station. Ask for one of the eight back-facing rooms, as they're quieter and cooler in summer (elevator, Niddastrasse 88, tel. 069/230-852, www.hoteltopas.de, hoteltopas@t-online.de). From the station, follow the same directions as for the Bristol Hotel (listed earlier), two doors away.

$ EasyHotel Frankfurt's tiny, no-frills rooms feel as if they were popped out of a plastic mold, right down to the ship's head-style "bathroom pod." Rates can be low if you book early, but are nonrefundable and you'll be charged for add-ons that are normally included at most other hotels (air-con, pay Wi-Fi, pay TV, elevator, pay parking, no breakfast but 20 percent discount at bakery next door, Düsseldorfer Strasse 19, www.easyhotel.com). Exit the station by track 24 and follow Düsseldorfer Strasse two blocks to the Platz der Republik tram stop, which is directly in front of the hotel.

Hostel: A block from the train station, **¢ Five Elements** is clean and modern and feels very safe inside. But because it's smack in the middle of the red light district, families might feel more comfortable elsewhere. Here, too, prices skyrocket during conventions (breakfast extra, private rooms available, elevator, Moselstrasse 40, tel. 069/2400-5885, www.5elementshostel.de, welcome@5elementshostel.de). From the station, exit the underground passage onto Taunusstrasse and go one block to the corner of Moselstrasse; the hostel is across the intersection to your left.

ELSEWHERE IN FRANKFURT

If you're in Frankfurt for one night, stay near the station—but if you're in town for a few days and want to feel like you belong, choose one of the following listings. Hotel Neue Kräme and Hotel Zentrum are near Römerberg, and the Maingau Hotel and the hostel are in the Sachsenhausen district, with lots of local shops and cafés (see "Eating in Frankfurt," later). For locations, see the "Frankfurt Hotels & Restaurants" map.

$$ Hotel Neue Kräme is a quiet little 21-room oasis tucked away above the center of Frankfurt's downtown action, just steps from Römerberg. Friendly staff welcome guests in this bright and cheerful place (two apartments with kitchen across street, elevator, Neue Kräme 23—look for blue-and-white *hotel* sign out

FRANKFURT

Frankfurt Hotels & Restaurants

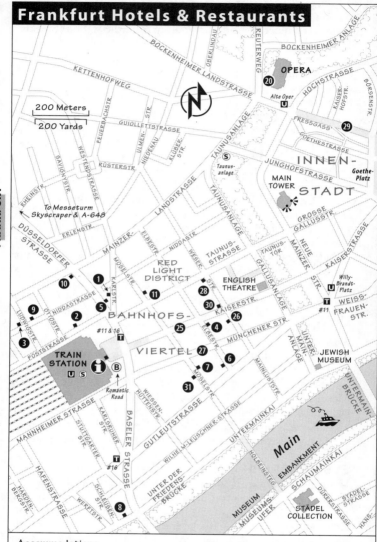

Accommodations

1. Hotel Concorde
2. Hotel Hamburger Hof
3. Bristol Hotel
4. Victoria Hotel
5. Manhattan Hotel
6. Holiday Inn Express Hauptbahnhof
7. Ibis Styles Frankfurt City
8. Ibis Hotel Frankfurt Centrum
9. Hotel Topas
10. EasyHotel Frankfurt
11. Five Elements Hostel
12. Hotel Neue Kräme
13. Hotel Zentrum
14. Maingau Hotel
15. Haus der Jugend Hostel

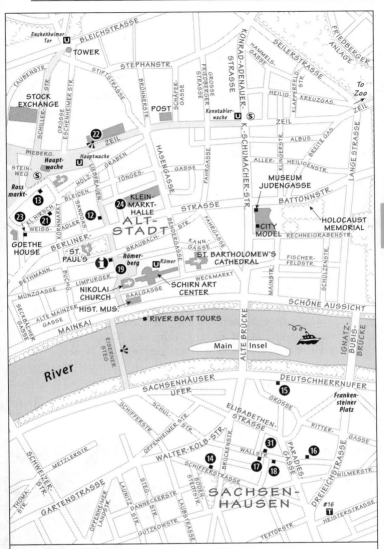

FRANKFURT

Eateries & Other

⑯ Dauth-Schneider
⑰ Atschel
⑱ Fichtekränzi
⑲ Römerberg Eateries
⑳ Restaurant Opéra
㉑ Leib & Seele
㉒ Galeria Kaufhof's Leonhard's Café & Restaurant

㉓ Café Karin
㉔ Kleinmarkthalle Eateries
㉕ Kaiserstrasse Eateries
㉖ L'Emir
㉗ Münchener Strasse Eateries
㉘ Indigo Restaurant
㉙ Fressgass' Eateries
㉚ REWE To Go Minimarket
㉛ Launderette (2)

front, tel. 069/284-046, www.hotel-neuekraeme.de, info@hotel-neuekraeme.de).

$$ Hotel Zentrum offers industrial-chic style hidden on the upper floors of a downtown building. With 29 colorful, modern rooms, it's in a great location near the Hauptwache (family rooms, elevator, free afternoon coffee and cake in lobby, Rossmarkt 7, tel. 069/5050-0190, www.hotel-zentrum.de, info@hotel-zentrum.de, manager Sascha).

$ Maingau Hotel, located across the river in the Sachsen-hausen district, is on a quiet residential street facing a neighborhood park. The 78 rooms are simple and bright. If you're looking for a little tranquility in an authentic residential setting, stay here (elevator, pay parking in nearby garage, Schifferstrasse 38, tel. 069/609-140, www.maingau.de, info@maingau.de). From the station, take tram #16 to the Lokalbahnhof/Textorstrasse stop; the hotel is three blocks away.

Hostel: The **¢ Haus der Jugend** is right along the river and is the only place I list where prices don't go up during conferences (membership required, private rooms available, lunch and dinner available, elevator, 2:00 curfew, Deutschherrnufer 12, tel. 069/610-0150, www.jugendherberge-frankfurt.de, info@hellofrankfurt.de). From the station, exit through the front door, turn right to the bus platforms, and take bus #46 (2/hour, direction: Mühlberg) to the Frankensteiner Platz stop, which is one door from the hostel.

Eating in Frankfurt

Instead of beer-garden ambience, Frankfurt entices visitors and locals to its Sachsenhausen district, across the river, where you'll find lots of characteristic apple-wine pubs (and plenty of other options). This cobbled and cozy neighborhood is the city's traditional eating-and-drinking zone—a great place to spend a warm summer evening.

Apfelwein, drunk around here since Charlemagne's time 1,200 years ago, became more popular in the 16th century, when local grapes were diseased. It enjoyed another boost two centuries later, when a climate change made grape-growing harder. Apple wine is about the strength of beer (5.5 percent alcohol), but like wine, it can be served spiced and warm in winter. This hard cider can be an acquired taste—good luck enjoying it. You'll see locals, who've spent a lifetime learning to like it, grasping their apple wine in *geripptes*—characteristic hatched glasses (which go back to its early days, when this tax-free drink was slurped by greasy-fingered sausage munchers on the streets).

Sachsenhausen is also a good place to sample local cuisine. The culinary pride of Frankfurt is *Grüne Sosse,* a green sauce made of sour cream blended with seven herbs (parsley, chives, watercress, sorrel, borage, chervil, and burnet); it's frequently served with beef, schnitzel, or halved hard-boiled eggs. Another widely available local specialty (for the adventurous) is *Handkäse mit Musik* ("hand cheese with music"—the "music" comes tomorrow), an aged, cylindrical ricotta-like cheese served with onions and vinegar. You can also satisfy your craving for *Leiterchen* here ("miniladders," or spare ribs—surprisingly meaty and salty).

APPLE-WINE PUBS IN SACHSENHAUSEN

The three apple-wine pubs I've listed below all have indoor and outdoor seating in a woodsy, rustic setting. Not just for tourists, these characteristic places are truly popular with Frankfurters, too. To reach them, take bus #46 from the train station (direction: Mühlberg) to Frankensteiner Platz. Or to walk from downtown (20 minutes), cross the river on the pedestrian-only Eiserner Steg bridge or Alte Brücke bridge. For locations, see the "Frankfurt Hotels & Restaurants" map.

$$ Dauth-Schneider has lots of tables outside on the shady, tree-covered square, a large indoor section, and a big and accessible menu. It's my first choice for eating outside on a balmy evening (daily 11:30-24:00, Neuer Wall 5, tel. 069/613-533). Families appreciate the big-city playground across the square from the outdoor tables.

$$ Atschel, across the street and a few doors down, is my Sachsenhausen choice for eating inside. They serve "Frankfurter Schnitzel" with green sauce and other local standards in a handsome dining room and cozy back garden (daily 12:00-24:00, kitchen closes at 22:30, cash only, Wallstrasse 7, tel. 069/619-201).

$$ Fichtekränzi, across the alley from Atschel, is open evenings only. It offers the typical specialties and some lighter fare, both in its cozy, bench-filled beer hall and outside under the trees. The atmosphere is young and relaxed—expect to share a table and make some new friends (Mon-Sat 17:00-23:00, Sun from 16:00, cash only, Wallstrasse 5, tel. 069/612-778).

Pub Crawl: Irish pubs and salsa bars clutter the pedestrian zone around Grosse Rittergasse and Frankensteiner Strasse; if you're looking for a place to do a pub crawl, this is it.

DINING DOWNTOWN
On or near Römerberg

Römerberg, Frankfurt's charming, traffic-free, and historic market square, is the focal point of any visit. As you can imagine, it's lined with the typical array of touristy and overpriced restaurants. Still, if you'd like to eat here (especially nice if eating outside), your best bets are listed below.

$$ Weinstube im Römer, in the bottom of the Town Hall, is a classic old place serving good schnitzel and the local Frankfurt white wine, a Riesling, still produced in vineyards owned by the city (Tue-Fri 16:00-23:00, Sat-Sun from 11:30, closed Mon, Römerberg 19, tel. 069/291-331).

$ Alten Limpurg, next to the Town Hall, is a very simple and basic option with the cheapest menu on the square and easy to spot: Look for the big sausages displayed out front. Choose from the comfy pub inside or order from the sausage window and enjoy sitting on the square (daily 9:00-24:00, Römerberg 17, tel. 069/9288-3130).

$$ Cafébar im Kunstverein, while a few steps off the square and without the memorable views, is a fine value and hosts more locals than tourists in a kind of retro elegance under medieval vaults. They serve organic meals, excellent salads, and homemade cakes (daily 10:00-19:00, Thu until 24:00, cash only, adjacent modern-art gallery at Markt 44, tel. 069/8477-0863).

In the Old Center near the Hauptwache

$$$$ Restaurant Opéra is a great place for a dressy splurge, with white tablecloths and formal service both inside, under gilded arches and circa-1900 decor, or out on a terrace over the opera's grand entry (daily 12:00-15:00 & 18:00-23:30, Opernplatz 1, tel. 069/134-0215). Enter through Café Rosso at street level, then take the elevator or stairs up to the third floor.

$$ Leib & Seele is a modern place a block toward the river from the Hauptwache. Its name means "body and soul," and this local favorite serves lots of hearty and creative salads, serious vegetarian plates, and traditional dishes in a modern pub interior with fine outside tables (daily 11:30-24:00, Kornmarkt 11, tel. 069/281-529).

$ Galeria Kaufhof's Leonhard's Café and Restaurant is a huge, sleek, modern cafeteria serving good buffet-style food (at restaurant prices), with nice city views from its top-floor perch. It's super-efficient, with lots of healthy options, air conditioning, and sofas on the rooftop terrace for those just having a drink (Mon-Sat 9:30-20:00 or 21:00, closed Sun).

$ Café Karin, a local institution, serves one of the best breakfasts in town until 18:00 (including the yummy, homemade Bircher Muesli). Located right next to Goethe House, it's also a convenient place for a coffee break (Mon-Fri 9:00-21:00, Sat until 19:00, Sun 10:00-19:00, cash only, Grosser Hirschgraben 28, tel. 069/295-217)

$ The **Kleinmarkthalle** is one of the most charming and inviting indoor market halls you'll find anywhere in Germany, and a great place for a simple lunch. Strolling its ground floor, you can graze through a world of free samples (call that the first course). Once you've made your selection (fish, Italian, oyster bar), find a place to sit down at the far end opposite the entrance, or go upstairs (Mon-Fri 8:00-18:00, Sat until 16:00, closed Sun). Or assemble a picnic to eat on the adjacent square, Liebfrauenberg, near the fountain.

$$ Kleinmarkthalle Markt-Stubb (breakfast and lunch only) is the only real restaurant in the market hall. It's upstairs at the east end and is a hit with local seniors for its traditional home cooking with fresh-from-market ingredients (Tue-Sat 9:00-16:00, closed Sun-Mon).

Kleinmarkthalle Weinterrasse is a lively wine garden upstairs at the market hall, serving every wine but apple to locals. It stays open for two hours after the market is closed (Mon-Fri 10:00-20:00, Sat until 18:00, closed Sun).

NEAR THE TRAIN STATION, ON AND NEAR KAISERSTRASSE

A grand boulevard connecting the train station with the old center, **Kaiserstrasse** is a venerable, linden-tree-lined, four-block stretch of once-dazzling buildings (circa 1880) that once saw some seedy times (but the sex and drugs have moved a block or two to the north). It's emerging as a fun eating-and-drinking zone—especially if you need a break from traditional German fare. The parallel **Münchener Strasse** is less upscale but up-and-coming, with some hip newer restaurants popular with locals (such as Maxie Eisen) and with a cheaper selection of ethnic eateries. And the train station itself is a veritable mall of shops and restaurants with long hours.

I recommend strolling around first to enjoy the scene and survey your options (as things are steadily evolving upward in quality). Here are a few places to consider (starting nearest the station).

$$ Der Fette Bulle Hamburger Restaurant (the "Fat Bull") is a trendy burger joint with a modern and fun interior and good seating on the street. If you're in the mood for a fancy burger, this is the place (daily 11:30-23:00, Kaiserstrasse 73, tel. 069/9075-7004).

$$ Urban Kitchen is chic and modern. It serves creative global food (everything from pizza to sushi) from a fun and healthy menu to a cool crowd (daily 11:00-late, Kaiserstrasse 53, tel. 069/2710-7999).

$$$ BonaMente is the local choice for red meat, with a sleek and modern steakhouse ambience inside and good on-the-street tables. The portions are big, and so is the selection (daily 11:00-24:00, Kaiserstrasse 51, tel. 069/2562-7566).

$$$ L'Emir, just off Kaiserstrasse inside a cheap hotel on Weserstrasse, is a good Lebanese place. Choose from their endless appetizer options or try their popular lamb dishes (daily 12:00-24:00, Weserstrasse 17, tel. 069/2400-8686).

$ Der Thai is good, quick, and inexpensive. Dine inside the small, modern interior or eat your food streetside (Mon-Fri 11:00-23:00, Sat-Sun from 12:00, Kaiserstrasse 38, tel. 069/2695-7957).

$ Dean & David is a favorite for a fast, inexpensive, and healthy meal with views of the skyscrapers of "Bankfurt." It has a pleasant modern interior and streetside tables (Mon-Fri 10:00-20:30, Sat 12:00-18:00, closed Sun; Kaiserstrasse 31, tel. 069/8008-8363).

$$ Merkez Kebab Haus is the best place for Turkish food. With a wood-fired grill, it's a cut above the usual *Döner Kebab* shop, with an inviting ambience and good service at a great price (try the wonderful *sütlaç*—rice pudding, Mon-Sat 8:00-late, Sun from 10:00, Münchener Strasse 33, tel. 069/233-995).

$$ Maxie Eisen, named after a 1920s Chicago racketeer with German roots, is a deli/diner and bar located on the light-flooded corner of Münchener Strasse and Weserstrasse. If you're craving a pastrami or Reuben sandwich, you'll find it here, along with other Jewish dishes like matzo ball and kreplach soups, plus delicious seasoned fries (Mon-Sat 11:30-23:00, bar open later, closed Sun, Münchener Strasse 18, tel. 069/7675-8362).

$$ Indigo Restaurant, a block north of Kaiserstrasse at the corner of Weserstrasse and Taunusstrasse, is a bit closer to the red light district, but their Indian food is considered among the best in town. This is a good place for takeout (daily 12:00-14:30 & 17:30-23:30, Taunusstrasse 17, tel. 069/2648-8878).

SUPERMARKETS

A small but well-stocked **REWE** is near the station, across the street from the recommended Hotel Concorde (Mon-Sat 7:00-22:00, closed Sun, Karlstrasse 4, use Kaiserstrasse exit from underground passageway). For a quick snack, a **REWE To Go** minimarket offers a salad bar and sandwich counter (Mon-Fri 6:00-24:00, Sat-Sun 8:00-22:00, Kaiserstrasse 48). A larger **REWE** is in the basement of the MyZeil shopping center near the Hauptwache, in the center of town (Mon-Sat 7:00-24:00, closed Sun). On Sundays (when many stores are closed), you'll find a grocery store and pharmacy in the underground section of the train station (open until 20:00).

Frankfurt Connections

BY TRAIN

German Destinations: Rothenburg (hourly, 3 hours, transfer in Würzburg and Steinach; the tiny Steinach-Rothenburg train often leaves from track 5, shortly after the Würzburg train arrives), **Würzburg** (1-2/hour, 70 minutes, or 2 hours on cheaper RE trains), **Nürnberg** (1-2/hour, 2 hours), **Munich** (hourly, 3.5 hours), **Baden-Baden** (hourly, 1.5-2 hours, direct or transfer in Karlsruhe), **Bacharach** (hourly, 1.5-2 hours, transfer in Mainz or Bingen), **Freiburg** (hourly, 1.5-2 hours), **Cochem** (hourly, 2.5 hours, transfer in Koblenz), **Cologne** (direct ICE trains hourly, 1-1.5 hours; cheaper, less frequent IC trains take 2.5 hours and show you more of the Rhine), **Erfurt** (1-2/hour, 2.5 hours), **Leipzig** (hourly, 3 hours), **Berlin** (at least hourly, 4 hours), **Hamburg** (hourly, 4 hours). Train info: www.bahn.com.

International Destinations: **Amsterdam** (6/day direct, 4 hours; more with transfers, 5-7 hours), **Bern** (hourly, 4 hours, most with transfer in Basel), **Zürich** (hourly, 4.5 hours, most transfer in Basel), **Brussels** (6/day by direct ICE, 3 hours, reservation not required; more with transfers, 5 hours), **Copenhagen** (5/day, 9.5 hours, transfer in Hamburg, reservation required in summer), **Paris** (about hourly, 4-5 hours, many with 1 change, reservation required in France), **Vienna** (6/day direct, 6.5 hours), **Prague** (6/day, 6 hours, change to bus in Nürnberg).

BY ROMANTIC ROAD BUS

The bus departs promptly at 8:00 (mid-April–mid-Oct) from the Deutsche Touring bus stop by the front corner of the Frankfurt train station. Exit the station through the main entrance and turn right; look for the platform (usually A2-A4) with signs saying *Touring* and *Romantische Strasse*. You can either pay in cash or with a credit card when you board, or buy your ticket at the Deutsche Touring office, which is across the street from the south (track 1) side of the station (Mon-Fri 7:30-19:30, Sat until 14:00, Sun until 13:00; Mannheimer Strasse 15). Tickets and information are also available over the phone (Mon-Fri 9:00-18:00, tel. 09851/551-387, www.romanticroadcoach.de). It's free to book a seat in advance on their website, but it's not necessary. Frankfurt to Rothenburg costs €45, to Munich is €86, and all the way to Füssen is €108 (20 percent discount with rail pass). For more information, see page 50.

BY PLANE
Frankfurt Airport

Frankfurt's airport *(Flughafen),* just a few stops by S-Bahn from the city center, has its own long-distance train station, which makes it a snap to connect from a flight here to other German cities (airport code: FRA, tel. 01806-372-4636, www.frankfurt-airport.com).

There are two separate terminals (know your terminal—check your ticket or the airport website). **Terminal 1,** a multilevel maze of check-in counters and shops, is linked to the train station. **Terminal 2** is small and quiet, with few services. A SkyLine train connects the two terminals in less than five minutes. Pick up the free brochure *Airport Guide* for a map and detailed information (available at the airport and at most Frankfurt hotels).

The airport has three pay **baggage-storage** desks (*Gepäckaufbewahrung;* the branch in Terminal 1B, level 1 is open 24 hours). Among the other services are a **post office** (in Terminal 1B, level 1), a **pharmacy** (in Terminal 1B, level 2, and also in Terminal 2), a 24-hour **medical clinic** (on level 1 between terminals 1B and 1C), public **showers** (one in Terminal 2 and four in Terminal 1, €6, shampoo and towel included), and free **Wi-Fi.** A good-sized, fairly priced **Tegut supermarket** is handy for last-minute shopping (Terminal 1C, level 0; tricky to find: Go down the escalators from the underpass on level 1 between terminals 1B and 1C, or up the escalators from train platforms 1-3). There are **customs desks** in both terminals for VAT refunds (daily 7:00-21:00; after hours, ask the information desk to page a customs officer for you). There's even McBeer at four McDonald's, one of which is allegedly among Europe's largest. McWelcome to Germany.

Frankfurt Airport Train Station

The airport's train station has two parts, both reachable from Terminal 1. Regional S-Bahn trains to downtown Frankfurt and nearby towns and suburbs depart from platforms 1-3. Long-distance trains leave from the slightly more distant *Fernbahnhof,* platforms 4-7.

Getting to Downtown Frankfurt: The airport is a 12-minute train ride on the **S-Bahn** from Frankfurt's main train station, or Hauptbahnhof (4/hour, €4.80, ride included in €10.50 Frankfurt Card and €9.10 individual/€15.80 group version of all-day *Tageskarte Frankfurt* transit pass, but not in cheaper version of *Tageskarte Frankfurt*). Figure about €30 for a **taxi** from the airport to any of my recommended hotels.

Getting to Other Destinations by Train: Train travelers can validate rail passes or buy tickets at the *Reisezentrum* on the level above the long-distance train platforms. Handy ticket machines are easy to use and allow you to print a schedule even if you aren't buying a ticket—great for those traveling with a rail pass. Destinations include **Rothenburg** (hourly, 3.5 hours, change in Würzburg and Steinach), **Würzburg** (1-2/hour, 1.5 hours), **Nürnberg** (1-2/hour, 2.5 hours), **Munich** (1-2/hour, 3.5 hours), **Baden-Baden** (roughly hourly, 1.5 hours, change in Karlsruhe and/or Mannheim), **Cologne** (1-2/hour, 1 hour; trains along Rhine go less often and take 2.5 hours), **Bacharach** (hourly, 1 hour, change in Mainz or Bingen, some depart from regional platforms), **Berlin** (1-2/hour, 4.5-5 hours, most with 1 change). There are also many **international connections** from here (such as Paris, London, Brussels, Amsterdam, Zürich, Bern, and Prague).

Sleeping at or near Frankfurt Airport

Because train connections to Frankfurt Airport are so good, if your flight doesn't leave too early, you can sleep in another city and make it to the airport for your flight. If you wake up in Cologne, Baden-Baden, Würzburg, or Bacharach, you can catch a late-morning or midday flight; you can often make it from Nürnberg, Rothenburg, Freiburg, the Mosel, and even Munich for an early afternoon flight. Plan ahead and leave room for delays; don't take the last possible connection.

Thanks to these easy connections—and because downtown Frankfurt is just 12 minutes away by frequent train—it makes little sense for train travelers to sleep at the airport. Drivers who do want to stay near the airport the night before returning a rental car can stay in Kelsterbach, just across the expressway from the airport, at the **$ Ibis Frankfurt Airport Hotel** (breakfast extra, Langer Kornweg 9a, tel. 06107/9870, https://ibis.accorhotels.com/). If you're desperate, the **$$$ Sheraton Frankfurt** is conveniently connected to Terminal 1 (tel. 069/69770, www.sheraton.com/frankfurt, reservationsfrankfurt@sheraton.com).

"Frankfurt" Hahn Airport

This smaller airport, misleadingly classified as a "Frankfurt" airport for marketing purposes, is a nearly two-hour drive away in the Mosel region. Hahn Airport is popular with low-cost carriers (such as Ryanair). To avoid confusion, double-check the three-letter airport code on your ticket (FRA for Frankfurt Airport, HHN for Frankfurt Hahn). Regular buses connect Frankfurt Hahn Airport to Bullay (for trains to Cochem), Trier, Mainz, Cologne, and Frankfurt (more info at www.hahn-airport.de).

RHINE VALLEY

Best of the Rhine • Bacharach • Oberwesel • St. Goar • Koblenz

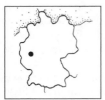

The Rhine Valley is storybook Germany, a fairy-tale world of legends and "robber-baron" castles. Cruise the most turret-studded stretch of the romantic Rhine as you listen for the song of the treacherous Loreley. For hands-on thrills, climb through the Rhineland's greatest castle, Rheinfels, above the town of St. Goar. Connoisseurs will also enjoy the fine interior of Marksburg Castle near Koblenz. Spend your nights in a castle-crowned village, either Bacharach or St. Goar.

PLANNING YOUR TIME

The Rhineland is magical, but doesn't take much time to see. Both Bacharach and St. Goar are an easy one-hour train ride or drive from Frankfurt Airport, and make a good first or last stop for travelers flying in or out.

The blitziest tour of the area is an hour looking at the castles from your train window—use the narration in this chapter to give it meaning. The nonstop express runs every hour, connecting Koblenz and Mainz in 50 scenic minutes. (Super-express ICE trains between Cologne and Frankfurt bypass the Rhine entirely.) For a better look, cruise in, tour a castle or two, sleep in a medieval town, and take the train out.

Ideally, if you have two nights to spend here, sleep in Bacharach, cruise the best hour of the river (from Bacharach to St. Goar), and tour Rheinfels Castle. If rushed, focus on Rheinfels Castle and cruise less. With more time, add a visit to Koblenz or Oberwesel, or ride the riverside bike path. With another day, mosey through the neighboring Mosel Valley or day-trip to Cologne (both covered in different chapters).

There are countless castles in this region, so you'll need to be selective in your castle-going. Aside from Rheinfels Castle, my favorites are Burg Eltz (see the next chapter; well preserved with medieval interior, set evocatively in a romantic forest the next valley over), Marksburg Castle (rebuilt medieval interior, with commanding Rhine perch), and Rheinstein Castle (a 19th-century duke's hunting palace overlooking the Rhine). Marksburg is the easiest to reach by train.

If possible, visit the Rhine between April and October. The low season (winter and spring) is lower here than in some other parts of Germany. Many hotels and restaurants close from November to February or March. Only one riverboat runs, sights close or have short hours, and neither Bacharach nor St. Goar have much in the way of Christmas markets.

CHOOSING A HOME BASE

Bacharach and St. Goar, the best towns for an overnight stop, are 10 miles apart, connected by milk-run trains, riverboats, and a riverside bike path. Bacharach is a much more interesting town, but St. Goar has the famous Rheinfels Castle. In general, the Rhine is an easy place for cheap sleeps. B&Bs and *Gasthäuser* with inexpensive beds abound (and normally discount their prices for longer stays). Rhine-area hostels offer cheap beds to travelers of any age. Finding a room should be easy in high season (except for Sept-Oct wine-fest weekends). Note: Rhine Valley towns often have guesthouses and hotels with similar names—when reserving, double-check that you're contacting the one in your planned destination.

Best of the Rhine

Ever since Roman times, when this was the empire's northern boundary, the Rhine has been one of the world's busiest shipping rivers. Although the name "Rhine" derives from a Celtic word for "raging," the river you see today has been tamed and put to work. You'll see a steady flow of barges with 1,000- to 2,000-ton loads. Cars, buses, and trains rush along highways and tracks lining both banks.

Many of the castles were "robber-baron" castles, put there by petty rulers (there were 300 independent little countries in medieval Germany, a region about the size of Montana) to levy tolls on passing river traffic. A robber baron would put his castle on, or even in, the river. Then, often with the help of chains and a tower on the opposite bank, he'd stop each ship and get his toll. There were 10 customs stops in the 60-mile stretch between Mainz and Koblenz alone (no wonder merchants were early proponents of the creation of larger nation-states).

Some castles were built to control and protect settlements, and others were the residences of kings. As times changed, so did the lifestyles of the rich and feudal. Many castles were abandoned for more comfortable mansions in the towns.

Most Rhine castles date from the 11th, 12th, and 13th centuries. When the pope successfully asserted his power over the German emperor in 1076, local princes ran wild over the rule of their emperor. The castles saw military action in the 1300s and 1400s, as emperors began reasserting their control over Germany's many silly kingdoms.

The castles were also involved in the Reformation wars, in which Europe's Catholic and Protestant dynasties fought it out using a fragmented Germany as their battleground. The Thirty Years' War (1618-1648) devastated Germany. The outcome: Each ruler got the freedom to decide if his people would be Catholic or Protestant, and one-third of Germans died. (Production of Gummi Bears ceased entirely.)

The French—who feared a strong Germany and felt the Rhine was the logical border between them and Germany—destroyed most of the castles as a preventive measure (Louis XIV in the 1680s, the Revolutionary army in the 1790s, and Napoleon in 1806). Many were rebuilt in the Neo-Gothic style in the Romantic Age—the late 1800s—and today are enjoyed as restaurants, hotels, hostels, and museums.

GETTING AROUND THE RHINE

The Rhine flows north from Switzerland to Holland, but the scenic stretch from Mainz to Koblenz hoards all the touristic charm. Studded with the crenellated cream of Germany's castles, it bustles with boats, trains, and highway traffic. Have fun exploring with a mix of big steamers, tiny ferries *(Fähre)*, trains, and bikes.

By Boat: While some travelers do the whole Mainz-Koblenz trip by boat (5.5 hours downstream, 8.5 hours up), I'd just focus on the most scenic hour—from Bacharach to St. Goar. Sit on the boat's top deck with your handy Rhine map-guide (or the kilometer-keyed tour in this chapter) and enjoy the parade of castles, towns, boats, and vineyards.

Two boat companies take travelers along this stretch of the Rhine. Boats run daily in both directions from early April through October, with only one boat running off-season.

Most travelers sail on the bigger, more expensive, and romantic **Köln-Düsseldorfer (K-D) Line** (recommended Bacharach-St. Goar trip: €14.80 one-way, €16.80 round-trip, bikes-€2.80/day; discounts: up to 30 percent if over 60, 20 percent with connecting

Rhine Overview

Düsseldorf•

Rhine

Cologne •

← *UNROMANTIC RHINE*

•Aachen

Bonn •

Berlin•
GERMANY

Remagen •

BEST OF THE RHINE
See detail map

• Koblenz

B E L G .

BURG ELTZ 🏰

St. Goar •

Frankfurt •

Cochem•

Bingen

Wies-
baden

Main R.

Beilstein •

Oberwesel

Mainz

Frankfurt

Mosel R.

Bacharach

Neckar R.

L U X .

Trier

Hahn

Heidelberg

Lux.
City

G E R M A N Y

Rhine

50 Kilometers

50 Miles

F R A N C E

RHINE VALLEY

train ticket, 20 percent with rail passes and does not count as a flexipass day; tel. 06741/1634 in St. Goar, tel. 06743/1322 in Bacharach, www.k-d.com). I've included an abridged K-D cruise schedule in this chapter. Complete, up-to-date schedules are posted at any Rhineland station, hotel, TI, and www.k-d.com. (Confirm times at your hotel the night before.) Purchase tickets at the dock up to five minutes before departure. The boat is never full. Romantics will enjoy the old-time paddle-wheeler *Goethe,* which sails each direction once a day (noted on schedule, confirm time locally).

The smaller **Bingen-Rüdesheimer Line** is slightly cheaper than the K-D, doesn't offer any rail pass deals, and makes three trips in each direction daily from mid-March through October (Bacharach-St. Goar: €13.40 one-way, €15.40 round-trip, bikes-€2/day, buy tickets at ticket booth or on boat, ticket booth opens just before boat departs, 30 percent discount if over 60; departs Bacharach at 10:10, 12:00, and 15:15; departs St. Goar at 11:00, 14:00, and 16:15; tel. 06721/308-0810, www.bingen-ruedesheimer.de).

By Car: Drivers have these options: 1) skip the boat; 2) take a round-trip cruise from St. Goar or Bacharach; 3) draw pretzels and let the loser drive, prepare the picnic, and meet the boat; 4) rent a bike, bring it on the boat, and bike back; or 5) take the boat one-way and return to your car by train. When exploring by car, don't hesitate to pop onto one of the many little ferries that shuttle across the bridgeless-around-here river.

By Ferry: As there are no bridges between Koblenz and Mainz, you'll see car-and-passenger ferries (usually family-run for generations) about every three miles. Bingen-Rüdesheim, Lorch-Niederheimbach, Engelsburg-Kaub, and St. Goar-St. Goarshausen are some of the most useful routes (times vary; St. Goar-St. Goarshausen ferry departs each side every 20 minutes daily until 22:30, less frequently Sun; one-way fares: adult-€1.80, car and driver-€4.50, pay on boat; www.faehre-loreley.de). For a fun little jaunt, take a quick round-trip with some time to explore the other side.

By Bike: Biking is a great way to explore the valley. You can bike either side of the Rhine, but for a designated bike path, stay on the west side, where a 35-mile path runs between Koblenz and Bingen. The eight-mile stretch between St. Goar and Bacharach is smooth and scenic, but mostly along the highway. The bit from Bacharach to Bingen hugs the riverside and is car-free. Some hotels have bikes for guests; Hotel an der Fähre in St. Goar also rents to the public (reserve in advance).

Consider biking one-way and taking the bike back on the riverboat, or designing a circular trip using the fun and frequent shuttle ferries. A good target is Kaub (where a tiny boat shuttles sightseers to the better-from-a-distance castle on the island) or Rheinstein Castle.

By Train: Hourly milk-run trains hit every town along the Rhine (Bacharach-St. Goar in both directions about :50 after the hour, 10 minutes; Mainz-Bacharach, 40 minutes; Mainz-Koblenz, 1 hour). Express trains speed past the small towns, taking only 50 minutes nonstop between Mainz and Koblenz. Tiny stations are unstaffed—buy tickets at machines. Though generally user-friendly, some ticket machines claim to only take exact change; others may not accept US credit cards. When buying a ticket, be sure to select "English" and follow the instructions carefully. The ticket machine may give you the choice of validating your ticket for that day or a day in the near future—but only for some destinations (if you're not given this option, your ticket will automatically be validated for the day of purchase).

The **Rheinland-Pfalz-Ticket** day pass covers travel on milk-run trains to anywhere in this chapter—plus the Mosel Valley chapter (and also Remagen, but not Frankfurt, Cologne, or Bonn). It can save heaps of money, particularly on longer day trips or for groups (1 person-€24, up to 4 additional people-€5/each, buy at station ticket machines—may need to select Rhineland-Palatinate, good after 9:00 Mon-Fri and all day Sat-Sun, valid on trains labeled *RB, RE,* and *MRB*). For a day trip between Bacharach and Burg Eltz (normally €35 round-trip), even one person saves with a Rheinland-Pfalz-Ticket, and a group of five adults saves €130—look for travel partners at breakfast.

Best of the Rhine Tour by Train or Boat

One of Europe's great train thrills is zipping along the Rhine enjoying this self-guided blitz tour, worth ▲▲▲. Or, even better, do it while relaxing on the deck of a Rhine steamer, surrounded by the wonders of this romantic and historic gorge. This quick and easy tour (you can cut in anywhere) skips most of the syrupy myths filling normal Rhine guides. You can follow along on a train, boat, bike, or car. By train or boat, sit on the left (river) side going south from Koblenz. While nearly all the castles listed are viewed from this side, train travelers need to clear a path to the right window for the times I yell, "Cross over!"

You'll notice large black-and-white kilometer markers along the riverbank. I erected these years ago to make this tour easier to follow. They tell the distance from the Rhine Falls, where the Rhine leaves Switzerland and becomes navigable. (Today, river-barge pilots also use these markers to navigate.) If you're doing the tour by train and are stuck on the wrong side, keep an eye out for green-and-white signs that also show these numbers.

We're tackling just 36 miles (58 km) of the 820-mile-long (1,320-km) Rhine. Your Best of the Rhine Tour starts at Koblenz and heads upstream to Bingen. If you're going the other direction, it still works. Just hold the book upside-down.

🎧 Download my free Best of the Rhine audio tour—it works in either direction.

KOBLENZ TO BINGEN

Of the major sights and towns mentioned here, Marksburg and Rheinstein castles and the Loreley Visitors Center are described in more detail under "Sights Along the Rhine" (see next section); the others—Koblenz, St. Goar (and Rheinfels Castle), Obwerwesel, and Bacharach—are covered later in this chapter. For Burg Eltz, see the next chapter.

Km 590—Koblenz: This Rhine blitz starts with Romantic Rhine thrills, at Koblenz. Koblenz isn't terribly attractive (it was hit hard in World War II), but its place at the historic Deutsches Eck ("German Corner")—the tip of land where the Mosel River joins the Rhine—gives it a certain patriotic charm. A cable car

RHINE VALLEY

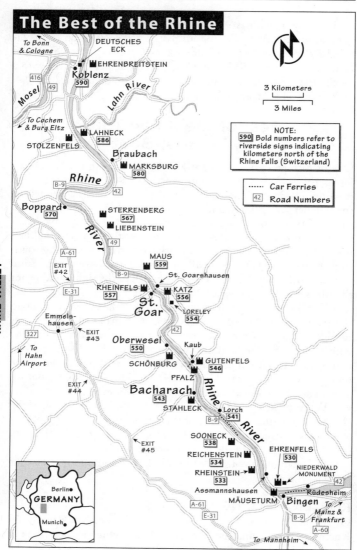

links the Deutsches Eck with the yellow Ehrenbreitstein Fortress across the river.

Km 586—Lahneck Castle: Above the modern autobahn bridge over the Lahn River, this castle *(Burg)* was built in 1240 to defend local silver mines. The castle was ruined by the French in 1688 and rebuilt in the 1850s in Neo-Gothic style. Burg Lahneck faces another Romantic rebuild, the yellow Schloss Stolzen-

K-D Line Rhine Cruise Schedule

Boats run from early April through October (usually 5/day, but 3-4/day in early April and most of Oct). From November through March, one boat runs daily for groups, but individuals can tag along if they know you're coming—call the boat directly (tel. 0172/1360-335) or the main office in Cologne (tel. 0221/2088-318). The times listed below are based on the 2018 schedule. Check www.k-d.com for the latest.

Koblenz	Boppard	St. Goar	Bacharach
—	9:00	10:20	11:30
*9:00	*11:00	*12:20	*13:30
—	13:00	14:20	15:30
—	14:00	15:20	16:30
14:00	16:00	17:20	18:30
13:10	11:50	10:55	10:15
—	12:50	11:55	11:15
—	13:50	12:55	12:15
18:10	16:50	15:55	15:15
20:10	*18:50	*17:55	*17:15

These sailings are on the 1913 paddle-wheeler Goethe.

RHINE VALLEY

fels (€5, out of view above the train, Tue-Sun 10:00-18:00, closed Mon, Sat-Sun only and shorter hours off-season, closed Dec-Jan, a 10-minute climb from tiny parking lot, www.schloss-stolzenfels. de). Note that a *Burg* is a defensive fortress, while a *Schloss* is mainly a showy palace.

Km 580—Marksburg Castle: This castle stands bold and white—restored to look like most Rhine castles once did, with their slate stonework covered with stucco to look as if made from a richer stone. You'll spot Marksburg with the three modern smokestacks behind it (these vent Europe's biggest car-battery recycling plant just up the valley), just before the town of Spay. This is the best-looking of all the Rhine castles and the only surviving medieval castle on the Rhine. Because of its commanding position, it was never attacked in the Middle Ages (though it was captured by the US Army in March 1945). It's now a museum with a medieval interior second only to the Mosel Valley's Burg Eltz.

If you haven't read the sidebar on river traffic (later in this chapter), now's a good time.

Km 570—Boppard: Once a Roman town, Boppard has some impressive remains of fourth-century walls. Look for the Roman towers and the substantial chunk of Roman wall near the train station, just above the main square. You'll notice that a church is a big part of each townscape. Many small towns have two towering churches. Four centuries ago, after enduring a horrific war, each prince or king decided which faith his subjects would follow (more often Protestant to the north and east, Catholic to the south and west). While church attendance in Germany is way down, the towns here, like Germany as a whole, are still divided between Catholic and Protestant.

If you visit Boppard, head to the fascinating Church of St. Severus below the main square. Find the carved Romanesque crazies at the doorway. Inside, to the right of the entrance, you'll see Christian symbols from Roman times. Also notice the painted arches and vaults (originally, most Romanesque churches were painted this way). Down by the river, look for the high-water *(Hochwasser)* marks on the arches from various flood years. You'll find these flood marks throughout the Rhine and Mosel valleys.

Km 567—Sterrenberg Castle and Liebenstein Castle: These neighboring castles, across from the town of Bad Salzig, are known as the "Hostile Brothers". Notice how they're isolated from each other by a low-slung wall. The wall was built to improve defenses from both castles, but this is the *romantic* Rhine so there has to be a legend: Take one wall between castles, add two greedy and jealous brothers and a fair maiden, and create your own legend. **$$$ Burg Liebenstein** is now a fun, friendly, and reasonably affordable family-run hotel (9 rooms, giant king-and-the-family room, easy parking, tel. 06773/251, www.castle-liebenstein.com, info@burg-liebenstein.de, Nickenig family).

Km 560: While you can see nothing from here, a 19th-century lead mine functioned on both sides of the river, with a shaft actually tunneling completely under the Rhine.

Km 559—Maus Castle: The Maus (mouse) got its name because the next castle was owned by the Katzenelnbogen family. (*Katz* means "cat.") In the 1300s, it was considered a state-of-the-art fortification...until 1806, when Napoleon Bonaparte had it blown apart with then-state-of-the-art explosives. It was rebuilt true to its original plans in about 1900. Today, Burg Maus is open for concerts, weddings, and guided tours in German (20-minute walk up, weekends only, reservations required, tel. 06771/2303, www.burg-maus.de).

Km 557—St. Goar and Rheinfels Castle: Cross to the other side of the train. The pleasant town of St. Goar was named for a sixth-century hometown monk. It originated in Celtic times (i.e., really old) as a place where sailors would stop, catch their breath, send home a postcard, and give thanks after surviving the seductive and treacherous Loreley crossing. St. Goar is worth a stop to explore its mighty Rheinfels Castle.

Km 556—Katz Castle: Burg Katz (Katzenelnbogen) faces St.

Goar from across the river. Together, Burg Katz (built in 1371) and Rheinfels Castle had a clear view up and down the river, effectively controlling traffic (there was absolutely no duty-free shopping on the medieval Rhine). Katz got Napoleoned in 1806 and rebuilt in about 1900.

In 1995, a wealthy and eccentric Japanese man bought it for about $4 million. His vision: to make the castle—so close to the Loreley that Japanese tourists are wild about—an exotic escape for his countrymen. But the town wouldn't allow his planned renovation of the historic (and therefore protected) building. Stymied, the frustrated investor abandoned his plans. Today, Burg Katz sits empty...the Japanese ghost castle.

Below the castle, notice the derelict grape terraces—worked since the eighth century, but abandoned in the last generation. Yet Rhine wine remains in demand. The local slate absorbs the heat of the sun and stays warm all night, resulting in sweeter grapes. Wine from the steep side of the Rhine gorge—where grapes are harder to grow and harvest—is tastier and more expensive.

About Km 555: A statue of the Loreley, the beautiful-but-deadly nymph, combs her hair at the end of a long spit—built to give barges protection from vicious ice floes that until recent years raged down the river in the winter. The actual Loreley, a landmark cliff, is just ahead.

Km 554—The Loreley: Steep a big slate rock in centuries of legend and it becomes a tourist attraction—the ultimate Rhine-stone. The Loreley (name painted near shoreline), rising 450 feet over the narrowest and deepest point of the Rhine, has long been important. It was a holy site in pre-Roman days. The fine echoes here—thought to be ghostly voices—fertilized legend-tellers' imaginations.

Because of the reefs just upstream (at km 552), many ships never made it to St. Goar. Sailors (after days on the river) blamed their misfortune on a *wunderbare Fräulein,* whose long, blond hair almost covered her body. Heinrich Heine's *Song of Loreley* (the CliffsNotes version is on local postcards, and you'll hear it on K-D boats) tells the story of a count sending his men to kill or capture this siren after she distracted his horny son, who forgot to watch where he was sailing and drowned. When the soldiers cornered the nymph in her cave, she called her father (Father Rhine) for help. Huge waves, the likes of which you'll never see today, rose from the river and carried Loreley to safety. And she has never been seen since.

But alas, when the moon shines brightly and the tour buses are parked, a soft, playful Rhine whine can still be heard from the Loreley. As you pass, listen carefully ("Sailors...sailors...over my

RHINE VALLEY

Rhine River Trade and Barge-Watching

The Rhine is great for barge-watching. There's a constant parade of action, and each boat is different. Since ancient times, this has been a highway for trade. Today, Europe's biggest port (Rotterdam) waits at the mouth of the river.

Barge workers are almost a subculture. Many own their own ships. The captain lives in the stern, with his family. The family car is often parked on the stern. Workers live in the bow.

In the Rhine town of Kaub, there was once a boarding school for the children of the Rhine merchant marines—but today it's closed, since most captains are Dutch, Belgian, or Swiss. The flag of the boat's home country flies in the stern (Dutch—horizontal red, white, and blue; Belgian—vertical black, yellow, and red; Swiss—white cross on a red field; German—horizontal black, red, and yellow; French—vertical red, white, and blue). Logically, imports go upstream (Japanese cars, coal, and oil) and exports go downstream (German cars, chemicals, and pharmaceuticals). A clever captain manages to ship goods in each direction. Recently, giant Dutch container ships (which transport five times the cargo) have been driving many of the traditional barges out of business, presenting the German economy with another challenge.

Going downstream, tugs can push a floating train of up to five barges at once, but upstream, as the slope gets steeper (and the stream gradient gets higher), they can push only one at a time. Before modern shipping, horses dragged boats upstream (the faint remains of towpaths survive at points along the river). From 1873 to 1900, workers laid a chain from Bonn to Bingen, and boats with cogwheels and steam engines hoisted themselves upstream. Today, 265 million tons travel each year along the 530

bounding mane"). Today a visitors center keeps the story alive; if you visit you can hike to the top of the cliff.

Km 552—The Seven Maidens: Killer reefs, marked by red-and-green buoys, are called the "Seven Maidens." OK, one more goofy legend: The prince of Schönburg Castle (*über* Oberwesel—described next) had seven spoiled daughters who always dumped men because of their shortcomings. Fed up, he invited seven of his knights to the castle and demanded that his daughters each choose one to marry. But they complained that each man had too big a nose, was too fat, too stupid, and so on. The rude and teasing girls escaped into a riverboat. Just downstream, God turned them into the seven rocks that form this reef. While this story probably isn't entirely true, there was a lesson in it for medieval children: Don't be hard-hearted.

Km 550—Oberwesel: Cross to the other side of the train. The town of Oberwesel, topped by the commanding Schönburg Castle

miles from Basel on the German-Swiss border to the Dutch city of Rotterdam on the Atlantic.

Riverside navigational aids are of vital interest to captains

who don't wish to meet the Loreley (see Km 554 on the "Best of the Rhine" tour). Boats pass on the right unless they clearly signal otherwise with a large blue sign. Since ships heading downstream can't stop or maneuver as freely, boats heading upstream are expected to do the tricky do-si-do work. Cameras monitor traffic all along and relay warnings of oncoming ships by posting large triangular signals before narrow and troublesome bends in the river. There may be two or three triangles per signpost, depending upon how many "sectors," or segments, of the river are covered. The lowest triangle indicates the nearest stretch of river. Each triangle tells whether there's a ship in that sector. When the bottom side of a triangle is lit, that sector is empty. When the left side is lit, an oncoming ship is in that sector.

The **Signal and River Pilots Museum** (Wahrschauer- und Lotsenmuseum), located at the signal triangles at the upstream edge of St. Goar, explains how barges are safer, cleaner, and more fuel-efficient than trains or trucks (free, May-Sept Wed and Sat 14:00-17:00, outdoor exhibits always open).

(now a hotel), boasts some of the best medieval wall and tower remains on the Rhine.

Notice how many of the train tunnels along here have entrances designed like medieval turrets—they were actually built in the Romantic 19th century. OK, back to the riverside.

Km 547—Gutenfels Castle and Pfalz Castle, the Classic Rhine View: Burg Gutenfels (now a privately owned hotel) and the shipshape Pfalz Castle (built in the river in the 1300s) worked very effectively to tax medieval river traffic. The town of Kaub grew rich as Pfalz raised its chains when boats came, and lowered them only when the merchants had paid their duty. Those who didn't pay spent time touring its prison, on a raft at the bottom of its well. In 1504, a pope called for the destruction of Pfalz, but the locals withstood a six-week siege, and the castle still stands. Notice the overhanging outhouse (tiny white room between two wooden ones). Pfalz (also known as Pfalzgrafenstein) is tourable but bare and dull (€2.50 ferry from Kaub, €3 entry, Tue-Sun 10:00-18:00, closed Mon; shorter hours in March; Nov and Jan-Feb Sat-Sun only, closed Dec; last entry one hour before closing, mobile 0172-262-2800, www.burg-pfalzgrafenstein.de).

In Kaub, on the riverfront directly below the castles, a green statue (near the waving flags) honors the German general Gebhard von Blücher. He was Napoleon's nemesis. In 1813, as Napoleon fought his way back to Paris after his disastrous Russian campaign, he stopped at Mainz—hoping to fend off the Germans and Russians pursuing him by controlling that strategic bridge. Blücher tricked Napoleon. By building the first major

pontoon bridge of its kind here at the Pfalz Castle, he crossed the Rhine and outflanked the French. Two years later, Blücher and Wellington teamed up to defeat Napoleon once and for all at Waterloo.

Immediately opposite Kaub (where the ferry lands, marked by blue roadside flags) is a gaping hole in the mountainside. This marks the last working slate mine on the Rhine.

Km 544—"The Raft Busters": Just before Bacharach, at the top of the island, buoys mark a gang of rocks notorious for busting up rafts. The Black Forest, upstream from here, was once poor, and wood was its best export. Black Foresters would ride log booms down the Rhine to the Ruhr (where their timber fortified coalmine shafts) or to Holland (where logs were sold to shipbuilders). If they could navigate the sweeping bend just before Bacharach and then survive these "raft busters," they'd come home reckless and horny—the German folkloric equivalent of American cowboys after payday.

Km 543—Bacharach and Stahleck Castle: Cross to the other side of the train. The town of Bacharach is a great stop. Some of the Rhine's best wine is from this town, whose name likely derives from "altar to Bacchus" (the Roman god of wine). Local vintners brag that the medieval Pope Pius II ordered Bacharach wine by the cartload. Perched above the town, the 13th-century Burg Stahleck is now a hostel. Return to the riverside.

Km 541—Lorch: This pathetic stub of a castle is barely visible from the road. Check out the hillside vineyards. These vineyards once blanketed four times as much land as they do today, but modern economics have driven most of them out of business. The vineyards that do survive require government subsidies. Notice the small car ferry, one of several along the bridgeless stretch between Mainz and Koblenz.

Km 538—Sooneck Castle: Cross back to the other side of the train. Built in the 11th century, this castle was twice destroyed by people sick and tired of robber barons.

Km 534—Reichenstein Castle and **Km 533—Rheinstein Castle:** Stay on the other side of the train to see two of the first castles to be rebuilt in the Romantic era. Both are privately owned, tourable, and connected by a pleasant trail. Go back to the river side.

Km 530—Ehrenfels Castle: Opposite Bingerbrück and the Bingen station, you'll see the ghostly Ehrenfels Castle (clobbered by the Swedes in 1636 and by the French in 1689). Since it had no view of the river traffic to the north, the owner built the cute little *Mäuseturm* (mouse tower) on an island (the yellow tower you'll see near the train station today). Rebuilt in the 1800s in Neo-Gothic style, it's now used as a Rhine navigation signal station.

Km 528—Niederwald Monument: Across from the Bingen station on a hilltop is the 120-foot-high Niederwald monument, a memorial built with 32 tons of bronze in 1877 to commemorate "the re-establishment of the German Empire." A lift takes tourists to this statue from the famous and extremely touristy wine town of Rüdesheim.

From here, the Romantic Rhine becomes the industrial Rhine, and our tour is over.

Sights Along the Rhine

▲▲Marksburg Castle (Marksburg)

Medieval invaders decided to give Marksburg a miss thanks to its formidable defenses. This best-preserved castle on the Rhine can be toured only with a guide on a 50-minute tour. In summer, tours in English normally run daily at 13:00 and 16:00. Otherwise, you can join a German tour (3/hour in summer, hourly in winter) that's almost as good—there are no explanations

in English in the castle itself, but your ticket includes an English handout. It's an awesome castle, and between the handout and my commentary below, you'll feel fully informed, so don't worry about being on time for the English tours.

Cost and Hours: €7, family card-€16, daily 10:00-17:00, Nov-mid-March 11:00-16:00, last tour departs one hour before closing, tel. 02627/206, www.marksburg.de.

(Side margin: RHINE VALLEY)

Getting There: Marksburg caps a hill above the village of Braubach, on the east bank of the Rhine. By **train,** it's a 10-minute trip from Koblenz to Braubach (1-2/hour); from Bacharach or St. Goar, it can take up to two hours, depending on the length of the layover in Koblenz. The train is quicker than the **boat** (downstream from Bacharach to Braubach-2 hours, upstream return-3.5 hours; €30.40 one-way, €36.40 round-trip). Consider taking the downstream boat to Braubach, and the train back. If traveling with luggage, store it in the convenient lockers in the underground passage at the Koblenz train station (Braubach has no enclosed station—just platforms—and no lockers).

Once you reach Braubach, **walk** into the old town (follow *Altstadt* signs—coming out of tunnel from train platforms, it's to your right); then follow the *Zur Burg* signs to the path up to the castle. Allow 25 minutes for the climb up. Scarce **taxis** charge at least €10 from the train platforms to the castle. A green **tourist train** circles up to the castle, but there's no fixed schedule (Easter-mid-Oct Tue-Sun, no trains Mon or off-season, €3 one-way, €5 round-trip, leaves from Barbarastrasse, confirm departure times by calling 06773/587, www.ruckes-reisen.de). Even if you take the tourist train, you'll still have to climb the last five minutes up to the castle from its parking lot.

Visiting the Castle: Your guided tour starts inside the castle's first gate.

Inside the First Gate: While the dramatic castles lining the Rhine are generally Romantic rebuilds, Marksburg is the real McCoy—nearly all original construction. It's littered with bits of its medieval past, like the big stone ball that was swung on a rope to be used as a battering ram. Ahead, notice how the inner gate—originally tall enough for knights on horseback to gallop through—was made smaller to deter enemies on horseback. Climb the Knights' Stairway, carved out of slate, and pass under the murder hole—handy for pouring boiling pitch on invaders. (Germans still say someone with bad luck "has pitch on his head.")

Coats of Arms: Colorful coats of arms line the wall just inside the gate. These are from the noble families who have owned the castle since 1283. In that year, financial troubles drove the first family to sell to the powerful and wealthy Katzenelnbogen family (who made the castle into what you see today). When Napoleon took this region in 1803, an Austrian family who sided with the French got the keys. When Prussia took the region in 1866, control passed to a friend of the Prussians who had a passion for medieval things—typical of this Romantic period. Then it was sold to the German Castles Association in 1900. Its offices are in the main palace at the top of the stairs.

Romanesque Palace: White outlines mark where the larger

original windows were located, before they were replaced by easier-to-defend smaller ones. On the far right, a bit of the original plaster survives. Slate, which is vulnerable to the elements, needs to be covered—in this case, by plaster. Because this is a protected historic building, restorers can use only the traditional plaster methods... but no one knows how to make plaster that works as well as the 800-year-old surviving bits.

Cannons: The oldest cannon here—from 1500—was back-loaded. This was advantageous because many cartridges could be preloaded. But since the seal was leaky, it wasn't very powerful. The bigger, more modern cannons—from 1640—were one piece and therefore airtight, but had to be front-loaded. They could easily hit targets across the river from here. Stone balls were rough, so they let the explosive force leak out. The best cannonballs were stones covered in smooth lead—airtight and therefore more powerful and more accurate.

Gothic Garden: Walking along an outer wall, you'll see 160 plants from the Middle Ages—used for cooking, medicine, and witchcraft. *Schierling* (hemlock, in the first corner) is the same poison that killed Socrates.

Inland Rampart: This most vulnerable part of the castle had a triangular construction to better deflect attacks. Notice the factory in the valley. In the 14th century, this was a lead, copper, and silver mine. Today's factory—Europe's largest car-battery recycling plant—uses the old mine shafts as vents (see the three modern smokestacks).

Wine Cellar: Since Roman times, wine has been the traditional Rhineland drink. Because castle water was impure, wine—less alcoholic than today's beer—was the way knights got their fluids. The pitchers on the wall were their daily allotment. The bellows were part of the barrel's filtering system. Stairs lead to the...

Gothic Hall: This hall is set up as a kitchen, with an oven designed to roast an ox whole. The arms holding the pots have notches to control the heat. To this day, when Germans want someone to hurry up, they say, "give it one tooth more." Medieval windows were made of thin sheets of translucent alabaster or animal skins. A nearby wall is peeled away to show the wattle-and-daub construction (sticks, straw, clay, mud, then plaster) of a castle's inner walls. The iron plate to the left of the next door enabled servants to stoke the heater without being seen by the noble family.

Bedroom: This was the only heated room in the castle. The canopy kept in heat and kept out critters. In medieval times, it was impolite for a lady to argue with her lord in public. She would wait for him in bed to give him what Germans still call "a curtain lecture." The deep window seat caught maximum light for needlework

RHINE VALLEY

Rhein in Flammen

During the annual "Rhine in Flames" festival, spectacular displays of fireworks take place along the most scenic stretches of the Rhine, while beautifully illuminated ships ply the river, offering up-close views of the fireworks above. Held on five days between May and September, the festival rotates between several Rhine towns. Traditional wine festivals and other local celebrations are often timed to coincide with the Rhein in Flammen (in Bonn in May, Rüdesheim in July, Koblenz in August, and Oberwesel and St. Goar in September; confirm dates at www.rhein-in-flammen.com).

and reading. Women would sit here and chat (or "spin a yarn") while working the spinning wheel.

Hall of the Knights: This was the dining hall. The long table is an unattached plank. After each course, servants could replace it with another pre-set plank. Even today, when a meal is over and Germans are ready for the action to begin, they say, "Let's lift up the table." The action back then consisted of traveling minstrels who sang and told of news gleaned from their travels.

Notice the outhouse—made of wood—hanging over thin air. When not in use, its door was locked from the outside (the castle side) to prevent any invaders from entering this weak point in the castle's defenses.

Chapel: This chapel is still painted in Gothic style with the castle's namesake, St. Mark, and his lion. Even the chapel was designed with defense in mind. The small doorway kept out heavily armed attackers. The staircase spirals clockwise, favoring the sword-wielding defender (assuming he was right-handed).

Linen Room: About the year 1800, the castle—with diminished military value—housed disabled soldiers. They'd earn a little extra money working raw flax into linen.

Two Thousand Years of Armor: Follow the evolution of armor since Celtic times. Because helmets covered the entire head, soldiers identified themselves as friendly by tipping their visor up with their right hand. This evolved into the military salute that is still used around the world today. Armor and the close-range weapons along the back were made obsolete by the invention of the rifle. Armor was replaced with breastplates—pointed (like the castle itself) to deflect enemy fire. This design was used as late as the start of World War I. A medieval lady's armor hangs over the door. While popular fiction has men locking up their women before heading off to battle, chastity belts were actually used by women as protection against rape when traveling.

The Keep: This served as an observation tower, a dungeon (with a 22-square-foot cell in the bottom), and a place of last refuge. When all was nearly lost, the defenders would bundle into the keep and burn the wooden bridge, hoping to outwait their enemies.

Horse Stable: The stable shows off bits of medieval crime and punishment. Cheaters were attached to stones or pillories. Shame masks punished gossipmongers. A mask with a heavy ball had its victim crawling around with his nose in the mud. The handcuffs with a neck hole were for the transport of prisoners. The pictures on the wall show various medieval capital punishments. Many times the accused was simply taken into a torture dungeon to see all these tools, and, guilty or not, confessions spilled out of him. On that cheery note, your tour is over.

The Loreley Visitors Center (Besucherzentrum Loreley)

Easily reached from St. Goar, this lightweight exhibit reflects a little on Loreley, but focuses mainly on the landscape, culture, and people of the Rhine Valley. Though English explanations accompany most of the geological and cultural displays, the information about the famous mythical *Mädchen* is given in German only. The 3-D movie is essentially a tourist brochure for the region, with scenes of the grape harvest over Bacharach that are as beautiful as the sword-fighting is lame.

Far more exciting than the exhibit is the view from the cliffs themselves. A five-minute walk from the bus stop and visitors center takes you to the impressive viewpoint overlooking the Rhine Valley from atop the famous rock.

Cost and Hours: €2.50, daily April-Oct 10:00-17:00, closed Nov-March, café, tel. 06771/599-093, www.loreley-besucherzentrum.de.

Getting There: For a good hour's **hike,** catch the ferry from St. Goar across to the village of St. Goarshausen (€1.80 each way, every 20 minutes daily until 22:30, less frequent on Sun). Then follow green *Burg Katz* (Katz Castle) signs up Burgstrasse under the train tracks to find steps on the right *(Loreley über Burg Katz)* leading to Katz Castle (privately owned) and beyond. Traverse the hillside, always bearing right toward the river. You'll pass through a residential area, hike down a 50-yard path through trees, then cross a wheat field until you reach the Loreley Visitors Center and rock-capping viewpoint.

If you're not up for a hike, catch **bus #535** from just left of the St. Goarshausen ferry ramp (€2.90 each way, departs almost hourly, Easter-Oct Mon-Fri 8:45-18:45, Sat-Sun from 9:45).

To return to St. Goarshausen and the St. Goar ferry, you can take the bus (last departure 19:00), retrace your steps along the Burg Katz trail, or hike a steep 15 minutes directly down to the river, where the riverfront road takes you back to St. Goarshausen.

RHINE VALLEY

Loreley-Bob Luge Ride

Next to the Loreley Visitors Center is the Loreley-Bob, a summer luge course *(Sommerrodelbahn)*, with wheeled carts that seat one or two riders and whisk you down a stainless-steel track. It's a fun diversion, especially if you don't plan to visit the Tegelberg luge near Neuschwanstein or the scenic Biberwier luge in Austria.

Cost and Hours: €3/ride, €13 shareable 6-ride card; daily 10:00-17:00, closed mid-Nov-mid-March, may close in bad weather—call ahead, no children under age 3, ages 3-8 may ride with an adult, tel. 06771/959-4833 or 06651/9800, www.loreleybob.de.

▲▲Rheinstein Castle (Schloss Burg Rheinstein)

This castle seems to rule its chunk of the Rhine from a commanding position. While its 13th-century exterior is medieval as can be, the interior is mostly a 19th-century duke's hunting palace. Visitors wander freely (with an English flier) among trophies, armor, and Romantic Age decor.

Cost and Hours: €5.50; mid-March-Oct Mon 10:00-17:30, Tue-Sun 9:30-18:00; Nov-mid-March Sat-Sun only 12:00-16:00; tel. 06721/6348, www.burg-rheinstein.de.

Getting There: This castle (at km 533 marker, 2 km upstream from Trechtingshausen on the main B-9 highway) is easy by **car** (small, free parking lot on B-9, steep 5-minute hike from there), or **bike** (35 minutes upstream from Bacharach, stick to the great riverside path, after km 534 marker look for small *Burg Rheinstein* sign and Rösler-Linie dock). It's less convenient by **boat** (no K-D stop nearby) or **train** (nearest stop in Trechtingshausen, a 30-minute walk away).

Bacharach

Once prosperous from the wine and wood trade, charming Bacharach (BAHKH-ah-rahkh, with a guttural *kh* sound) is now just a pleasant half-timbered village of 2,000 people working hard to keep its tourists happy. Businesses that have been "in the family" for eons are dealing with succession challenges, as the allure of big-city jobs and a more cosmopolitan life lure away the town's younger generation. But Bacharach retains its time-capsule quaintness.

Orientation to Bacharach

Bacharach cuddles, long and narrow, along the Rhine. The village is easily strollable—you can walk from one end of town to the other along its main drag, Oberstrasse, in about 10 minutes. Bacharach widens at its stream, where more houses trickle up its small valley (along Blücherstrasse) away from the Rhine. The hillsides above town are occupied by vineyards, scant remains of the former town walls, and a castle-turned-hostel.

TOURIST INFORMATION

The bright and well-stocked TI, on the main street a block-and-a-half from the train station, will store bags and bikes for day-trippers (April-Oct Mon-Fri 9:00-17:00, Sat-Sun 10:00-15:00; Nov-March Mon-Fri 9:00-13:00, closed Sat-Sun; from the train station, exit right and walk down the main street with the castle high on your left—the TI will be on your right at Ober-

RHINE VALLEY

strasse 10; tel. 06743/919-303, www.bacharach.de or www.rhein-nahe-touristik.de, Herr Kuhn and his team).

HELPFUL HINTS

Carry Cash: Although more places are accepting credit cards, come prepared to pay cash for most things in the Rhine Valley.

Shopping: The **Jost** German gift store, across the main square from the church, carries most everything a souvenir shopper could want—from beer steins to cuckoo clocks—and can ship purchases to the US (RS% with €10 minimum purchase: 10 percent with cash, 5 percent with credit card; open daily 9:00-18:00, closed Nov-Feb; Blücherstrasse 4, tel. 06743/909-7214).

Laundry: The **Sonnenstrand campground** may let you use their facilities even if you're not staying there, but priority goes to those who are. Call ahead (tel. 06743/1752).

Picnics: You can pick up picnic supplies at **Tomi's,** a basic grocery store (Mon-Fri 8:00-12:30 & 14:00-18:00, Sat 8:00-12:30, closed Sun, Koblenzer Strasse 2). For a gourmet picnic, call the recommended **Rhein Hotel** to reserve a "picnic bag" complete with wine, cheese, small dishes, and a hiking map (€15/person, arrange a day in advance, tel. 06743/1243).

Bike Rental: Some hotels loan bikes to guests. For bike rental in town, head to **Rent-a-Bike Weber** (€10/day, Koblenzer Stras-

se 35, tel. 06743-1898, mobile 0175-168073, heidi100450@
aol.com).

Parking: It's simple to park along the highway next to the train
tracks or, better, in the big public lot by the boat dock (€4 from
9:00 to 18:00, pay with coins at *Parkscheinautomat,* display
ticket on dash, free overnight).

Local Guides: Thomas Gundlach happily gives 1.5-hour town
walks to individuals or small groups for €35. History buffs
will enjoy his "war tour," which focuses on the town's survival
from 1864 through World War II. He also offers 4- to 10-hour
hiking or biking tours for the more ambitious (mobile 0179-
353-6004, thomas_gundlach@gmx.de). Also good is **Birgit
Wessels** (€45/1.5-hour walk, tel. 06743/937-514, wessels.
birgit@t-online.de). The **TI** offers 1.5-hour tours in English
with various themes, including a night tour (prices vary, gather a group). Or take my self-guided town walk or walk the
walls—both are described next.

Taxi: Call Dirk Büttner at 06743/1653.

Bacharach Town Walk

• *Start this self-guided walk at the Köln–Düsseldorfer ferry dock (next
to a fine picnic park).*

Riverfront: View the town from the parking lot—a modern
landfill. The Rhine used to lap against Bacharach's town wall, just
over the present-day highway. Every few years the river floods, covering the highway with several feet of water. Flat land like this is
rare in the Rhine Valley, where towns are often shaped like the
letter "T," stretching thin along the riverfront and up a crease in
the hills beyond.

Reefs farther upstream forced boats to unload upriver and re-
load here. Consequently, in the Middle Ages, Bacharach was the
biggest wine-trading town on the Rhine. A riverfront crane hoisted huge kegs of prestigious "Bacharach" wine (which, in practice,
was from anywhere in the region). Today, the economy is based on
tourism.

Look above town. The **castle** on the hill is now a hostel. Two
of the town's original 16 towers are visible from here (up to five if
you look really hard). The bluff on the right, with the yellow flag, is
the **Heinrich Heine Viewpoint** (the end-point of a popular hike).
Old-timers remember when, rather than the flag marking the town
as a World Heritage site, a swastika sculpture 30 feet wide and tall
stood there. Realizing that it could be an enticing target for Allied
planes in the last months of World War II, locals tore it down even
before Hitler fell.

RHINE VALLEY

Nearby, a stone column in the park describes the Bingen to Koblenz stretch of the Rhine gorge.

• *Before entering the town, walk upstream through the...*

Riverside Park: The park was originally laid out in 1910 in the English style: Notice how the trees were planted to frame fine town views, highlighting the most pic-turesque bits of architecture. Erected in 2016, a Picasso-esque sculpture by Bacharach artist Liesel Metten—of three figures sharing a bottle of wine (a Riesling, perhaps?)—celebrates three men who brought fame to the area through poetry and prose: Victor Hugo, Clemens Brentano, and Hein-rich Heine. Other new elements of the park are designed to bring people to the riverside and combat flooding.

The dark, sad-looking monu-ment—its "eternal" flame long snuffed out—is a **war memorial**. The German psyche is permanently scarred by war memories. Today, many Germans would rather avoid monuments like this, which recall the dark periods be-fore Germany became a nation of pacifists. The military Maltese cross—flanked by classic German helmets—has a W at its center, for Kaiser Wilhelm. On the opposite side, each panel honors sons of Bacharach who died for the Kaiser: in 1864 against Denmark, in 1866 against Austria, in 1870 against France, in 1914 during World War I. Review the family names below: You may later rec-ognize them on today's restaurants and hotels.

• *Look upstream from here to see (in the distance) the...*

Trailer Park and Campground: In Germany, trailer vacation-ers and campers are two distinct subcultures. Folks who travel in motorhomes, like many retirees in the US, are a nomadic bunch, cruising around the countryside and paying a few euros a night to park. Campers, on the other hand, tend to set up camp in one place—complete with comfortable lounge chairs and TVs—and stay put for weeks, even months. They often come back to the same spot year after year, treating it like their own private estate. These camping devotees have made a science out of relaxing. Tourists are welcome to pop in for a drink or meal at the campground café (see "Activities in Bacharach," later).

• *Continue to where the park meets the playground, and then cross the highway to the fortified riverside wall of the Catholic church, decorated with...*

High-Water Marks: These recall various floods. Before the

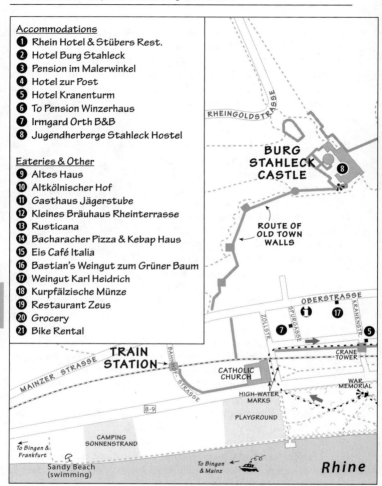

Accommodations
❶ Rhein Hotel & Stübers Rest.
❷ Hotel Burg Stahleck
❸ Pension im Malerwinkel
❹ Hotel zur Post
❺ Hotel Kranenturm
❻ To Pension Winzerhaus
❼ Irmgard Orth B&B
❽ Jugendherberge Stahleck Hostel

Eateries & Other
❾ Altes Haus
❿ Altkölnischer Hof
⓫ Gasthaus Jägerstube
⓬ Kleines Bräuhaus Rheinterrasse
⓭ Rusticana
⓮ Bacharacher Pizza & Kebap Haus
⓯ Eis Café Italia
⓰ Bastian's Weingut zum Grüner Baum
⓱ Weingut Karl Heidrich
⓲ Kurpfälzische Münze
⓳ Restaurant Zeus
⓴ Grocery
㉑ Bike Rental

1910 reclamation project, the river extended out to here, and boats would tie up at mooring rings that used to be in this wall.

• *From the church, go under the 1858 train tracks (and past more high-water marks) and hook right up the stairs at the yellow floodwater yardstick to reach the town wall. Atop the wall, turn left and walk under the long arcade. After 30 yards, on your left, notice a...*

Well: Rebuilt as it appeared in the 17th century, this is one of seven such wells that brought water to the townsfolk until 1900. Each neighborhood's well also provided a social gathering place and the communal laundry. Walk 50 yards past the well along the wall to an alcove in the medieval tower with a view of the war memorial in the park. You're under the crane tower *(Kranenturm)*. After barrels of wine were moved overland from Bingen, avoiding

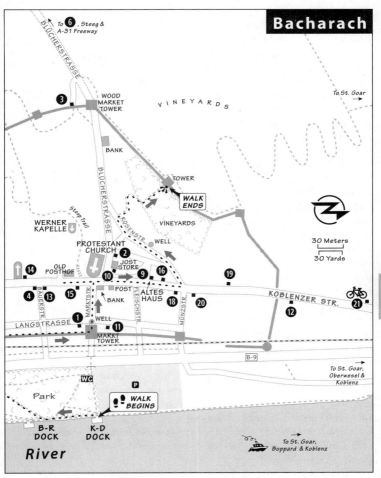

dangerous stretches of river, the precious cargo could be lowered by cranes from here into ships to continue more safely down the river. The Rhine has long been a major shipping route through Germany. In modern times, it's a bottleneck in Germany's train system. The train company gives hotels and residents along the tracks money for soundproof windows.

• *Continue walking along the town wall. Pass the recommended Rhein Hotel just before the...*

Markt Tower: This marks one of the town's 15 original 14th-century gates and is a reminder that in that century there was a big wine market here.

• *Descend the stairs closest to the Rhein Hotel, pass another well, and follow Marktstrasse away from the river toward the town center, the two-tone church, and the town's...*

Main Intersection: From here, Bacharach's main street (Oberstrasse) goes right to the half-timbered red-and-white Altes Haus (which we'll visit later) and left 400 yards to the train station. Spin around to enjoy the higgledy-piggledy building styles. The town has a case of the doldrums: The younger generation is moving to the big cities and many long-established family businesses have no one to take over for their aging owners. In the winter the town is particularly dead.

• *To the left (south) of the church, a golden horn hangs over the old...*

Posthof: Throughout Europe, the postal horn is the symbol of the postal service. In olden days, when the postman blew this, traffic stopped and the mail sped through. This post station dates from 1724, when stagecoaches ran from Cologne to Frankfurt and would change horses here, Pony Express-style. Notice the cornerstones at the Posthof entrance, protecting the venerable building from reckless carriage wheels. If it's open, inside the old oak doors (on the left) is the actual door to the post office that served Bacharach for 200 years. Find the mark on the wall labeled *Rheinhöhe 30/1-4/2 1850*. This recalls a historic flood caused by an ice jam at the Loreley just downstream. Notice also the fascist eagle in the alcove on the right (from 1936; a swastika once filled its center). The courtyard was once a carriage house and inn that accommodated Bacharach's first VIP visitors.

Two hundred years ago, Bacharach's main drag was the only road along the Rhine. Napoleon widened it to fit his cannon wagons. The steps alongside the church lead to the ruins of the 15th-century Werner Chapel and the castle.

• *Return to the church, passing the recommended Italian ice-cream café (**Eis Café Italia**), where friendly Mimo serves his special invention: Riesling wine-flavored gelato.*

Protestant Church: Inside the church (daily 10:00-18:00, closed Nov-March, English info on a stand near door), you'll find grotesque capitals, brightly painted in medieval style, and a mix of round Romanesque and pointed Gothic arches. The church was fancier before the Reformation wars, when it (and the region) was Catholic. Bacharach lies on the religious border of Germany and, like the country as a whole, is split between Catholics and Protestants. To the left of the altar, some medieval (pre-Reformation) frescoes survive where an older Romanesque arch was cut by a pointed Gothic one.

If you're considering bombing the town, take note: A blue-and-white plaque just outside the church's door warns that, according to the Hague Convention, this historic building shouldn't be targeted in times of war.

• *Continue down Oberstrasse to the...*

Altes Haus: Dating from 1389, this is the oldest house in town. Notice the 14th-century building style—the first floor is made of stone, while upper floors are half-timbered (in the ornate style common in the Rhine Valley). Some of its windows still look medieval, with small, flattened circles as panes (small because that's all that the glass-blowing technology of the time would allow), pieced together with molten lead (like medieval stained glass in churches). Frau Weber welcomes visitors to enjoy the fascinating ground floor of the recommended Altes Haus restaurant, with its evocative old photos and etchings (consider eating here later).

• *Keep going down Oberstrasse to the...*

Old Mint (Münze): The old mint is marked by a crude coin in its sign. As a practicality, any great trading town needed coinage, and since 1356, Bacharach minted theirs here. Now, it's a restaurant and bar, **Kurpfälzische Münze,** with occasional live music. Across from the mint, the recommended **Bastian** family's wine garden is another lively place in the evening (see "Nightlife in Bacharach" and "Wine Tasting," later). Above you in the vineyards stands a lonely white-and-red tower—your final destination.

• *At the next street, look right and see the mint tower, painted in the medieval style, and then turn left. Wander 30 yards up Rosenstrasse to the well. Notice the sundial and the wall painting of 1632 Bacharach with its walls intact. Study the fine slate roof over the well: The town's roof tiles were quarried and split right here in the Rhineland. Continue another 30 yards up Rosenstrasse to find the tiny-stepped lane on the right leading up into the vineyard and to the...*

Tall Tower: The slate steps lead to a small path through the vineyard that deposits you at a viewpoint atop the stubby remains of the medieval wall and a tower. The town's towers jutted out from the wall and had only three sides, with the "open" side facing the town. Towers were covered with stucco to make them look more impressive, as if they were made of a finer white stone. If this tower's open, hike up to climb the stairs for the best view. (The top floor has been closed to give nesting falcons some privacy.)

Romantic Rhine View: Looking south, a grand medieval town spreads before you. For 300 years (1300-1600), Bacharach was big (population 4,000), rich, and politically powerful.

From this perch, you can see the ruins of a 15th-century chapel and six surviving **city towers.** Visually trace the wall to the Stahleck Castle. The castle was actually the capital of Germany for a couple of years in the 1200s. When Holy Roman Emperor Frederick Barbarossa went away to fight the Crusades, he left his brother (who lived here) in charge of his vast realm. Bacharach was home to one of the seven electors who voted for the Holy Roman Emperor in 1275. To protect their own power, these prince electors did their best to choose the weakest guy on the ballot. The elector from Bacharach helped select a two-bit prince named Rudolf von Habsburg (from a no-name castle in Switzerland). However, the underestimated Rudolf brutally silenced the robber barons along the Rhine and established the mightiest dynasty in European history. His family line, the Habsburgs, ruled much of Central and Eastern Europe from Vienna until 1918.

Plagues, fires, and the Thirty Years' War (1618-1648) finally did in Bacharach. The town has slumbered for several centuries. Today, the castle houses commoners—40,000 overnights annually by hostelers.

In the mid-19th century, painters such as J. M. W. Turner and writers such as Victor Hugo were charmed by the Rhineland's romantic mix of past glory, present poverty, and rich legend. They put this part of the Rhine on the old Grand Tour map as the "Romantic Rhine." Hugo pondered the chapel ruins that you see under the castle: In his 1842 travel book, *Excursions Along the Banks of the Rhine,* he wrote, "No doors, no roof or windows, a magnificent skeleton puts its silhouette against the sky. Above it, the ivy-covered castle ruins provide a fitting crown. This is Bacharach, land of fairy tales, covered with legends and sagas." If you're enjoying the Romantic Rhine, thank Victor Hugo and company.

• *Our walk is done. To get back into town, just retrace your steps. Or, to extend this walk, take the level path away from the river that leads along the once-mighty wall up the valley to the next tower, the...*

Wood Market Tower: Timber was gathered here in Bacharach and lashed together into vast log booms known as "Holland rafts" (as big as a soccer field) that were floated downstream. Two weeks later the lumber would reach Amsterdam, where it was in high demand as foundation posts for buildings and for the great Dutch shipbuilders. Notice the four stones above the arch on the uphill side of the tower—these guided the gate as it was hoisted up and down.

• *From here, cross the street and go downhill into the parking lot. Pass the recommended* **Pension im Malerwinkel** *on your right, being careful not to damage the old arch with your head. Follow the creek past a delightful little series of half-timbered homes and cheery gardens known as* **"Painters' Corner"** *(Malerwinkel). Resist looking into some weirdo's peep show (on the right) and continue downhill back to the village center.*

Activities in Bacharach

Walk Along the Old Town Walls

A steep and rocky but clearly marked walking path follows the remains of Bacharach's old town walls and makes for a good hour's workout. There are benches along the way where you can pause and take in views of the Rhine and Bacharach's slate roofs. The TI has maps that show the entire route. The path starts near the train station, climbs up to the hostel in what was Stahleck Castle (serves lunch from 12:00-13:30), descends into the side valley, and then continues up the other side to the tower in the vineyards before returning to town. To start the walk at the train station, find the house at Oberstrasse 2 and climb up the stairway to its left. Then follow the *Stadtmauer-Rundweg* signs. Good bilingual signposts tell the history of each of the towers along the wall—some are intact, one is a private residence, and others are now only stubs.

Swimming, Eating, and Drinking at Camping Sonnenstrand

This campground, a 10-minute walk upstream from Bacharach, has a sandy beach with water as still as a lake, and welcomes non-campers (especially if you buy a drink at their café). On hot summer days you can enjoy a dip in the Rhine at the beach at your own risk (free, no lifeguard—beware of strong current). This is a chance to see Euro-style camping, which comes with a sense of community. Campers are mostly Dutch, English, Belgian, and German, with lots of kids (and a playground). The **$ terrace café** overlooking the campsites and the river is the social center and works well for a drink or meal (inside or outside with river view, daily 17:00-21:00, closed Nov-March, tel. 06743/1752, www.camping-rhein.de).

RHINE VALLEY

Sleeping in Bacharach

The only listings with parking are Pension im Malerwinkel, Pension Winzerhaus, and the hostel. For the others, you can drive in to unload your bags and then park in the public lot (see "Helpful Hints," earlier). If you'll arrive after 20:00, let your hotel know in advance (many hotels with restaurants stay open late, but none have 24-hour reception desks).

$$ Rhein Hotel, overlooking the river with 14 spacious and comfortable rooms, is classy, well-run, and decorated with modern flair. This place has been in the Stüber family for six generations and is decorated with works of art by the current owner's siblings. The large family room downstairs is über stylish, while the quaint "hiker room" on the top floor features terrific views of both the town and river. You can sip local wines in the renovated room where owner Andreas was born (river- and train-side rooms come with quadruple-paned windows and air-con, in-room sauna, packages available including big three-course dinner, ask about "picnic bags" when you check in, free loaner bikes, directly inland from the K-D boat dock at Langstrasse 50, tel. 06743/1243, www.rhein-hotel-bacharach.de, info@rhein-hotel-bacharach.de). Their recommended Stübers Restaurant is considered the best in town.

$$ Hotel Burg Stahleck, above a cozy café in the town center, rents five big, bright rooms, more chic than shabby. Birgit treats guests to homemade cakes at breakfast (family rooms, view room, free parking, cheaper rooms in guesthouse around the corner, Blücherstrasse 6, tel. 06743/1388, www.urlaub-bacharach.de, info@urlaub-bacharach.de).

$ Pension im Malerwinkel sits like a grand gingerbread house that straddles the town wall in a quiet little neighborhood so charming it's called "Painters' Corner" *(Malerwinkel).* The Vollmer family's super-quiet 20-room place is a short stroll from the town center. Here guests can sit in a picturesque garden on a brook and enjoy views of the vineyards (cash only, family rooms, elevator, no train noise, bike rentals, easy parking; from  Oberstrasse, turn left at the church, walkers can follow the path to the left just before the town gate but drivers must pass through the gate to find the hotel parking lot, Blücherstrasse 41; tel. 06743/1239, www.im-malerwinkel.de, pension@im-malerwinkel.de, Armin and Daniela).

$ Hotel zur Post, refreshingly clean and quiet, is conveniently located right in the town center with no train noise. Its 12 rooms are a good value. Run by friendly and efficient Ute, the hotel offers more solid comfort than old-fashioned character, though the lovely wood-paneled breakfast room has a rustic feel (family room, Oberstrasse 38, tel. 06743/1277, www.hotel-zur-post-bacharach.de, h.zurpost@t-online.de).

$ Hotel Kranenturm, part of the medieval town wall, has 16 rooms with rustic castle ambience and *Privatzimmer* funkiness right downtown. The rooms in its former *Kranenturm* (crane tower) have the best views. While just 15 feet from the train tracks, a combination of medieval sturdiness and triple-paned windows makes the riverside rooms sleepable (RS%, family rooms, Rhine views come with train noise—earplugs on request, back rooms are quieter, closed Jan-Feb, Langstrasse 30, tel. 06743/1308, mobile 0176-8056-3863, www.kranenturm.com, hotel.kranenturm@gmail.com).

RHINE VALLEY

$ Pension Winzerhaus, a 10-room place run by friendly Sybille and Stefan, is just outside the town walls, directly under the vineyards. The rooms are simple, clean, and modern, and parking is a breeze (cash only, family room, laundry service, parking, nondrivers may be able to arrange a pickup at the train station—ask in advance, Blücherstrasse 60, tel. 06743/1294, www.pension-winzerhaus.de, winzerhaus@gmx.de).

¢ Irmgard Orth B&B rents three bright rooms, two of which share a small bathroom on the hall. Charming Irmgard speaks almost no English, but is exuberantly cheery and serves homemade honey with breakfast (cash only, Spurgasse 2, tel. 06743/1553—speak slowly; she prefers email: orth.irmgard@gmail.com).

¢ Jugendherberge Stahleck hostel is a 12th-century castle on the hilltop—350 steps above Bacharach—with a royal Rhine view. Open to travelers of any age, this gem has 36 rooms, eight with private showers and WCs. The hostel offers hearty all-you-can-eat buffet dinners (18:00-19:30 nightly); in summer, its bistro serves drinks and snacks until 22:00. If you arrive at the

RHINE VALLEY

train station with luggage, it's a minimum €10 taxi ride to the hostel—call 06743/1653 (pay Wi-Fi, reception open 7:00-20:00—call if arriving later, tel. 06743/1266, www.diejugendherbergen.de, bacharach@diejugendherbergen.de, Samuel). If driving, don't go in the driveway; park on the street and walk 200 yards.

Eating in Bacharach

RESTAURANTS
Bacharach has several reasonably priced, atmospheric restaurants offering fine indoor and outdoor dining. Most places don't take credit cards.

The recommended Rhein Hotel's **$$$ Stübers Restaurant** is Bacharach's best top-end choice. Andreas Stüber, his family's sixth-generation chef, creates regional plates prepared with a slow-food ethic. The menu changes with the season and is served at river- and track-side seating or indoors with a spacious wood-and-white-tablecloth elegance. Consider the William Turner pâté starter plate, named after the British painter who liked Bacharach. Book in advance for the special Tuesday slow-food menu (discount for hotel guests, always good vegetarian and vegan options, daily 17:00-21:30 plus Sun 11:30-14:15, closed mid-Dec-Feb, call or email to reserve on weekends or for an outdoor table when balmy, family-friendly with a play area, Langstrasse 50, tel. 06743/1243, info@rhein-hotel-bacharach.de). Their Posten Riesling is well worth the splurge and pairs well with both the food and the atmosphere.

$$$ Altes Haus, the oldest building in town (see the "Bacharach Town Walk," earlier), serves classic German dishes within Bacharach's most romantic atmosphere. Find the cozy little dining room with photos of the opera singer who sang about Bacharach, adding to its fame (Thu-Tue 12:00-14:30 & 18:00-21:30, Mon dinner only, limited menu and closes at 18:00 on weekends, closed Wed and Dec-Easter, dead center by the Protestant church, tel. 06743/1209).

$$$ Altkölnischer Hof is a family-run place with outdoor seating right on the main square, serving Rhine specialties that burst with flavor. This restored 18th-century banquet hall feels formal and sophisticated inside, with high ceilings and oil paintings depicting the building's history. Reserve an outdoor table for a more relaxed meal, especially on weekends when locals pack the place (Tue-Sun 12:00-14:30 & 17:30-21:00, closed Mon and Nov-Easter, Blücherstrasse 2, tel. 06743/947-780, www.altkoelnischer-hof.de).

CASUAL OPTIONS

$$ Gasthaus Jägerstube is every local's nontouristy, good-value hangout. It's a no-frills place run by a former East German family determined to keep Bacharach's working class well-fed and watered. Next to the WC is a rare "party cash box." Regulars drop money into their personal slot throughout the year, Frau Tischmeier banks it, and by year's end...there's plenty in the little savings account for a community party (Wed-Mon March-Nov 11:00-22:00, food served until 21:30; Dec-Feb from 15:00, food served until 20:30; closed Tue year-round; Marktstrasse 3, tel. 06743/1492, Tischmeier family).

$$ Kleines Brauhaus Rheinterrasse is a funky microbrewery serving hearty meals, fresh-baked bread, and homemade beer under a 1958 circus carousel that overlooks the town and river. Sweet Annette cooks while Armin brews, and the kids run free in this family-friendly place. For a sweet finish, try the "beer-liquor," which tastes like Christmas. Don't leave without putting €0.20 in the merry-go-round-in-a-box in front of the Rhine Theater next door (Tue-Sun 13:00-22:00, closed Mon, at the downstream end of town, Koblenzer Strasse 14, tel. 06743/919-179). The little flea market in the attached shed seems to fit right in.

$$ Rusticana, draped in greenery, is an inviting place serving homestyle German food and apple strudel that even the locals swear by. Sit on the delightful patio or at cozy tables inside (daily 11:00-20:00, credit cards accepted, Oberstrasse 40, tel. 06743/1741).

$ Bacharacher Pizza and Kebap Haus, on the main drag, is the town favorite for *döner kebabs,* cheap pizzas, and salads. Imam charges the same to eat in or take out (daily 11:00-22:00, Oberstrasse 43, tel. 06743/3127).

Camping Sonnenstrand, a 10-minute walk from town, has a café (dinner only) with great river views inside and out (see "Activities in Bacharach," earlier).

Gelato: Right on the main street, **Eis Café Italia** is run by friendly Mimo Calabrese, who brought gelato to town in 1976. He's known for his refreshing, not-too-sweet Riesling-flavored gelato. He also makes one with rose petals from a nearby farm. Eat in or take it on your evening stroll (no tastes offered, homemade, Waldmeister flavor is made with forest herbs—top secret, daily 13:00-19:00, closed mid-Oct-March, Oberstrasse 48).

WINE TASTING

Bacharach is proud of its wine. Two places in town—Bastian's rowdy and rustic Grüner Baum, and the more sophisticated Weingut Karl Heidrich—offer visitors an inexpensive tasting memory. Each creates carousels of local wines that small groups of travelers (who don't mind sharing a glass) can sample and compare. Both places offer light plates of food if you'd like a rustic meal.

At **$$ Bastian's Weingut zum Grüner Baum,** pay €29.50 for a wine carousel of 12 glasses—nine different white wines, two reds, and one lonely rosé—and a basket of bread. Your mission: Meet up here after dinner with others who have this book. Spin the Lazy Susan, share a common cup, and discuss the taste. The Bastian family insists: "After each wine, you must talk to each other" (daily 12:00-22:00, Nov-Dec closed Mon-Wed, closed Jan-Feb, just past Altes Haus, tel. 06743/1208). To make a meal of a carousel, consider the *Käseschmaus* (seven different cheeses—including *Spundekäse,* the local soft cheese—with bread and butter). Along with their characteristic interior, they have three nice terraces (front for shade, back for sun, and a courtyard).

$$ Weingut Karl Heidrich is a fun family-run wine shop and *Stube* in the town center, where Markus and daughters Magdalena and Katharina proudly share their family's centuries-old wine tradition, explaining its fine points to travelers. They offer a variety of €14.50 carousels with six wines, English descriptions, and bread—ideal for the more sophisticated wine taster—plus light meals and a meat-and-cheese plate (Thu-Mon 12:00-22:00, kitchen closes at 21:00, closed Tue-Wed and Nov-mid-April, Oberstrasse 16, will ship to the US, tel. 06743/93060, info@weingut-karl-heidrich.

de). With advance notice, they'll host a wine tasting and hike for groups (€185/up to 15 people).

Nightlife in Bacharach

Bacharach goes to bed early, so your options are limited for a little after-dinner action. But a handful of local bars/restaurants and two wine places (listed in "Wine Tasting," earlier) are welcoming and can be fun in the late hours.

$$ Kurpfälzische Münze (Old Mint) has live music some nights, ranging from jazz and blues to rock to salsa, and pairs local wines with meat-and-cheese plates and other local specialties (daily 12:00-24:00, Nov-March from 18:00). **Gasthaus Jägerstube** (described earlier) is a good pick for those who want to mix with a small local crowd. **$$ Restaurant Zeus**'s delicious Greek fare, long hours, and outdoor seating add a spark to the city center after dark (daily 17:30-24:00, cash only, Koblenzer Strasse 11, tel. 06743/909-7171). For something a bit off the beaten path try **Jugendherberge Stahleck**—Bacharach's hostel—where the bistro serves munchies and drinks with priceless views until 22:00 in summer (listed earlier, under "Sleeping in Bacharach").

Bacharach Connections

BY TRAIN

Milk-run trains stop at Rhine towns each hour starting as early as 6:00, connecting at Mainz and Koblenz to trains farther afield. Trains between St. Goar and Bacharach depart at about :50 after the hour in each direction (buy tickets from the machine in the unstaffed stations, carry cash since some machines won't accept US credit cards).

The durations listed below are calculated from Bacharach; for St. Goar, the difference is only 10 minutes. From Bacharach (or St. Goar), to go anywhere distant, you'll need to change trains in Koblenz for points north, or in Mainz for points south. Milk-run connections to these towns depart hourly, at about :50 past the hour for northbound trains, and at about :05 past the hour for southbound trains (with a few more on the half hour). Train info: www.bahn.com.

From Bacharach by Train to: St. Goar (hourly, 10 minutes), **Moselkern** near Burg Eltz (hourly, 1.5 hours, change in Koblenz), **Cochem** (hourly, 2 hours, change in Koblenz), **Trier** (hourly, 3 hours, change in Koblenz), **Cologne** (hourly, 2 hours with change in Koblenz, 2.5 hours direct), **Frankfurt Airport** (hourly, 1 hour, change in Mainz or Bingen), **Frankfurt** (hourly, 1.5 hours, change in Mainz or Bingen), **Rothenburg ob der Tauber** (every 2 hours,

4.5 hours, 3-4 changes), **Munich** (hourly, 5 hours, 2 changes), **Berlin** (every 2 hours with a transfer in Frankfurt, 5.5 hours; more with 2-3 changes), **Amsterdam** (hourly, 5-7 hours, change in Cologne, sometimes 1-2 more changes).

ROUTE TIPS FOR DRIVERS

This area is a logical first (or last) stop in Germany. If you're using Frankfurt Airport, here are some tips.

Frankfurt Airport to the Rhine: Driving from Frankfurt to the Rhine or Mosel takes about an hour (follow blue autobahn signs from airport—major cities are signposted).

The Rhine to Frankfurt: From St. Goar or Bacharach, follow the river to Bingen, then autobahn signs to *Mainz*, then *Frankfurt*. From there, head for the airport *(Flughafen)* or downtown (signs to *Messe*, then *Hauptbahnhof*, to find the parking under Frankfurt's main train station—see "Arrival in Frankfurt—By Car" on page 79).

Oberwesel

Oberwesel (OH-behr-vay-zehl), with more commerce than St. Goar and Bacharach combined, is just four miles from Bacharach. Oberwesel was a Celtic town in 400 BC, then a Roman military station. It's worth a quick visit, with a charming main square, a fun-to-walk medieval wall, and the best collection of historic Rhine artifacts I've found within the Rhine Valley. From the river, you'll notice its ship's masts rising from terra firma—a memorial to the generations of riverboat captains and sailors for whom this town is famous. Like most towns on the Rhine, Oberwesel is capped by a castle (Schönburg, now a restaurant, hotel, and youth hostel with a small museum). The other town landmark is its 130-foot-tall crenellated Ochsenturm (Oxen Tower), standing high and solitary overlooking the river.

Oberwesel is an easy stop by boat, train, bike, or car from Bacharach. There's free parking by the river (as is often the case in small towns, you must display a plastic clock—see page 217).

Exploring Oberwesel is a breeze when you follow my self-guided walk. Start out by picking up a map from the **TI** on the main square (closed Sun, 10-minute walk from the train station at Rathausstrasse 3—from the station turn right and follow Liebfrauenstrasse to Marktplatz, tel. 06744/710-624, www.oberwesel. de). Maps are also available at the Kulturhaus and Stadtmuseum Oberwesel, and posted around town—just snap a photo of one to use as a guide.

Oberwesel Walk

I've laced together Oberwesel's sights with this self-guided walk. Allow at least an hour without stops. Here's an overview: Starting at the Marktplatz, you'll visit the museum and hike the lower wall to the Ochsenturm at the far end of town, then climb to the top of the town and walk the upper wall, passing through the Stadtmauergarten and Klostergarten (former monastery) before returning to the Marktplatz, where you can get a bite to eat at one of several cafés.

• *Begin at the Marktplatz in front of the TI.*

Marktplatz: For centuries this has been Oberwesel's social and commercial center. That tradition continues today in the Marktplatz's tourist-friendly cafés and wine bars. If you're here in the summer, you can't miss the oversized wine glass declaring that Oberwesel is a winegrowers' town. Around harvest time, the city hosts a huge wine festival and elects a "Wine Witch." Why? It's pure marketing. After World War II, the Rhine's wine

producers were desperate to sell their wine, so they hosted big parties and elected a representative. All the other towns picked wine queens, but Oberwesel went with a witch instead.

• *Continue along the main drag, passing several cafés, until you see the entrance (marked* Eingang*) for the museum on the left.*

Kulturhaus and Stadtmuseum Oberwesel: This is the region's best museum on local history and traditions, with lots of artifacts and interesting exhibits. The ground floor retraces the history of Oberwesel, from the Romans to the 19th-century Romantics.

Upstairs you'll learn how salmon were once fished here, and timber traders lashed together huge rafts of wood and floated them to the Netherlands to sell. You'll see dramatic photos of the river when it was jammed with ice, and review wine witches from the past few decades (€3, Tue-Fri 10:00-17:00, Sat-Sun from 14:00, closed Mon; Nov-March Tue-Fri until 14:00, closed Sat-Mon; borrow the English descriptions, Rathausstrasse 23, tel. 06744/7147-26, www.kulturhaus-oberwesel.de).

• *Return to the Marktplatz, turn toward the river and walk to the...*

Town Wall: The walls in front of you are some of the best-preserved walls in the Middle Rhine Valley, thanks to the work of a group of local citizen volunteers.

• *Turn right on Rheinstrasse, climb the narrow steps on the left to the top of the wall, and start walking downstream (left), toward the leaning tower.*

Hospitalgassenturm (Hospital Tower) and Vineyards: This tower was initially constructed to rest on the wall. But it was too heavy. In an attempt to "fix it," they straightened out the top.

Notice the vineyards along the banks of the Rhine. They've been part of the landscape here for centuries. Recently, many vintners have been letting the vineyards go untended, as they are just too expensive to keep up. The hope is that a younger generation will bring new energy to the Rhineland's vineyards. But the future of these fabled vineyards remains uncertain.

• *Continue walking until you come to the...*

Werner-Kapelle (Hospital Chapel): This chapel was built into the wall in the 13th century and remains part of the hospital district to this day. The sick lay in bed here with their eyes on the cross, confident that a better life awaited them in heaven. Today this chapel serves the adjacent, more modern hospital (free, daily 9:00-17:00).

• *Continue walking along the wall to reach the next tower. Climb up if you'd like.*

Steingassenturm: This tower is named for the first paved road in town, just ahead. Inside the tower, notice the little holes about six feet up. This is where they placed the scaffolding during construction. If you climb to the top, consider how many Romantic painters and poets in centuries past enjoyed this same view.

As Victor Hugo wrote, "This is the warlike Oberwesel whose old walls are riddled with the havoc of shot and shells. Upon them you easily recognize the trace of the huge cannon balls of the bishops of Treves, the Biscayans of Louis XIV, and the revolutionary grape shot of France. At the present day Oberwesel resembles an old veteran soldier turned winemaker, and what excellent wine he produces."

RHINE VALLEY

• Carry on toward the two towers in the distance. Just before the break in the wall, stop to take in the view.

View of the Katzenturm (Cat Tower) and Ochsenturm (Oxen Tower): These were among the 16 towers that once protected Oberwesel. The farthest tower, Ochsenturm, was built in the 14th century as a lookout and signal tower, but its eight-sided design and crenellated top were also a status symbol for the archbishop, declaring his power to all who passed here along the Rhine. The tower still impresses passersby today.

Take a moment here, with all the ships and trains going by, to think about transportation on the Rhine across the centuries. The Rhine has been a major transportation route since Roman times, when the river marked the northern end of the empire. The Rhineland's many castles and fortifications, like the one above Oberwesel, testify to its strategic importance in the Middle Ages. The stretch from Koblenz to Bingen was home to no fewer than 16 greedy dukes and lords—robber barons running two-bit dukedoms, living in hilltop castles and collecting tolls from merchant vessels passing by in the river below.

Between you and the river are: a bike lane (once a towpath for mighty horses pulling boats upstream), a train line (one of the first in Germany), and the modern road (built in the 1950s). Until modern times there was just one small road through Oberwesel—the one you walked along to get to the center of town.

Have you heard the trains passing by? Increasing rail traffic has made nearly constant train noise quite an issue for Rhinelanders. It's estimated that, on average, a train barrels down each side of the Rhine every three minutes. That's 500 trains a day. Landowners complain that it's nearly impossible to sell a piece of property along this stretch due to the train noise.

• A set of stairs takes you down to street level. Notice the white church on the hilltop to your left—that's where you're headed, to continue this walk with a visit to the upper town walls. To get there, walk straight ahead along Niederbachstrasse. Go under the arch and make an immediate left to walk through the Kölnischer Torturm (Cologne Gate Tower). Follow Kölnische Turmgasse two blocks to find a staircase to your right, leading up to the church. Ascend the stairs and stop at the top to enjoy the view.

St. Martin's Church: Built in the 14th century, this is one of two major churches in town and is known to townspeople as the "white church." Although it looks like sandstone, it's actually made of more readily available slate. Notice the picturesque little church-caretaker's house to the left, then ascend the small set of stairs to the church.

• *Walk around the left side of the church and peek inside. Then continue around the back of the building through the gate to the gardens overlooking the Rhine.*

Gardens: The church garden to the right, with the green cross, was planted in the 17th century. The garden to the left is much more modern; step into it to enjoy this secret oasis. Before leaving the garden, turn around and notice the tower attached to the back of the church. Set on a hilltop, the tower was part of the town's defensive wall—built long before the church. Later, when it came time to build a church, the townsfolk incorporated the tower into the new structure.

• *Exiting the gardens, head through the gate across from the church entrance, cross the street, and merge onto the dirt path bordering the outside of the upper town wall. Follow the wall to the first of two towers.*

Michelfeldturm I and II: This stretch is the oldest part of the town wall. Of the 23 original towers, 16 remain today. If you're looking for a summer home along the Rhine, here's a real-estate tip. The city leases these towers for €1 for 100 years. The hitch? You have to agree to restore them. Notice the house set atop the first tower.

• *Continue walking until you come to the next tower.*

Kuhhirtenturm (Cowherder's Tower): This is now a private home with a fanciful drawbridge. If the bridge is down you'll know they're home. According to local folklore, a teenage son of the tower's owners once had a rowdy graduation party here. With all the noise, neighbors complained. But when the police came, they just hoisted up the drawbridge and partied on.

• *Enjoy the views along this last stretch of the wall. To the left you'll see the Rathaus (Town Hall), with the clock on top. That's where this walk ends. Pass the Pulverturm (Powder Tower) and start downhill, stopping just beyond the miniature house.*

View of Schönburg Castle: You can't help but take in the castle view from here. There's been a castle in Oberwesel since the 10th century. Destroyed by the French in 1689, it stood in ruins for 200 years before being rebuilt. Today it houses a hotel/restaurant, youth hostel, and small museum. While there's not much to see at the castle itself, the hike to reach it (along the Elfenley trail) is scenic.

• *Turning away from the castle, continue downhill and take the first set of stairs to your left, bordering a vineyard. At the bottom of the stairs follow the path past the beautiful backyard gardens. Continue down another small set of stairs, passing a well on your left, and then immediately ascend another set of stairs (along Rasselberg). When you reach the ivy-lined wall, enter the gardens to your left.*

Stadtmauergarten (Town Wall Gardens): These beautiful gardens were made possible by a local lad who left town to pursue his fortune but never forgot where he came from. Upon his retirement, he returned to Oberwesel to establish a private foundation and spent his last years back in his old childhood home...our next stop.

• *Exit the gardens, turn left, and walk downhill. At the dead-end, turn right and walk until you see the cross (on the left) at the next intersection. Take a left and walk to the entrance of the monastery.*

Klostergarten (Monastery Garden): For 600 years Franciscan monks lived, worked, and prayed here. During Napoleon's reign this monastery was vacated and later fell victim to fire. The poor took refuge in what was left and built their homes inside the former cloister, sacristy, and other remnants. At its peak, after World War II, about 70 people were living here. Only a dozen remain today in this very unique (and cramped) living space.

• *Feel free to enter and explore a bit, but be respectful and remember that this is a private residence. When you reach the information board (in English) beside the church entrance, you know you're done. Retrace your steps back to the entrance and walk downhill until you reach the Marktplatz.*

St. Goar

St. Goar (sahnkt gwahr) is a classic Rhine tourist town. Its hulk of a castle overlooks a half-timbered shopping street and leafy riverside park, busy with sightseeing ships and contented strollers. Rheinfels Castle, once the mightiest on the river, is the single best Rhineland ruin to explore. While the town of St. Goar itself is less interesting than Bacharach, be sure

to explore beyond the shops: Thoughtful little placards scattered around town explain factoids (in English) about each street, lane, and square. St. Goar also makes a good base for hiking or biking the region. A tiny car ferry will shuttle you back and forth across the busy Rhine from here. (If you run out of things to see, a great pastime in St. Goar is simply chatting with friendly Heike at the K-D boat kiosk.) For train connections, see "Bacharach Connections," earlier.

Orientation to St. Goar

St. Goar is dominated by its mighty castle, Rheinfels. The village—basically a wide spot in the road at the foot of Rheinfels' hill—isn't much more than a few hotels and restaurants. From the riverboat docks, the main drag—Heerstrasse, a dull pedestrian mall without history—cuts through town before ending at the road up to the castle.

TOURIST INFORMATION

The helpful St. Goar TI, which stores bags for free, is on the main pedestrian street (Mon-Fri 9:00-13:00 & 14:00-18:00, Sat-Sun 10:00-13:00; shorter hours and closed Sat-Sun off-season; from train station, go downhill around church and turn left after the recommended Hotel Am Markt, Heerstrasse 127; tel. 06741/383, www.st-goar.de).

HELPFUL HINTS

Picnics: St. Goar's waterfront park has benches perfect for a picnic. You can buy picnic fixings on the pedestrian street at the tiny **St. Goarer Stadtladen** grocery store (Tue-Fri 8:00-19:00, Sat until 16:00, closed Sun-Mon, Heerstrasse 106) or at the recommended **Café St. Goar.**

Shopping: The Montag family runs two shops (one specializes in steins and the other in cuckoo clocks), both at the base of the castle hill road. The stein shop under Hotel Montag has Rhine guides and fine steins. The other shop boasts "the largest free-hanging cuckoo clock in the world" (RS%—10 percent discount, €10 minimum purchase; both locations open daily 9:00-18:00, shorter hours Nov-April). They'll ship your souvenirs home—or give you a VAT form to claim your tax refund at the airport if you're carrying your items with you. A couple of other souvenir shops are across from the K-D boat dock.

Laundry: Helmut Dubrulle can pick up and drop off your laundry, or you can drop it off. There's no self-service (Mon-Fri 9:00-12:30, also Tue and Thu-Fri 14:00-17:00, closed Sat-Sun, one street above the main drag between the train station and TI, Herpellstrasse, tel. 06741-512).

Bike Rental: Call ahead to reserve a bike at **Hotel an der Fähre,**

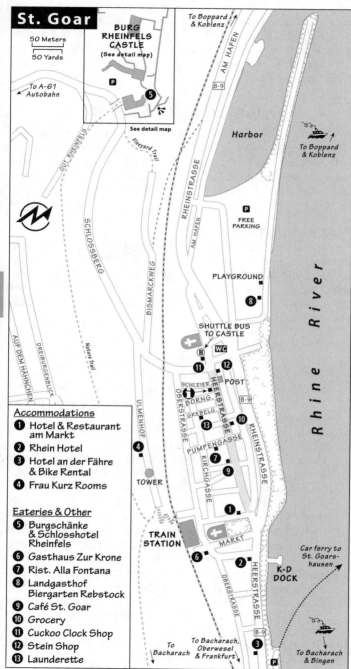

St. Goar

50 Meters
50 Yards

BURG RHEINFELS CASTLE
(See detail map)

To A-61 Autobahn

See detail map

To Boppard & Koblenz

AM HAFEN

B-9

Harbor

To Boppard & Koblenz

Vineyard Trail

RHEINSTRASSE

AM HAFEN

P FREE PARKING

GUT RHEINFELS

SCHLOSSBERG

BISMARCKWEG

RHINE VALLEY

AUF DEM HÄHNCHEN

DREIBURGENBLICK

Nature Trail

PLAYGROUND

Rhine River

SHUTTLE BUS TO CASTLE

WC

B

SCHLEIER

HEERSTRASSE

POST

BORNG.

OBERSTRASSE

ULMENHOF

GREBELG.

B-9

PUMPENGASSE

KIRCHGASSE

RHEINSTRASSE

TOWER

MARKT

TRAIN STATION

HEERSTRASSE

OBERSTRASSE

Car ferry to St. Goarshausen

K-D DOCK

To Bacharach

To Bacharach, Oberwesel & Frankfurt

B-9

To Bacharach & Bingen

Accommodations
1 Hotel & Restaurant am Markt
2 Rhein Hotel
3 Hotel an der Fähre & Bike Rental
4 Frau Kurz Rooms

Eateries & Other
5 Burgschänke & Schlosshotel Rheinfels
6 Gasthaus Zur Krone
7 Rist. Alla Fontana
8 Landgasthof Biergarten Rebstock
9 Café St. Goar
10 Grocery
11 Cuckoo Clock Shop
12 Stein Shop
13 Launderette

which rents wheels to the public (€10/day, pickup after 10:00, Heerstrasse 47, tel. 06741/980-577).

Parking: A free lot is at the downstream end of town, by the harbor. For on-street parking by the K-D boat dock and recommended hotels, get a ticket from the machine *(Parkscheinautomat)* and put it on the dashboard (€4/day, daily 9:00-18:00, coins only, free overnight). Make sure you press the button for a day ticket.

Sights in St. Goar

Rheinfels Castle is St. Goar's only real sight. For day trips from here, see "Sights Along the Rhine," earlier.

▲▲▲Rheinfels Castle (Burg Rheinfels)

Perched proudly atop the hill above St. Goar, the ruins of this once mightiest of Rhine River castles still exude a hint of menace. Built

in the 13th century, Rheinfels ruled the river for more than 500 years. The castle you see today, though impressive and an evocative sight to visit, is but a shadow of its former sprawling self. This hollow but interesting shell offers your single best hands-on ruined-castle experience on the river. The free castle map shows which areas are accessible without a guided tour, and my self-guided tour below covers most everything worth seeing.

Cost and Hours: €5, family card-€10, daily 9:00-18:00, Nov-mid-March possibly Sat-Sun only 11:00-17:00 (call ahead), last entry one hour before closing—weather permitting.

Information: Tel. 06741/7753, in winter 06741/383, www.st-goar.de.

Tours: Due to a multiyear restoration, parts of the castle grounds, including the tunnels, can only be seen with a guided tour. Tours are run in both German and English but determined on the day by who shows up; to arrange an English tour for a group, call 1-2 days in advance. If you plan to take a tour, you must bring a flashlight for the dark tunnels.

Services: A handy WC is immediately across from the ticket booth (men take note of the guillotine urinals—stand back when you pull to flush). There are also WCs in the hotel across from the entrance.

Getting to the Castle: A **taxi** up from town costs €5 (tel. 06741/7011). Or take the shuttle bus (€2 one-way, generally April-

RHINE VALLEY

RHINE VALLEY

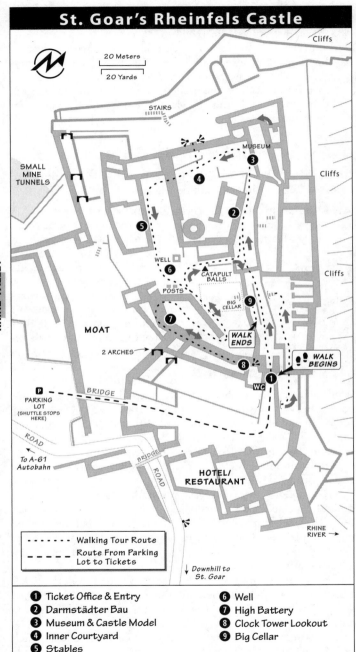

St. Goar's Rheinfels Castle

Cliffs

20 Meters
20 Yards

STAIRS

SMALL
MINE
TUNNELS

Cliffs

MUSEUM

❸

❹

❷

❺

Cliffs

WELL

❻

CATAPULT
BALLS

POSTS

BIG
CELLAR

❾

MOAT

❼

WALK
ENDS

2 ARCHES

❽

WALK
BEGINS

❶

WC

P

PARKING
LOT
(SHUTTLE STOPS
HERE)

BRIDGE

ROAD

To A-61
Autobahn

BRIDGE

ROAD

HOTEL/
RESTAURANT

RHINE
RIVER

Walking Tour Route

Route From Parking
Lot to Tickets

↓ Downhill to
St. Goar

❶ Ticket Office & Entry
❷ Darmstädter Bau
❸ Museum & Castle Model
❹ Inner Courtyard
❺ Stables
❻ Well
❼ High Battery
❽ Clock Tower Lookout
❾ Big Cellar

Oct daily 10:55-16:55, departs roughly every 30 minutes or when full). The shuttle departs from the Catholic church just past the top end of the pedestrian street. **Parking** at the castle costs €1/hour, cash only.

To **walk** up to the castle, simply follow the main road up through the railroad underpass at the top end of the pedestrian street (5 minutes). But it's more fun to **hike** the nature trail: Start at the St. Goar train station. Take the underpass under the tracks at the north end of the station, climb the steep stairs uphill, turn right (following *Burg Rheinfels* signs), and keep straight along the path just above the old city wall. Small red-and-white signs show the way, taking you to the castle in 15 minutes.

Background: Burg Rheinfels *was* huge—for five centuries, it was the biggest castle on the Rhine. Built in 1245 to guard a toll station, it soon earned the nickname "the unconquerable fortress." In the 1400s, the castle was thickened to withstand cannon fire. Rheinfels became a thriving cultural center and, in the 1520s, was visited by the artist Albrecht Dürer and the religious reformer Ulrich Zwingli. It saw lots of action in the Thirty Years' War (1618-1648), and later became the strongest and most modern fortress in the Holy Roman Empire. It withstood a siege of 28,000 French troops in 1692. But eventually the castle surrendered to the French without a fight, and in 1797, the French Revolutionary army destroyed it. For years, the ruined castle was used as a source of building stone, and today—while still mighty—it's only a small fraction of its original size.

◐ Self-Guided Tour: Rather than wander aimlessly, visit the castle by following this tour. We'll start at the museum, then circulate through the courtyards, up to the highest lookout point, finishing in a big cellar. To walk around the fortified ramparts, and to access the dark tunnels that require a flashlight, you'll need to book a tour (see earlier). If it's damp, be careful of slippery stones.

Pick up the free map and use its commentary to navigate from red signpost to red signpost through the castle. My self-guided tour route is similar to the one marked on the castle map. That map, the one in this book, and this tour all use the same numbering system. (You'll notice that I've skipped a couple stops—just walk on by signs for ❷ *Darmstädter Bau and* ❺ *Stables.*)

• *Buy your ticket and walk through the castle's clock tower, labeled* ❶ Uhrturm. *Continue straight, passing a couple points of interest (which we'll visit later), until you get to the* ❸ *museum.*

Museum and Castle Model: The pleasant museum is located in the only finished room of the castle. It features a sweeping history exhibit with good English descriptions and Romantic Age etchings that give a sense of the place as it was in the 19th century (daily 10:00-12:30 & 13:00-17:30, closed Nov-mid-March).

RHINE VALLEY

The seven-foot-tall carved stone immediately to the right inside the door (marked *Flammensäule*)—a tombstone from a nearby Celtic grave—is from 400 years before Christ. There were people here long before the Romans...and this castle.

The massive fortification was the only Rhineland castle to withstand Louis XIV's assault during the 17th century. At the far left end of the room is a model reconstruction of the castle, showing how much bigger it was before French Revolutionary troops destroyed it in the 18th century. Study this. Find where you are. (Hint: Look for the tall tower.) This was the living quarters of the original castle, which was only the smallest ring of buildings around the tiny central courtyard (13th century). The ramparts were added in the 14th century. By 1650, the fortress was largely complete. Since its destruction by the French in the late 18th century, it's had no military value. While no WWII bombs were wasted on this ruin, it served St. Goar as a stone quarry for generations. The basement of the museum shows the castle pharmacy and an exhibit of Rhine-region odds and ends, including tools, an 1830 loom, and photos of icebreaking on the Rhine. While once routine, icebreaking hasn't been necessary here since 1963.

• *Exit the museum and walk 20 yards directly out, slightly uphill and halfway into the castle courtyard. At the first opening on the right, step up for a peek out at the...*

Corner of Castle: Look right. That's the original castle tower. A three-story, half-timbered building originally rose beyond the tower's stone fortification. The two stone tongues near the top supported the toilet. (Insert your own joke here.) Lean and look left.

Thoop...You're Dead: Notice the smartly placed crossbow slits. While you're lying there, notice the stonework. The little round holes were for the scaffolds they used as they built up, which indicate that this stonework is original.

• *Pick yourself up and walk back into the inner courtyard, (❹ Innenhof).*

Medieval Castle Courtyard: Five hundred years ago, the entire castle encircled this courtyard. The place was self-sufficient and ready for a siege, with a bakery, pharmacy, herb garden, brewery, well (top of yard), and livestock. During peacetime, 300-600 people lived here; during a siege, there would be as many as 4,000. The walls were plastered and painted white. Bits of the original 13th-century plaster survive.

• *Continue through the courtyard under the Erste Schildmauer (first*

shield wall) sign, turn left, and walk straight toward the two old wooden upright posts. Find the pyramid of stone catapult balls on your left just before you reach the posts.

Castle Garden: Catapult balls like these were too expensive not to recycle—they'd be retrieved after any battle. Across from the balls is a well (❻ *Brunnen*)—essential for any castle during the age of sieges. Look in. Thirsty? The old posts are for the ceremonial baptizing of new members of the local trading league. While this guild goes back centuries, it's now a social club that fills this court with a huge wine party every year on the third weekend of September.

• *Climb uphill to the castle's highest point by walking along the cobbled path (look for the* To the Tower *sign) up past the high battery (❼ Hohe Batterie) to the castle's best viewpoint—up where the German flag waves (signed ❽ Uhrturm).*

Highest Castle Tower Lookout: Enjoy a great view of the river, the castle, and the forest. Remember, the fortress once covered five times the land it does today. Notice how the other castles (across the river) don't poke above the top of the Rhine canyon. That would make them easy for invading armies to see.

RHINE VALLEY

From this perch, survey the Rhine Valley, cut out of slate over millions of years by the river. The slate absorbs the heat of the sun, making the grapes grown here well-suited for wine. Today the slate is mined to provide roofing. Imagine St. Goar himself settling here 1,500 years ago, establishing a place where sailors—thankful to have survived the treacherous Loreley—would stop and pray. Imagine the frozen river of years past, when the ice would break up and boats would huddle in man-made harbors like the one below for protection. Consider the history of trade on this busy river—from the days when castles levied tolls on ships, to the days when boats would be hauled upstream with the help of riverside towpaths, to the 21st century when 300 ships a day move their cargo past St. Goar. And imagine this castle before the French destroyed it...when it was the mightiest structure on the river, filled with people and inspiring awe among all who passed.

• *Return to the catapult balls, walk downhill and through the tunnel, and pause to look back up and see the original 13th-century core of the castle. Now go right toward the entrance, first veering down to see the...*

Big Cellar: This ❾ *Grosser Keller* was a big pantry. When the castle was smaller, this was the original moat—you can see the rough lower parts of the wall. The original floor was 13 feet deeper. The drawbridge rested upon the stone nubs on the left. When the castle expanded, the moat became this cellar. Halfway up the walls on the entrance side of the room, square holes mark spots where timbers made a storage loft, perhaps filled

with grain. In the back, an arch leads to the wine cellar (probably blocked off) where finer wine was kept. Part of a soldier's pay was wine...table wine. This wine was kept in a single 180,000-liter stone barrel (that's 47,550 gallons), which generally lasted about 18 months.

The count owned the surrounding farmland. Farmers got to keep 20 percent of their production. Later, in more liberal feudal times, the nobility let them keep 40 percent. Today, the German government leaves the workers with 60 percent...and provides a few more services.

• *You're free. Climb out, turn right, and leave. For coffee on a terrace with a great view, visit Schlosshotel Rheinfels, opposite the entrance.*

Sleeping in St. Goar

For parking advice, see "Helpful Hints," earlier.

$ Hotel am Markt, run by Herr and Frau Marx and their friendly staff, is a decent value with all the modern comforts. It features 15 rustic rooms in the main building (think antlers with a pastel flair), 10 classier rooms right next door, and a good restaurant. It's a stone's throw from the boat dock and train station (family rooms, some rooms with river view, two apartments also available, closed Nov-Feb, pay parking, Markt 1, tel. 06741/1689, http://hotel-sankt-goar.de, dashotel@t-online.de).

$ Rhein Hotel, on the other side of the church from Hotel am Markt and run with enthusiasm by young and energetic Gil Velich, has 10 bright and stylish rooms in a spacious building (some rooms with river view and balconies, family rooms, pay laundry, closed mid-Nov-March, Heerstrasse 71, tel. 06741/981-240, www.rheinhotel-st-goar.de, info@rheinhotel-st-goar.de).

$ Hotel an der Fähre is a simple place on the busy road at the end of town, immediately across from the ferry dock. It rents 12 cheap and colorful rooms (cash only, some view rooms, cheapest rooms with shared bath, street noise but double-glazed windows, parking, closed Nov-Feb, Heerstrasse 47, tel. 06741/980-577, www.

hotel-stgoar.de, info@hotel-stgoar.de, friendly Alessya). They also offer rental bikes by reservation (see "Helpful Hints," earlier).

$ Frau Kurz has been housing my readers since 1988. With the help of her daughter, Jeanette, she offers St. Goar's best B&B, renting three delightful rooms (sharing 2.5 bathrooms) with bathrobes, a breakfast terrace with castle views, a garden, and homemade marmalade (cash only, free and easy parking, ask about apartment with kitchen, Ulmenhof 11, tel. 06741/459, www.gaestehaus-kurz.de, fewo-kurz@kabelmail.de). If you're not driving, it's a steep five-minute hike from the train station: Exit left from the station, take an immediate left under the tracks, and go partway up the zigzag stairs, turning right through an archway onto Ulmenhof; #11 is just past the tower.

Eating in St. Goar

$$ Hotel Restaurant am Markt serves tasty traditional meals with plenty of game and fish (specialties include marinated roast beef and homemade cheesecake) at fair prices with good atmosphere and service. Choose cozy indoor seating, or dine outside with a river and castle view (daily 9:00-21:00, closed Nov-Feb, Markt 1, tel. 06741/1689).

$$$ Burgschänke is easy to miss on the ground floor of Schlosshotel Rheinfels (the hotel across from the castle entrance—enter through the souvenir shop). It offers the only reasonably priced lunches up at Rheinfels Castle, is family-friendly, and has a Rhine view from its fabulous outdoor terrace (*Flammkuchen* and regional dishes, Sun-Thu 11:00-21:00, Fri-Sat until 21:30, tel. 06741/802-806).

The **$$$$ Schlosshotel Rheinfels** dining room is your Rhine splurge, with an incredible indoor view terrace in an elegant, dressy setting. Call to reserve for weekends or if you want a window table (daily 7:00-11:00, 12:00-14:00 & 18:00-21:00, tel. 06741/8020, www.schloss-rheinfels.de).

$$ Gasthaus Zur Krone is the local choice for traditional German food in a restaurant off the main drag. There's no river view, but it's cozy and offers some outdoor seating on weekends (Thu-Tue 11:00-14:30 & 18:00-21:00, closed Wed, cash only, next to the train station and church at Oberstrasse 38, tel. 06741/1515).

$$ Ristorante Alla Fontana, tucked away on a back lane and busy with locals, serves the best Italian food in town at great prices in a lovely dining room or on a leafy patio (Tue-Sun 11:30-14:00 & 17:30-21:30, closed Mon, cash only, dinner reservations smart, Pumpengasse 5, 06741/96117).

$$ Landgasthof Biergarten Rebstock is hidden on the far end of town on the banks of the Rhine. They serve schnitzel and plenty of beer and wine. A nice playground and minigolf course on either side keeps the kids busy (April-Oct long hours daily—weather permitting, Am Hafen 1, tel. 06741/980-0337).

$ Café St. Goar is the perfect spot for a quick lunch or *Kaffee und Kuchen*. They sell open-face sandwiches, strudel, tiny cookies, and a variety of cakes to satisfy any appetite. Grab something for a picnic or enjoy seating on the pedestrian-only street out front (Mon-Sat 9:00-18:00, Sun from 10:00, Heerstrasse 95, tel. 06741/1635).

Koblenz

The main town on this stretch of the Romantic Rhine is Koblenz—situated where the Mosel River flows into the Rhine. The word "Koblenz" comes from the Roman word for confluence—a reminder that 2,000 years ago, this was the northern border of the Roman Empire. The city has long been a strategic base. A transportation hub with a key bridge and a mighty fortress, it was heavily bombed in World War II. The city feels rebuilt today and has little of the charm that most are looking for when they visit the Rhineland. All I would do here is check out the modern center (Zentralplatz, with its Forum Confluentes and Rhineland museum), trek out to the Deutsches Eck ("German Corner") for a little Deutschland patriotism, ride the cable car over the Rhine (from the Deutsches Eck to the castle), and tour the Ehrenbreitstein Fortress, if only for the views.

The **TI** is inside the Forum Confluentes cultural center on Zentralplatz (daily 10:00-18:00, tel. 0261/19433, www.koblenz-touristik.de).

Arrival in Koblenz: If you're driving a **car,** go directly to the Deutsches Eck and park. If arriving by **train,** walk (or catch bus #1) from the station through the town center to the Deutsches Eck, with a stop at Zentralplatz on the way. K-D Rhine sightseeing **boats** stop right at the Deutsches Eck (2-3/day, 3.5 hours upstream to St. Goar, 2.5 hours downstream from St. Goar, www.k-d.com).

Sights in Koblenz

Zentralplatz and Forum Confluentes

The city's once bombed-out center now sparkles with sleek modern architecture. On the main square, Zentralplatz, you'll find the striking Forum Confluentes. This bright, modern cultural center houses the TI; the Romanticum, an interactive museum with fun Romantic-era portrayals of Rhine towns and exhibits on the Rhineland culture; and the Mittelrhein Museum, with art from medieval to modern. You can also catch an elevator ride to the roof terrace for sweeping city views. (Romanticum-€6, daily 10:00-18:00, tel. 0261/19433; Mittelrhein-€6, Tue-Sun 10:00-18:00, closed Mon; elevator-€1, daily 9:00-20:00; Zentralplatz 1, tel. 0261/129-2520, www.forum-confluentes.de). It's a short walk from here to the Deutsches Eck.

Deutsches Eck

The actual tip of land where the two rivers meet is the legendary "Deutsches Eck"—the "German Corner." For many Germans, this spot stirs their nationalistic spirit. While *"Deutschland über alles"* ("Germany above all"—a line from the German national anthem) is often associated with Hitler and German expansionism in the 20th century, the phrase actually refers to the fragmentation of German-speaking states before unity in 1871. The *Song of Germany* celebrated the notion of the little German states uniting in one German nation.

When Germany finally was united, it was the Johnny-come-lately of European superpowers and scrambled to establish its legitimacy. The allure of this strategic spot made it a natural staging ground to symbolize unity. Notice how the flags of the many German states all converge on the flag of a united Germany at the tip of the peninsula. While, historically, there was a lack of clarity about the French/German border (and under Napoleon, it was actually right here), today the "German Corner" is seen not as a border but as the heart of a great nation. Beyond the flag-lined plaza is a reconstructed memorial to Kaiser Wilhelm. Germans come here to feel good about their country while enjoying the organ grinders and buskers playing accordions in this park-like atmosphere.

Seilbahn Cable Car

Koblenz's cable car runs above the Rhine River, stretching a half-mile from the Deutsches Eck to the Ehrenbreitstein Fortress high above. As you glide over the river you'll get fine views of the point where the Rhine and the Mosel rivers converge. This is the only convenient way to get from the city to the fortress.

Cost and Hours: €7.20 one-way, €9.90 round-trip, €13.80 round-trip combo-ticket with fortress entry; daily 9:30-19:00, Nov-March Sat-Sun only 9:30-17:30; tel. 0261/2016-5850, www.seilbahn-koblenz.de.

Ehrenbreitstein Fortress

While a castle has stood on this strategic point much longer, what you see today is not your classic Rhine castle standing tall, but a squat and sprawling, bombshell-hardened 19th-century fortress. The exhibit is poorly signposted, with little English describing a vast space that is not very inviting. As you enter you'll get a map with 20 points of (little) interest. But the views are grand and it's a chance to roam free in a castle.

Cost and Hours: €7, €13.80 combo-ticket with round-trip cable-car ride, daily 10:00-18:00, Nov-March until 17:00, tel. 0261/6675-4000, www.diefestungehrenbreitstein.de.

MOSEL VALLEY

Cochem • Burg Eltz • Beilstein

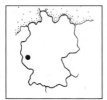

The misty Mosel is what some visitors hope the Rhine will be—peaceful, sleepy, romantic villages slipped between impossibly steep vineyards and the river; fine wine; a sprinkling of castles (Burg Eltz is tops); and lots of friendly small pensions. Boat, train, and car traffic here is a trickle compared with the roaring Rhine. While the swan-speckled Mosel (MOH-zehl in German; Moselle/moh-ZEHL in French) moseys 300 miles from France's Vosges mountain range to Koblenz (where it dumps into the Rhine), the most scenic piece of the valley lies between the towns of Bernkastel-Kues and Cochem. I'd savor only this section. Cochem and Trier are easy day trips from each other (an hour by train, 60 miles by car). Cochem is the handiest home base, unless you have a car and want the peace of Beilstein.

GETTING AROUND THE MOSEL VALLEY

By Train and Bus: Fast trains zip you between Koblenz, Cochem, Bullay, and Trier in a snap. Other destinations require changing to a slow train or bus. Beilstein is a 20-minute ride on bus #716 from Cochem (see "Getting to Beilstein," later). Burg Eltz is a scenic 1.5-hour hike or €28 taxi ride from the tiny Moselkern train station (or about a €55 taxi ride from Cochem). For bus times, pick up printed schedules at train stations and TIs, or check the regional transit website (www.vrminfo.de) or Germany's train timetable (www.bahn.com).

By Boat: Thanks to its many locks, Mosel cruises feel more like canal-boat rides than the cruises on the mighty Rhine. The Kolb Line has the most frequent departures, and cruises the most scenic stretch of the Mosel (tel. 02673/1515, www.moselrundfahrten.

de). A simple and fun outing is the one-hour cruise between **Cochem** and **Beilstein,** passing through the Fankel lock (4-5/day in each direction May-Oct, weekends only in April, no boats off-season, first departure from Cochem at about 10:30, last departure from Beilstein at about 17:30, €12 one-way, €16 round-trip). Another option is the boat in the other direction (downstream) from **Cochem** to **Treis-Karden** (3/day, runs mid-July-Aug daily; May-mid-July and Sept-Oct Wed and Sat-Sun only; no boats off-season; 40 minutes, €11 one-way, €14 round-trip).

From Karden, you can get to Burg Eltz via a long hike (2 hours, steep in places), train-and-hike combination, weekend bus (May-Oct only, 4/day, www.burg-eltz.de), or taxi ride—though it's generally easier to reach Burg Eltz from the Moselkern train station. Kolb also runs one-hour **sightseeing cruises** and two-hour "Tanz Party" **dancing cruises** from Cochem (€11 sightseeing cruises 5/day Easter-Oct; €18 dancing cruises with live music at 20:15, May-Oct Sat only, Aug-Sept also Tue).

The K-D (Köln-Düsseldorfer) line sails the lower Mosel, between **Cochem** and **Koblenz**—but only Friday to Sunday, and only once a day in each direction (€38.20 one-way, May-Sept only, none off-season, Koblenz to Cochem 9:45-15:00, Cochem to Koblenz 15:40-20:00; 20 percent discount with a German rail pass and does not count as the use of a flexipass day, possible discounts with Eurail pass—ask; tel. in Cochem 02671/980-023, www.k-d.com).

Each year in May or June, the Mosel locks close for a week or more of maintenance, and none of the boats listed here run. In 2019, this is scheduled to happen May 21-28.

By Car: Two-lane roads run along both riverbanks. While these riverside roads are a delight, the river valley is very windy. Overland shortcuts can "cut the corners" and save you serious time—especially between Burg Eltz and Beilstein (see page 179) and if you're driving between the Mosel and the Rhine (note the Brodenbach-Boppard shortcut). Both Koblenz and Trier have car-rental agencies. A mile-long, 500-foot-high, €456 million expressway bridge (called Hochmoselbrücke) is being built near the town of Ürzig, just southwest/upstream of Cochem and Beilstein. It may be completed in 2019.

By Bike: Biking along the Mosel is all the rage among Dutch and German tourists. You can rent bikes in most Mosel towns (I've listed options in both Cochem and Beilstein). A fine bike path follows the river from Koblenz to Zell (some bits share the road with

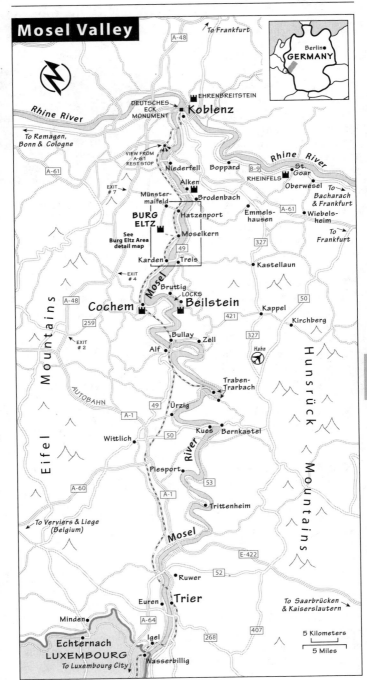

Mosel Valley

To Frankfurt

A-48

GERMANY
Berlin

Rhine River

DEUTSCHES ECK MONUMENT

EHRENBREITSTEIN

Koblenz

To Remagen, Bonn & Cologne

A-61

VIEW FROM A-61 REST STOP

EXIT #7

Niederfell

Boppard

Rhine River

B-9

St. Goar

RHEINFELS

Oberwesel

Alken

To Bacharach & Frankfurt

Münster-maifeld

Brodenbach

Emmels-hausen

A-61

Wiebels-heim

BURG ELTZ

See Burg Eltz Area detail map

Hatzenport

To Frankfurt

Moselkern

327

Mosel

49

Karden

Treis

Kastellaun

EXIT #4

Bruttig

LOCKS

Cochem

259

Beilstein

Kappel

50

421

Kirchberg

327

EXIT #2

Bullay

Zell

Alf

Hahn

AUTOBAHN

Traben-Trabach

A-1

49

Ürzig

River

Hunsrück Mountains

Eifel Mountains

Wittlich

50

Kues

Bernkastel

Piesport

A-60

A-1

53

To Verviers & Liege (Belgium)

Trittenheim

Mosel

E-422

52

Ruwer

Trier

Euren

To Saarbrücken & Kaiserslautern

Minden

A-64

Igel

268

407

Echternach

LUXEMBOURG
To Luxembourg City

Wasserbillig

5 Kilometers

5 Miles

MOSEL VALLEY

cars). Allow one hour between Cochem and Beilstein. Many pedal one-way, then relax on a return cruise or train ride.

By Ferry: About a dozen small car-and-passenger ferries *(Fähre)* cross the Mosel between Koblenz and Trier.

By Plane: The confusingly named Frankfurt Hahn Airport, a popular hub for low-fare airlines such as Ryanair, is actually located near the Mosel (airport code: HHN, www.hahn-airport.de). You can ride bus #750 from the airport to Bullay (about €8, runs every 2 hours, 50 minutes) where you can take a train to Cochem (10 minutes). Groups of five or more should book ahead for this bus (tel. 0800-724-1370, www.airportshuttle-mosel.de/AirportHahn).

HELPFUL HINTS

Wine Festivals: Throughout the Mosel region on summer weekends and during the fall harvest, wine festivals with oompah bands, dancing, and colorful costumes are powered by good food and wine. You'll find a wine festival in some nearby village any weekend, June through September (see calendar at www.mosellandtouristik.de). The tourist season lasts from April through October. Things close down tight through the winter.

Carry Cash: Although more places are accepting credit cards, come prepared to pay cash for many services in the Mosel Valley—including food, hotels, and transportation—especially at Burg Eltz and in smaller villages along the river,

Helpful Guidebook: The booklet *The Castles of the Moselle* (sold at TIs) offers information on castles from Koblenz to Trier—including Burg Eltz, Cochem, and Metternich in Beilstein. It also has some drawings of what the now-ruined castles once looked like.

Cochem

With a majestic castle and picturesque medieval streets, Cochem (KOHKH-ehm) is the hub of the middle Mosel. Home to 5,000 people, it's a larger, more bustling town than Beilstein, Bacharach, or St. Goar. Duck into a damp wine cellar to sample the local white wine (*Weinprobe* means "wine tasting"). Stroll pleasant paths along the idyllic riverbank, hike through vineyards for a panoramic view, or just grab a bench and watch Germany at play. River-cruise passengers clog the old town during the day, but evenings are peaceful.

Orientation to Cochem

Long and skinny Cochem stretches along both banks of the Mosel. The main part of town, on the west bank, sits below vineyards and the town's showpiece castle. From the river, the town bunny-hops up various small valleys.

TOURIST INFORMATION

The information-packed TI is by the bridge at the main bus stop on Endertplatz. Find out about special events, wine tastings, public transportation to Burg Eltz, and area hikes. Consider the six-foot-long *Mosellauf* poster/brochure (Mon-Sat 9:00-17:00, Sun 10:00-15:00; Sat until 15:00 and closed Sun May-mid-July; off-season shorter hours and closed Sat-Sun; Endertplatz 1, tel. 02671/60040, www.ferienland-cochem.de).

ARRIVAL IN COCHEM

By Train: Cochem's train station is often unstaffed and has no lockers, but you can pay to leave your bags at the Gleis 9 café off the station hall (Mon-Fri 7:30-19:00, Sat-Sun from 10:00).

To reach town, make a hard right out of the station and walk about 10 minutes along cobbled Ravenéstrasse, keeping to the right at the busy intersection past the supermarket. You'll soon see a safe crosswalk; take it to find the TI and bus station (both on your left, before the bridge). To continue to the main square (Markt) and colorful medieval town center, continue under the bridge (with pay WC on your left), then stay straight to follow Bernstrasse.

By Car: Drivers can park in a lot behind the train station (€5/day, reach it by circling around on Ravenéstrasse and Pinnerstrasse). There's also a multistory garage just up Endertstrasse from the bridge (€8/day).

HELPFUL HINTS

Festival: Cochem's biggest wine festival is held the last weekend in August. High season for wine aficionados lasts from August through October.

Laundry: Frau Huntscha at **Wäscherei Huntscha** will wash, dry, and fold your clothes, and the location is handy, but she speaks no English (Mon-Tue and Thu-Fri 9:00-14:30, Sat from 10:00, closed Wed and Sun, entrance just down the alley around Ravenéstrasse 31 opposite the supermarket, tel. 02671/3493).

Bike Rental: Consider taking a bike on the boat or train and pedaling back. **Radverleih Schaltwerk,** between the station and TI, offers helmets with rentals (€10/day, €20/day for electric bikes; Mon-Fri 9:00-13:00 & 14:00-18:00, Sat 9:00-13:00, Sun 10:00-12:30—except closed Sun Nov-March; drop-off after 18:00 possible, Ravenéstrasse 18, tel. 02671/603-500). The ticket office at the **K-D boat dock** also rents bikes (€9/day, €18/day for electric bikes, daily May-Sept 9:00-18:00, tel. 02671/980-023).

Tours: To explore Cochem town, consider one of the TI's tour offerings: one-hour walking tours run twice a week at 11:00 (€3.50, Mon and Sat March-Dec, Sept-Oct also Wed); night watchman tours run on Saturdays (€5, at 20:30; tel. 02671/60040, www.ferienland-cochem.de).

Taxi: Taxis usually wait at the taxi stand in front of the church on Moselpromenade; if not, call 02671/8080.

Sights in Cochem

Cochem Castle (Reichsburg Cochem)

This pretty, pointy castle on a hill above town is the work of overly imaginative 19th-century restorers. Like many castles along the Rhine and Mosel, Cochem's—dating from the year 1000—was blown up by French troops in 1689. For almost two hundred years it stood in ruins (much like Beilstein's) until it caught the attention of Louis Ravené, a rich Berliner who'd made a fortune in the steel industry. He bought the castle dirt-cheap in 1868 and

spared no expense in turning it into a luxurious private residence furnished with tasteful antiques. Today, the castle can only be visited on a 40-minute tour (these run more frequently in German, but guides pass out a helpful English info sheet that makes the visit worthwhile). You'll see seven beautiful rooms, complete with antlers on the wall and hidden doors leading to secret passages. The other 43 rooms are empty, as Ravené's descendants took most of their stuff with them in 1942 when they were forced to sell the castle to the Nazi government (which then used it as a training

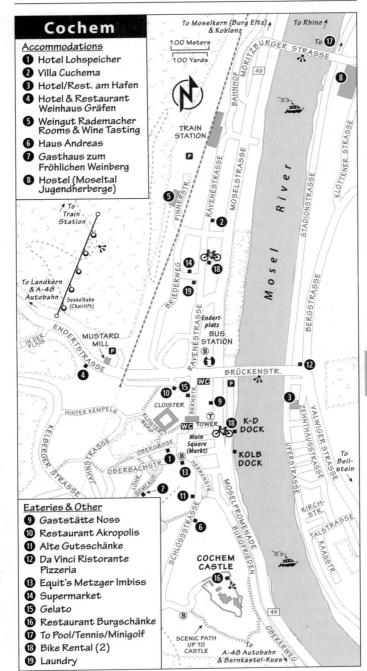

Cochem

<u>Accommodations</u>

① Hotel Lohspeicher
② Villa Cuchema
③ Hotel/Rest. am Hafen
④ Hotel & Restaurant Weinhaus Gräfen
⑤ Weingut Rademacher Rooms & Wine Tasting
⑥ Haus Andreas
⑦ Gasthaus zum Fröhlichen Weinberg
⑧ Hostel (Moseltal Jugendherberge)

<u>Eateries & Other</u>

⑨ Gaststätte Noss
⑩ Restaurant Akropolis
⑪ Alte Gutsschänke
⑫ Da Vinci Ristorante Pizzeria
⑬ Equit's Metzger Imbiss
⑭ Supermarket
⑮ Gelato
⑯ Restaurant Burgschänke
⑰ To Pool/Tennis/Minigolf
⑱ Bike Rental (2)
⑲ Laundry

To Moselkern (Burg Eltz) & Koblenz
To Rhine
To ⑰

100 Meters
100 Yards

N

TRAIN STATION

To Train Station

To Landkern & A-48 Autobahn

Sesselbahn (Chairlift)

MUSTARD MILL

BAHNHOF MORITZBURGER STRASSE
49
PINNERSTR.
RAVENESTRASSE
MOSELSTRASSE
STADIONSTRASSE
KLOTTENER STRASSE

M o s e l   R i v e r

BRIEDERWEG
RAVENESTRASSE
Endert-platz BUS STATION
BERGSTRASSE

BRÜCKENSTR.

WC

CLOISTER
TOWER
WC
Main Square (Markt)
K-D DOCK
KOLB DOCK

HINTER KEMPELN
KELBERGER STRASSE
JAHNSTRASSE
KLOSTERBERG
BERNSTR.
OBERGASSE
OBERBACHSTR.
UERSENSTR.
SCHLAUF
LOHSTR.
SCHLOSSSTRASSE
MOSELPROMENADE BURGFRIEDEN
ZEHNTHAUSSTRASSE
VALWIGER STRASSE
UFERSTRASSE
KIRCH-STR.
TALSTRASSE
KAASSTR.

COCHEM CASTLE

⑯

49

SCENIC PATH UP TO CASTLE
To A-48 Autobahn & Bernkastel-Kues

IN DER FLAIN
ENDERTSTRASSE

To Beilstein

MOSEL VALLEY

center for lawyers). Since 1978 the castle has been owned by the town of Cochem.

Cost and Hours: €6, daily, first tour at 9:00, last tour at 17:00, English tours generally at 12:00 and 15:00, tours run irregularly mid-Nov-mid-March—see schedule on website, tel. 02671/255, www.reichsburg-cochem.de.

Eating: $$ Restaurant Burgschänke serves lunch and offers scenic views of the Mosel Valley (daily 10:00-18:00, closed Nov-mid-March, tel. 02671/255).

Getting There on Foot: *Zur Burg* signs point the way up. From the old town's main square (Markt), with your back to the tower, the quickest way is to walk a block straight ahead on Herrenstrasse and then turn right up Schlossstrasse (10- to 15-minute huff and puff with views of the castle above vineyards). Along the way, you'll see a golden mosaic of St. Christopher, the patron saint of travelers.

A 25-minute scenic route is to continue along Herrenstrasse, which changes its name to Burgfrieden and then turns into a path winding up to the castle from behind. Even if you ride the bus up to the castle (explained next), this trail is the prettiest way to get back down (look for the *Zur Mosel und zur City* sign below the castle).

Getting There by Bus: If you've already *probed* a little *Wein* and would rather ride up, consider the shuttle bus that runs to the castle from the bus station (next to the TI) or the main square—though you still have to walk the last five minutes uphill (bus #781, €2.50 one-way, €4 round-trip, 1-3/hour, May-Oct only, first bus up weekdays at 10:30 and weekends at 10:10, last bus down at 18:00, look for *Reichsburg Shuttle-Bus* sign at bus station, tel. 02671/7647, www.reichsburg-cochem.de).

Chairlift and Hikes

For great views, ride the *Sesselbahn* (chairlift), which ascends the hill on the opposite side of town from the castle (€4.90 one-way, €6.90 round-trip, daily 10:00-18:00, longer hours July-Aug, shorter hours on rainy days, closed off-season, tel. 02671/989-065, www.cochemer-sesselbahn.de). There's a pricey restaurant at the top, along with a short, rocky path that leads to the Pinnerkreuz overlook. Instead of riding to the top, you can scramble up the narrow path under the lift for 20 minutes of heart-pounding, aerobic excitement. Or take the long, winding trail up to the same point from behind the train station (find trailhead past Weingut Rademacher just beyond the station parking lot).

For the best of all worlds, ride the lift up, take in the view from the restaurant, follow the path to the station *(Bahnhof)*, then down through the forest and then the vineyards to a wine tasting at Weingut Rademacher (described next).

Wine Tasting

At **Weingut Rademacher,** near the train station, you can taste four local wines for €6 (usually open April-Oct Mon-Sat 10:00-18:30, closed Sun, different hours during festivals, call ahead to confirm, open by arrangement Nov-March, Pinnerstrasse 10, tel. 02671/4164, www.weingut-rademacher.de; they also rent rooms—see "Sleeping in Cochem," later). Other wine cellars in town also offer tastings.

If you have a car, consider going upriver to the town of **Zell,** famous for its Schwarze Katze ("Black Cat") wine. That's where English-speaking Peter Weis runs **F. J. Weis** winery and gives a clever, entertaining tour of his 60,000-bottle-per-year wine cellar (€18, includes tasting, book ahead by phone, April-mid-Nov daily 10:00-18:00, open by arrangement mid-Nov-March, tel. 06542/41398, mobile 0172-780-7153, www.weingut-weis.de). You'll find his *Weinkeller* south of Zell, 200 yards past the bridge toward Bernkastel (on the riverside at Notenau 30). Peter also rents two luxurious **$$** apartments with kitchen facilities (breakfast extra).

Mustard Mill (Historische Senfmühle)

Just down the road from the chairlift, you can see one of the oldest mills (c. 1810) of its kind still operating in Europe. Run by Wolfgang Steffens and his helpful staff, they use only natural spices and follow centuries-old recipes to produce some of Germany's best mustard. You may also want to try their homemade spirits or, for a unique treat, look for the Roter-Weinbergs-Pfirsich Likör—a local cordial made from the small, tart "red peaches" that are unique to the Mosel Valley.

Cost and Hours: Free mustard tasting of 8-10 varieties plus jams and chutney, 30-minute guided tours in German only-€2.50, daily 10:00-18:00, Enderstrasse 18, tel. 02671/607665, www.senfmuehle.net.

Swimming, Tennis, and Golf

Cochem's leisure center (Freizeitzentrum) offers an array of family-friendly activities: an indoor wave pool, an outdoor pool, a sauna, tennis courts, and minigolf (30 minutes on foot from the center of town, or take bus #702 from outside the TI, 9/day Mon-Fri).

Cost and Hours: Indoor pool-€7/3 hours, generally Tue-Sun 10:00-19:00, closed Mon; hours and prices vary for other activities; 10 minutes beyond youth hostel at Moritzburger Strasse 1, tel. 02671/97990, www.moselbad.de.

MOSEL VALLEY

Cruise

The Kolb Line offers one-hour sightseeing cruises and schmaltzy two-hour dancing cruises with live music (see "Getting Around the Mosel Valley—By Boat," earlier in this chapter).

Sightseeing Train

A little green-and-yellow tourist train leaves from under the bridge at the TI and does a 20-minute sightseeing loop through town with commentary in German and English. Since Cochem is such a pedestrian-friendly town, this is worth it only on a rainy day, or if you're bored and lazy.

Cost and Hours: €6, includes a coupon for a souvenir glass of wine in the train company's nearby wine shop, 1-2/hour, daily 10:00-17:00, Nov-March weekends only.

Sleeping in Cochem

Cochem is a good base for train travelers. Most of my recommendations are within a 10- to 15-minute walk or a €6 taxi ride from the station. August is very tight on rooms, with various festivals and generally inflated prices.

$$ Hotel Lohspeicher, an upscale-rustic hotel just off the main square on a street with tiny steps, is for those willing to pay a bit extra for quality lodgings in the thick of things. Its nine high-ceilinged rooms have modern comforts, and the owner is a gourmet chef who offers cooking classes as well as hiking and biking excursions—book in advance (includes classy breakfast in a fine stone-and-timber room, elevator, pay parking, Obergasse 1, tel. 02671/3976, www.lohspeicher.de, service@lohspeicher.de, Ingo and Anna Beth).

$$ Villa Cuchema's 12 fresh and beautifully decorated rooms fill a handsome 1904 row house two convenient blocks from the station, along the street leading into town. Guests enjoy a pleasant roof terrace overlooking the river (laundry, local wines/beers available, free parking—entrance on Moselstrasse, Ravenéstrasse 34, tel. 02671/910-224, www.villa-cuchema.de, info@villa-cuchema.de; energetic Peter and Ann-Kathrin).

$$ Hotel am Hafen, across the bridge from the TI, offers a mellow atmosphere with views over the river to Cochem. Some of the 18 rooms have balconies (restaurant/terrace with seafood specialties, limited free parking, pay parking garage, closed Dec-Jan, Uferstrasse 3, tel. 02671/97720, www.hotelamhafen.de, info@hotelamhafen.com).

$ Hotel & Restaurant Weinhaus Gräfen, run by the friendly and helpful Vatlav family, has a mix of 14 comfortable rooms, a nicely decorated terrace, and a recommended restaurant downstairs (family rooms, elevator, discounted parking at nearby public garage; near chairlift at Endertstrasse 27, tel. 02671/4453, www. weinhaus-graefen.de, info@weinhaus-graefen.de).

$ Weingut Rademacher rents six simple ground-floor rooms that share a lounge with a fridge and a microwave. It's wedged between vineyards and train tracks, with a pleasant garden (free parking—exit station at rear and walk diagonally across the municipal parking lot to Pinnerstrasse 10; tel. 02671/4164, www. weingut-rademacher.de, info@weingut-rademacher.de). Their wine tastings—free for guests—are open to the public (described earlier, under "Sights in Cochem").

$ Haus Andreas has 10 clean rooms at fair prices in the old town (cash only, pay Wi-Fi, pay parking but free lot nearby, Schlossstrasse 9, reception is often across the street in shop at #16, tel. 02671/1370 or 02671/5155, www.hausandreas.de, info@ hausandreas.de, kind Frau Pellny speaks a little English). From the main square, take Herrenstrasse, after a block, angle right up the steep hill on Schlossstrasse.

¢ Gasthaus zum Fröhlichen Weinberg, near a quiet, colorful courtyard just above the main square, is a relaxed jumble of nine clean, inexpensive rooms, some with low ceilings and tiny bathrooms and most with sunny balconies. Topped by a fun roof garden with a view over town, it's run by friendly Jutta and her mother, who makes jam from vineyard peaches fresh from the garden (cash only, fan available, family rooms, lots of stairs, pay parking, Schlaufstrasse 11, tel. 02671/4193, www.zum-froehlichen-weinberg.de, weinberg-cochem@t-online.de). From the main square, go up Oberbachstrasse (in the far-right corner if coming from the station) and then left up tiny Schlaufstrasse.

Cochem's **¢ hostel (Moseltal Jugendherberge)** is a huge, family-friendly complex just across the river from the train station, with picnic tables, a grill pit, a playground, and a sundeck over the Mosel (private rooms available, box lunches available, game room, bar, restaurant, fills up—reserve in advance, Klottener Strasse 9, tel. 02671/8633, www.diejugendherbergen.de/cochem, cochem@ diejugendherbergen.de). To reach it from the train station, take an immediate left up the hill and walk parallel to the train tracks until you reach the "new bridge" on your right; the hostel is to the right immediately after the bridge.

Eating in Cochem

In addition to the following listings, cafés at both the castle and the chairlift serve lunch (see "Sights in Cochem," earlier) and there are plentiful pizza, Turkish, and Asian options in the old town.

$$$ Gaststätte Noss is one of several restaurants along the riverside promenade. It's open later than most—and supplies meat from its own butcher shop. Don't confuse it with the hotel of the same name; look for the awning draped in vines, which cover the sign (Fri-Wed 10:00-20:00, open later Fri-Sun, closed Thu, Mosel-promenade 4, tel. 02671/7067).

$$$ Hotel am Hafen's restaurant is a comfortable, well-respected riverfront eatery that specializes in seafood. From their terrace you can enjoy gorgeous views of the river and castle (indoor and outdoor seating, daily 12:00-21:00, Uferstrasse 3, tel. 02671/97720).

$$$ Restaurant Akropolis sits hidden away upstairs in a cozy room with a modern take on an old Greek cave house. Their extensive menu ranges from simple gyros and souvlaki to pricier steak, lamb, and seafood dishes. Try to score a seat under the twinkling ceiling that imitates the night sky (daily 11:30-14:30 & 17:00-22:00, reservations smart, Liniustrasse 7, tel. 02671 9153780, www.akropolis-cochem.de).

$$ Alte Gutsschänke, better known as "Arthur's place," is where locals go for a glass of wine in a cozy cellar. Seating is at long, wooden, get-to-know-your-neighbor tables (extensive wine list and very basic pub food, Easter-Oct Tue-Fri from 18:00, Sat-Sun from 14:00, closed Mon and in winter, just uphill from the old town's Markt square at Schlossstrasse 6, tel. 02671/8950).

$$ Hotel & Restaurant Weinhaus Gräfen is where you can meet the locals while enjoying freshly prepared traditional food (Fri-Wed 10:00-22:00, closed Thu and last 2 weeks of Nov and Feb, below recommended hotel at Endertstrasse 27, tel. 02671/4453).

$$ Da Vinci Ristorante Pizzeria serves good, reasonably priced Italian fare at its hard-to-miss location just across the bridge from the TI. Grab a seat on the covered terrace for city, river, and castle views while rubbing elbows with locals and fellow travelers (Tue-Sun 17:30-22:00, Fri and Sun also 12:00-14:00, closed Mon except mid-July-Aug, Bergstrasse 1, tel. 02671/916-195).

$ Equit's Metzger Imbiss is a great and inexpensive alternative for lunch or an early dinner. Local butcher Thomas Equit offers tasty sausages, schnitzel, and other regional dishes—as well as burgers—for a reasonable price. The interior is modern, clean, and very inviting. In summer, the big front windows are opened up, and you'll feel like you're sitting right on the main square (daily 10:00-18:00, cash only, Markt 10, tel. 02671/910-710).

Picnics: The **Diewald supermarket** stocks everything you need for a fabulous picnic (Mon-Fri 7:30-20:00, Sat 8:00-18:00, closed Sun). Located between the train station and TI, it's just off Ravenéstrasse, up a little side street at #33, behind a clothing store.

Gelato: For good quality, inexpensive scoops, **Gelateria**

MOSEL VALLEY

Fratelli Bortolot brings a taste of Italy to the Rhine. They run a sprawling café on the corner facing the Brückenstrasse bridge, but stick to their smaller shop closer to the main square just inside the old town (daily 11:00-late, Bernstrasse 25).

Cochem Connections

From Cochem by Train to: Moselkern (for hike to Burg Eltz; hourly, 16 minutes), **Trier** (2/hour, 1 hour), **Frankfurt Airport** (hourly, 2.5 hours, change in Koblenz and sometimes Mainz), **Cologne** (hourly, 2.5 hours, most change in Koblenz), **Bacharach** (hourly, 2 hours, change in Koblenz), **Rothenburg** (every 1-2 hours, 6 hours, 4 changes), **Berlin** (roughly hourly, 7 hours, 1-2 changes), **Paris** (roughly every 2 hours, 4-5 hours, transfer in Saarbrücken or in Trier and Luxembourg). Train info: www.bahn.com. Bus info: Tel. 02671/8976, www.vrminfo.de.

Burg Eltz

My favorite castle in all of Europe—worth ▲▲▲—lurks in a mysterious forest. It's been left intact for 700 years and is decorated and furnished throughout much as it was 500 years ago. Thanks to smart diplomacy, clever marriages, and lots of luck, Burg Eltz (pronounced "boorg elts") was never destroyed (it survived one five-year siege). It's been in the Eltz family for 850 years. The scenic 1.5-hour walk up the Elz Valley to the castle makes a great half-day outing if you're staying anywhere along the Mosel—and a worthwhile day trip if you're staying on the Rhine.

MOSEL VALLEY

GETTING THERE

The castle is a pleasant 1.5-hour **walk** from the nearest train station, in the little village of Moselkern—the walk is not only easy, it's the most fun and scenic way to visit the castle.

Alternatively, if the weather is bad, or you prefer not to walk, you can take a **taxi** (or, on summer weekends only, the **bus**) to the castle from the village of Karden (see "By Bus from the Treis-Karden Station," later).

Cars (and taxis) park in a lot near, but not quite at, Burg Eltz.

MOSEL VALLEY

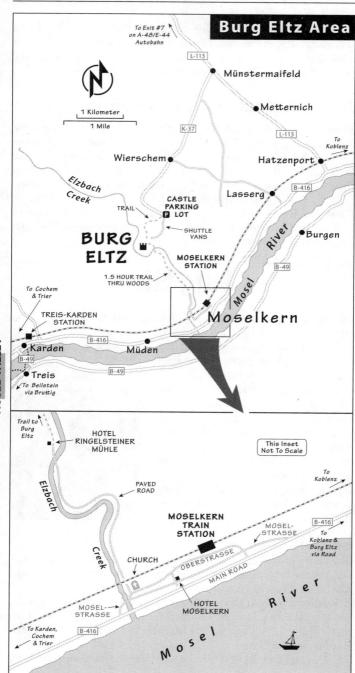

From the lot, hike 15 minutes downhill to the castle or wait (10 minutes at most) for the red castle shuttle bus (€2 each way).

Each of your options is explained next.

Hiking from Moselkern

The hike between the Moselkern train station and Burg Eltz runs through a magical pine forest, where sparrows carry crossbows, and maidens, disguised as falling leaves, whisper "watch out." You can do the hike in 75 minutes at a steady clip, but allow an extra 20 minutes or so to enjoy the scenery. The trail is mostly gentle, except for a few uneven parts that are slippery when wet and the steep flight of stairs leading up to the castle at the end. The overall elevation gain from the river to the castle is less than 400 feet.

Getting to Moselkern: To start the hike, take the slow milk-run train (hourly) to Moselkern from Cochem (16 minutes, €4.90). If you're returning to Cochem, buy a €9.80 round-trip ticket; groups of at least three can get a €19.20 *Mini-gruppenkarte* (covers round-trips for up to 5 people, not valid week-days before 9:00). You can reach Moselkern by train from towns on the Rhine (including Cologne and Bacharach) with a change at Koblenz.

Storing Luggage: The Moselkern train station is unstaffed and has no lockers, phones, or taxis. You can store luggage at Hotel Moselkern, on the river a five-minute walk from the station (see "Sleeping near Burg Eltz," later); call the hotel in advance to make arrangements (tel. 02672/1303). There's no charge for storage, but consider thanking them by eating at their restaurant (food served 12:00-21:00, reasonable prices) or buying a drink at the hotel bar.

The Hike: The path up to the castle begins at the other end of Moselkern village from the station. Turn right from the station along Oberstrasse, cross the intersection with Weinbergsstrasse, and continue straight along narrow Oberstrasse. In about five minutes, you'll pass the village church. Keep going straight a few houses past the church; then, as the street ends, turn right through the underpass. On your left is the Elzbach stream that you'll fol-low all the way up to the castle. Follow the road straight along the stream through a mostly residential neighborhood. Just before the road crosses the stream on a stone bridge, take either the footpath (stay right) or the bridge—they join up again later.

About 30 minutes into your walk, the road ends at the parking lot of the Hotel Ringelsteiner Mühle. Stay to the right of the hotel and continue upstream along the easy-to-follow trail, which starts out paved but soon changes to dirt. From here, it's another 45 minutes through the forest to the castle.

Hiking from Karden (with Optional Boat Trip)

If you don't mind a longer hike, consider a boat ride to the village of Karden, then walk to Burg Eltz from there. (Karden is also on the train line between Cochem and Moselkern.) This two-hour hike is steep in places, and harder to follow and less shady than the hike from Moselkern.

Getting to Karden: Kolb Line riverboat cruises run between Cochem and Karden three times a day in July-Aug and less frequently in spring and fall (see "Getting Around the Mosel Valley" near the beginning of this chapter). Make sure to get off the boat in Karden (not in Treis, across the river). If you come by train, get off at the Treis-Karden stop, which is in Karden but serves both villages.

Storing Luggage: The elegant Schloss-Hotel Petry, across from the Treis-Karden station, is happy to guard your bags if you eat at their **$$$** restaurant (lunch daily 12:00-14:00, St. Castorstrasse 80, tel. 02672/9340, www.schloss-hotel-petry.de).

The Hike: The path from Karden to Burg Eltz starts at the far end of Karden village, beyond the white-towered St. Castor's church (follow *Burg Eltz* signs). Get a trail map (available locally), and be prepared for full sun when the hike travels through open fields.

Shortcuts: To ride the boat but avoid the lengthy hike to Burg Eltz, you can either hop the hourly train from Treis-Karden to Moselkern and take the shorter 1.5-hour hike from there (described earlier); take the bus from the Treis-Karden station straight up to Burg Eltz on weekends (May-Oct only, described next); or take a taxi from Karden to the castle (see later).

By Bus from the Treis-Karden Station

From May through October on Saturdays and Sundays only, bus #330 runs to Burg Eltz from the Treis-Karden railway station (4/day, 40 minutes; leaves Treis-Karden station at 9:10, 11:15, 15:10, and 17:15; leaves Burg Eltz at 10:30, 12:30, 16:30, and 18:30; confirm times at Cochem TI, with bus operator at tel. 02671/8976, or at www.burg-eltz.de). To make the best use of your time, take the 9:10 or 15:10 bus from Treis-Karden to Burg Eltz, and return to Treis-Karden on either the 12:30 or 18:30 bus. This allows you about 2.5 hours to explore the castle.

By Taxi

You can taxi to the castle from **Cochem** (30 minutes, about €55 one-way for up to 4 people, Cochem taxi tel. 02671/8080), **Moselkern** (€28 one-way, taxi tel. 02672/1407), or **Karden** (€30 one-way, taxi tel. 02672/1407). Remember: Even with a taxi, you'll still have a 15-minute walk from the parking lot to the castle. If you're planning to taxi from Moselkern, call ahead and ask the taxi to meet your train at Moselkern station. Consider taxiing up to Burg Eltz and then enjoying the hike downhill back to the train station in Moselkern.

By Car

Be Careful: Signs direct drivers to two different "Burg Eltz" parking lots—some deceptively take drivers far from the castle, while

others get you right there. From Koblenz, leave the river at Hatzenport, following the white *Burg Eltz* signs through the towns of Münstermaifeld and Wierschem. From Cochem, follow the *Münstermaifeld* signs from Moselkern. The castle parking lot (€2/day, daily 9:00-18:30) is just over a mile past Wierschem. (Note that the *Eltz* signs at Moselkern lead to Hotel Ringelsteiner Mühle and the trailhead for the hike to the castle—see next. To drive directly to the castle, ignore the *Eltz* signs until you reach Münstermaifeld.)

Drive/Hike Combo: If you're driving but would enjoy walking part of the path from Moselkern up to the castle, drive to Moselkern, follow the *Burg Eltz* signs up the Elz Valley, park at the Hotel Ringelsteiner Mühle (buy ticket from machine), and hike about 45 minutes up the trail to the castle (full hike described earlier).

Shortcut to Beilstein: If driving from Burg Eltz to Beilstein, you'll save 30 minutes with this shortcut: Cross the river at Treis-Karden, go through town, and bear right at the swimming pool (direction: Bruttig-Fankel). This overland route deposits you in Bruttig, a scenic three-mile riverside drive from Beilstein.

ORIENTATION TO BURG ELTZ

Cost and Hours: €10 castle entry (includes guided tour and treasury), April-Oct daily from 9:30, last tour departs at 17:30, closed Nov-March. Pick up the free English descriptions at entry. Tel. 02672/950-500, www.burg-eltz.de.

Tours: The only way to see the castle is with a 40-minute tour (included with admission). Guides speak English and thoughtfully collect English speakers into tour groups—well worth waiting for (usually a 30-minute wait at most; visit treasury in the meantime).

Bring Cash: The castle (including the parking lot and café) doesn't accept credit cards—only cash. There's no ATM, so make sure you bring enough. (There's one exception: If you spend at least €30 at the ticket desk they will accept Visa and MasterCard.)

Eating: The **$** castle café downstairs serves lunch, with soups and bratwurst-and-fries cuisine (April-Oct daily 9:30-16:30; snacks available upstairs until 18:00, cash only).

VISITING THE CASTLE

Elz is the name of a stream that runs past the castle through a deep valley before emptying into the Mosel. The first record of a *Burg* (castle) on the Elz is from 1157. By about 1490, the castle looked like it does today, with the homes of three big landlord families gathered around a tiny courtyard within one formidable fortification. Today, the excellent tour winds you through two of those homes, while the third is still the residence of the castellan (the man who maintains the castle).

This is where members of the **Eltz family** stay when they're not at one of their other feudal holdings. The elderly countess of Eltz—whose husband's family goes back 33 generations here (you'll see a photo of their family)—enjoys flowers. Each week for 40 years, she made the grand arrangements that adorned the public castle rooms. Nowadays a local florist continues the tradition.

It was a comfortable castle for its day: 80 rooms made cozy by 40 fireplaces and wall-hanging tapestries. Many of its 20 toilets were automatically flushed by a rain drain. The delightful **chapel** is on a lower floor. Even though "no one should live above God," this chapel's placement was acceptable because it filled a bay window, which flooded the delicate Gothic space with light. The three families met—working out common problems

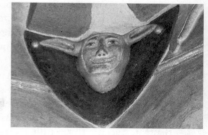

as if sharing a condo complex—in the large "conference room." A carved jester and a rose look down on the big table, reminding those who gathered that they were free to discuss anything ("fool's freedom"—jesters could say anything to the king), but nothing discussed could leave the room (the "rose of silence"). In the **bedroom,** have fun with the suggestive decor: the jousting relief carved into the canopy, and the fertile and phallic figures hiding in the lusty green wall paintings.

Near the exit, the **treasury** fills the four higgledy-piggledy floors of a cellar with the precious, eccentric, and historic mementos of this family that once helped elect the Holy Roman Emperor and, later, owned a sizable chunk of Croatia (Habsburg favors). The silver and gold work—some of Germany's best—is worth a close look with the help of an English flier.

SLEEPING NEAR BURG ELTZ

Although I prefer the bustle of Cochem or the charm of Beilstein, staying in tiny, sleepy Moselkern is a workable option. You can set off to Burg Eltz right after breakfast to beat the heat on a warm day. **$ Hotel Moselkern,** set alongside the river a five-minute walk from the train station, has 25 comfortable rooms in a solid, 1970s-era building. All rooms have balconies, most of them overlooking the river (cash only, elevator, restaurant with outdoor seating, free parking, bowling alley in basement, tel. 02672/1303, www.hotel-moselkern.de, hotel-moselkern@t-online.de, Wanda Ketsila).

Beilstein

Just upstream from Cochem is the quaintest of all Mosel towns. Cozy Beilstein (BILE-shtine) is Cinderella-land touristy but tranquil, except for its territorial swans. Beilstein has no food shops, ATMs (bring cash), or public restrooms (you'll have to use a café's or restaurant's). It does have one bus stop, one  mailbox, and 180 residents who run about 30 guesthouses and eateries. It's nicknamed the "Sleeping Beauty of the Mosel" because until about 1900, it was inaccessible except by boat. Beilstein also has no TI, but there is an information board by the bus stop, and cafés and guesthouses can give you town info.

PLANNING YOUR TIME

Car travelers use Beilstein as a base, day-tripping from here to Cochem, Trier, Burg Eltz, and the Rhine. Overnighting in Beilstein without a car is doable, as long as you check the bus and boat schedules in advance and plan carefully. If you're staying in Cochem and using public transportation, you can day-trip to Beilstein: Take the bus to Beilstein, follow my self-guided walk up to the castle, have lunch, and then return by boat. While the town is peaceful and a delight in the evening, midday crowds in peak season can trample all its charm and turn it into a human traffic jam. In the winter (mid-Nov until Easter), Beilstein is dead as a doornail.

GETTING TO BEILSTEIN

Beilstein has no train station, but it's easy to reach from Cochem—either on **bus #716** (May-Oct hourly Mon-Fri, 8-10/day Sat, less frequent Sun and Nov-April, 20 minutes; last bus departs between 21:00-22:00 except Sun 18:00-19:00, €3.80, www.vrminfo.de), by **taxi** (about €20), or by one-hour **river cruise** (4-5/day in each direction May-Oct, weekends-only in April, no boats off-season, first departure from Cochem at about 10:30, last departure from Beilstein at about 17:30, €12 one-way, €16 round-trip). If **driving,** there's a free lot along the river just upstream from town, under the castle hill. Parking spaces closer-in cost €1/hour during the day (4-hour maximum, use coins to buy ticket from *Parkscheinautomat* machine by town info board).

Two helpful tips: When looking up schedules on www.bahn.com (the Deutsche Bahn website), Beilstein's bus stop appears as "Moselstrasse (Beilstein)." On weekends when bus #716 runs infrequently and the Ellenz Fähre ferry is running (see "Beilstein's Riverfront," later), you can reach Beilstein from Cochem via bus #711 along the other side of the river. (This alternative is slightly more expensive, and the ferry's irregular hours and early closing time complicate it, so I prefer taking the direct #716 bus.) If you go this way, take bus #711 to the Ellenz Fähre stop, then ride the ferry across the river to Beilstein.

Beilstein Walk

Explore the narrow lanes, ancient wine cellar, resident swans, and ruined castle by following this short self-guided walk.
• *Stand along the riverfront, by the town info board.*

Beilstein's Riverfront

In 1963, the big road and the Mosel locks were built, making the river peaceful today. Before then, access to Beilstein was limited to a tiny one-way lane and the small ferry. Originally, the ferry was motorless and the cables that tethered it allowed the craft to cross the river powered only by the current and an angled rudder. However, since the river was tamed by locks, the current is so weak that the ferry needs its motor. Today, the funky little **Ellenz Fähre** ferry shuttles people, bikes, and cars constantly (€1.50, Easter-Oct daily 9:00-18:00, no ferries off-season, wave to summon ferry if captain has paused on opposite bank).

The campground across the river is typical of German campgrounds—nearly all of its residents set up their trailers and tents at Easter and use them as summer homes until October, when the regular floods chase them away for the winter. If you stood where you are now through the winter, you'd have cold water up to your crotch five times.

Look inland. The town was given market rights in 1310 and was essentially an independent city-state for centuries (back when

there were 300 such petty kingdoms and dukedoms in what we now call "Germany"). The Earl of Beilstein ruled from his castle above town. He built the Altes Zollhaus in 1634 to levy tolls from river traffic. Today, the castle is a ruin, the last monk at the once-mighty monastery (see the big church high on the left) retired in 2009, and the town's economy is based only on wine and tourists.

Beilstein is so well preserved because it was essentially inaccessible by road until about 1900. And its tranquility is a result of Germany's WWI loss, which cost the country the regions of Alsace and Lorraine (now part of France, these provinces have flip-flopped between the two nations since the Thirty Years' War). Before World War I, the Koblenz-Trier train line—which connects Lorraine to Germany—was the busiest in the country, tunneling through the grape-laden hill across the river in what was the longest train tunnel in Germany. The construction of a supplemental line designed to follow the riverbank (like the lines that crank up the volume on the Rhine) was stopped in 1914. After Alsace and Lorraine went to France in 1918, the new line no longer made any sense, and the plans were scuttled.

• *Follow the main "street" up into town. You'll notice blue plaques on the left marking the high-water (Hochwasser) points of historic floods. At the first corner, after the Wirtshaus Alte Stadtmauer, go left and find house #13 in the corner.*

Former Synagogue

In the 1300s, several Jewish families were invited to Beilstein after being persecuted and expelled from towns on the Rhine. By 1840, a quarter of the town's 300 inhabitants were Jewish. The synagogue (which dates from

MOSEL VALLEY

1310) and the adjacent rabbi's home were at #13. The medallion above the door shows the Star of David embedded in the double-headed eagle of the Holy Roman Emperor, indicating that the Jews would be protected by the emperor. This was perhaps of some comfort, but not reliable. Of the town's many Jews, most moved away (to larger German towns or abroad) in the 1800s and early 1900s. Others assimilated, marrying Gentiles and raising their children as Christians (among these was the Lipmann family, whose descendants run the riverfront hotels). By 1933, only one Jewish family was left in Beilstein to deal with the Nazis. There are no practicing Jews in town today. The cemetery above the castle is another interesting Jewish sight (see "Beilstein's Castle," later).

• *Continue right (uphill) from the synagogue, and then with the church high above, go right again. You'll reach a long flight of stairs (marked Klostertreppe) that leads to the monastery. Look up (it's only worth actually going up the stairs if you like good views, Baroque churches...or you're a hungry masochist).*

Although the last Carmelite monk retired several years ago, Rome maintains a handsome but oversized-for-this-little-town **Catholic church** that runs a restaurant with a great view. It's a screwy situation that seems to make locals uncomfortable when you ask them about it.

• *Continue back to the main street, called...*

Bachstrasse ("Creek Street")

The town's main drag runs straight inland through Beilstein, passing through the tunnel you see to the left. It covers up the brook that once flowed through town and used to provide a handy 24/7 disposal service. Today, Bachstrasse is lined with wine cellars. The only way for a small local vintner to make any decent money these days is to sell his wine directly to customers in inviting little places like these.

• *Cross Bachstrasse and walk a few steps ahead to the...*

Market Square (Marktplatz)

For centuries, neighboring farmers sold their goods on Marktplatz. The *Zehnthaus* (tithe house) was the village IRS, where locals would pay one-tenth *(Zehnte)* of their produce to their landlord (either the Church or the earl). Pop into the **Zehnthauskeller.** Stuffed with peasants' offerings 400 years ago, it's now packed with vaulted medieval ambience. It's fun at night for candlelit wine-tasting, soup and cold cuts, and schmaltzy music (often live Fri and Sat). The adjacent **Bürgerhaus** (above the fountain) had nothing to do with medieval fast food. First the village church, then the residence of the *Bürger* (like a mayor), and later the communal oven and the village grade school, today it's where locals hold a big party or wedding (upstairs) and a venue for local craftspeople to show their goodies (below). **Haus Lipmann** (on the riverside, now a recommended hotel and restaurant) dates from 1727. It was built by the earl's family as a residence after the French destroyed his castle. Haus Lipmann's main dining hall was once the knights' hall.

• *Leave the square going uphill and follow the main street through the tunnel and up to the top end of town. Then bear right up the stairs (follow signs for Burgruine Metternich) to...*

Beilstein's Castle

Beilstein once rivaled Cochem as the most powerful town on this part of the Mosel. Like so much around here, it was destroyed by

the French in 1689. Its castle (officially named Burg Metternich) is a sorry ruin today, but those who make the steep 10-minute climb are rewarded with a postcard Mosel view and a chance to hike even higher to the top of its lone surviving tower for a 360-degree view (€2.50, daily 9:00-18:00, closed Nov-Easter, view café/restaurant, tel. 02673/93639, www.burgmetternich.de).

For more exercise and an even better **viewpoint,** exit through the turnstile at the rear of the castle. Take the uphill (left-hand)

road, and after 100 yards, fork right. Here you'll find the ultimate "castle/river bend/carpets of vineyards" photo op. The derelict vineyard in front of you is a sign of recent times—the younger generation is abandoning the family plots, opting out of all that hard winemaking work.

From this viewpoint, continue another 100 yards farther up the road to the small but poignant **Jewish cemetery** *(Jüdische Friedhof).*

To reach the viewpoint and the cemetery without going through the castle, continue up the road past the castle entrance, then follow the signs for *Jüdische Friedhof.*

• *From here, you can return to the castle gate, ring the bell (Klingeln), and show your ticket to get back in and retrace your steps; or continue on the road, which curves and leads downhill (a gravel path at the next bend on the left leads back into town).*

MOSEL VALLEY

Activities in Beilstein

Biking and Boating

Boats come and go several times a day for extremely relaxing river trips (for details, see "Getting Around the Mosel Valley" at the beginning of this chapter). While scenic, these rides can take longer than you'd like because of the locks. I prefer a riverside bike ride (perhaps combined with a boat trip). Biking is very popular along the Mosel, and roads are accompanied by smooth and perfectly flat bike lanes. The lanes are separate from the car traffic, letting you really relax as you pedal through gorgeous riverside scenery. To rent a quality bike in Beilstein, visit Herr Nahlen (€9/day, daily 9:00-12:00, return bikes between 16:00 and 19:00, no rentals Nov-March, reservations smart for groups, Bachstrasse 47, tel. 02673/1840, www.fahrradverleih-in-beilstein.de).

Five-Hour Trip to Zell and Back: You could rent a bike in Beilstein, catch the 9:20 boat to Zell (2.5-hour ride), enjoy that pretty town, and cycle 15 miles back to Beilstein along the sleepy and windy riverside bike path.

Hour-and-a-Half Loop: For a shorter bike trip, ride the little ferry across the river from Beilstein, explore the campground, continue left past Poltersdorf, cycle under vineyards to Senhals, cross the bridge to Senheim, and return to Beilstein on the other side of the river. At the edge of Mesenich, leave the road and take the peaceful bike lane along the river, explore another campground, and head for Beilstein, with its castle in the distance encouraging you home.

Sleeping in Beilstein

Beilstein's hotels shut down from at least December through mid-March. All the listings here are just steps from the bus stop and boat dock, except for Hotel Lipmann am Klosterberg. All accept credit cards except Gasthaus Winzerschenke an der Klostertreppe.

$$$ Hotel Lipmann Altes Zollhaus is run by one of three Lipmann sisters carrying on an eight-generation-long tradition in town. The nine bright rooms right on the riverfront feel fresh and cheery (closed mid-Nov-Easter, tel. 02673/1850, www.hotel-lipmann.de, lipmann@t-online.de, family rooms, free parking at Hotel Lipmann Am Klosterberg, also has a restaurant—see "Eating in Beilstein," later).

$$ Hotel Lipmann Am Klosterberg, run by Joachim Lipmann and his wife Marlene, is a big, modern place with 16 comfortable rooms at the extremely quiet top of town (elevator, easy free parking, Auf dem Teich 8, up the main street 200 yards then a sharp left before the stairs to the castle, same contact info as Altes Zollhaus).

$$ Hotel Haus Lipmann is your chance to live in a medieval mansion with hot showers and TVs. A prizewinner for atmosphere, it's been in the Lipmann family since 1795. The creaky wooden staircase and the elegant dining hall, with long wooden tables surrounded by antlers, chandeliers, and feudal weapons, will get you in the mood for your castle sightseeing, but the riverside terrace may mace your momentum. There are six guest rooms in the main building, six larger rooms in an equally old building next door, and, across the square, four **$$$$** spacious, sleek studios with luxe bathrooms and an elevator. David and his wife Anja work hard for their guests (some rooms with Mosel views, family rooms, closed Nov-Easter, Marktplatz 3, tel. 02673/1573, www.hotel-haus-lipmann.com, hotel.haus.lipmann@t-online.de).

$ Gasthaus Winzerschenke an der Klostertreppe is welcoming and a great value, with four sharp rooms right at the bottom of the stairs to the church cloister (cash only, family rooms, closed Nov-Easter, take a few steps up the main street and take second left—after the second building—onto Fürst-Metternich-Strasse, reception in restaurant, tel. 02673/1354, www.winzerschenke-beilstein.de, winzerschenke-beilstein@t-online.de, young and eager Stefanie and Christian Sausen).

$ Hotel Gute Quelle, straddling the main street and the square, offers half-timbers, a good restaurant, and 13 inviting rooms up a narrow stairway, plus seven more in an annex across the street (free Gäste-Ticket for guests—good for buses and trains between Koblenz and Traben-Trarbach, closed Nov-mid-March, Marktplatz 34, tel. 02673/1437, www.hotel-gute-quelle.de, info@hotel-gute-quelle.de, helpful Susan speaks Irish). The hotel also has five bigger, very quiet family rooms and an apartment that sleeps up to four in an adjacent building.

Eating in Beilstein

You'll have no problem finding a characteristic dining room or a relaxing riverview terrace in Beilstein.

$$ Restaurant Haus Lipmann serves good, fresh food with daily specials on a glorious, leafy riverside terrace. For a wonderful trip memory, enjoy a slow meal here while watching the lazy riverside action and the changing light on the distant vineyards (daily 10:00-21:30, last meal order at 20:00, closed Nov-Easter).

The daughters Lippman run two **$$$** restaurants and a **$$** wine bar all within steps of each other. **Hotel Lipmann Altes Zollhaus,** run by Julia, serves specialties cooked on a lava-stone grill (Thu-Tue 11:00-22:00, closed Wed). You could toss a dinner roll across to **Alte Stadtmauer,** run by Kristina, with a relaxed terrace overlooking the river (Wed-Mon 11:00-22:00, closed Tue and mid-Nov-Easter). And **Zehnthauskeller** on the Marktplatz is *the* place for wine tasting, a light meal, and lively *Schlager* music (kitschy German folk-pop). Hang with old locals on holiday, sitting under a dark medieval vault or out in the Marktplatz (try the *Flammkuchen*—German version of white pizza, Tue-Sun 11:00-22:00, closed Mon and Nov-Easter, run by Joachim Lipmann's other daughter Sabine).

The recommended **$$ Hotel Gute Quelle** runs a popular restaurant with classic, well-presented German dishes (daily 11:00-21:00, closed Nov-mid-March, Marktplatz 34).

COLOGNE & THE UNROMANTIC RHINE

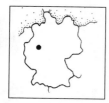

Romance isn't everything. Cologne (Köln— pronounced "kurln"—in German) is an urban Jacuzzi that keeps the Rhine churning. It's home to Germany's greatest Gothic cathedral, one of the country's best collections of Roman artifacts, a world-class art museum, and a healthy dose of German urban playfulness.

Peaceful Bonn, which offers good people-watching and fun pedestrian streets, used to be the capital of West Germany. The small town of Remagen had a bridge that helped defeat Hitler in World War II, and unassuming Aachen, near the Belgian border, was once the capital of Europe.

Cologne

Germany's fourth-largest city, Cologne has a compact, lively center. The Rhine was the northern boundary of the Roman Empire, and, 1,700 years ago, Constantine—the first Christian emperor—made what was then called "Colonia" the seat of a bishopric. (Five hundred years later, under Charlemagne, Cologne became the seat of an archbishopric.) With 40,000 people within its walls, Cologne was the largest German city and an important

cultural and religious center throughout the Middle Ages. Today, the city is most famous for its toilet water: Eau de Cologne was first made here by an Italian chemist in 1709.

During World War II, bombs destroyed 95 percent of Cologne—driving its population from 800,000 down to an estimated 30,000 at its lowest ebb. But with the end of the war, the city immediately began putting itself back together (the population rebounded to about 400,000 by Christmas 1945). Today, it's a bustling commercial and cultural center that still respects its rich past.

PLANNING YOUR TIME

Cologne makes an ideal on-the-way stop; it's a major rail junction, and its top sights are clustered near the train station. With a couple of hours, you can toss your bag in a locker, take my self-guided town walk, zip through the cathedral, and make it back to the station for your train. If you're planning that short of a stop, make sure you'll be here when the whole church is open (in between its services—see the sight listing for times). More time (or an overnight) allows you to delve into a few of the city's fine museums and take in an old-time beer pub.

Orientation to Cologne

Cologne's core was bombed out, then rebuilt in mostly modern style with a sprinkling of quaint. The city has two areas that matter to visitors: One is the section right around the train station and cathedral. Here you'll find most sights and most of my recommended hotels, plus the TI and plenty of eateries and services. Hohe Strasse, Cologne's pedestrian shopping street, begins near the cathedral. The other area—called the "old town"—is between the river and the Alter Markt, a few blocks to the south. After the war, this section was rebuilt in the old style, and today pubs and music clubs pack the restored buildings.

TOURIST INFORMATION

Cologne's energetic TI is opposite the cathedral entrance (Mon-Sat 9:00-20:00, Sun 10:00-17:00, Kardinal-Höffner-Platz 1, tel. 0221/346-430, www.koelntourismus.de). For information on Cologne's museums, visit www.museenkoeln.de.

City Bus Tours: The TI sells tickets and is the departure point for city bus tours offered by two competing companies (1.5-hour tour-€15; hop-on, hop-off tour-€18; departures at least hourly in summer, most have recorded commentary in both German and English, but Kölner CityTour has live guides every 2 hours—see www.cityfahrten.de).

ARRIVAL IN COLOGNE

Cologne couldn't be easier to visit—its three important sights cluster within two blocks of the TI and train station. This super pedestrian zone is a constant carnival of people.

By Train: Cologne's busy train station has everything you need: drugstore, bookstore, food court, juice bar, grocery store, pricey 24-hour "McClean" pay WC with showers, travel center (*Reisezentrum,* long hours daily), and high-tech lockers (next to *Reisezentrum;* insert coins or bills and wait for door to open; your luggage—up to four pieces—is transferred to storage via an underground conveyor belt and retrieved when you reinsert your ticket). Exiting the front of the station (the end near track 1), you'll find yourself smack-dab in the shadow of the cathedral. Up the steps and to the right is the cathedral's main entrance (TI across street).

By Car: Drivers should follow signs to *Zentrum,* then continue to the huge Parkhaus am Dom garage under the cathedral (€2.40/hour, €24/day). The lot outside the garage has a cheaper day rate (€4/hour, €15/day). There's also the Parkhaus am Heumarkt, centrally located at the south end of the old town area (€2.50/hour, €20/day).

By Boat: If you're arriving on a K-D Line boat, exit the boat to the right, then walk along the waterside park until just before the train bridge, when the cathedral comes into view on the left.

HELPFUL HINTS

Closed Day: Note that most museums are closed on Monday (though the cathedral remains open). The cathedral is off-limits to sightseers during services.

Sightseeing Cards: The **MuseumCard** is valid for two consecutive days (or a Sun and Tue, as museums close Mon). It covers all local public transit on the first day and includes the Roman-Germanic Museum, Museum Ludwig, and Wallraf-Richartz Museum, plus several lesser museums (but not the cathedral sights). If you're visiting all three museums, this card will save you money (€18/person, €30 family pass includes 2 adults and 2 kids up to age 18, sold at participating museums, www.museenkoeln.de). Skip the **KölnCard;** its small discounts aren't worth it.

Festivals: Though **Carnival** is celebrated all over Germany, Cologne's celebration is famously exuberant. Join the locals as they dress up, feast, and exchange *Bützje*—innocent pursed-lip kisses. Festivities start on the Thursday before Ash Wednesday and culminate with a huge parade on the following Monday ("Rose Monday," or *Rosenmontag*). The parade draws musicians from all over Germany, and families line the parade route to grab pieces of candy tossed off the floats (www.

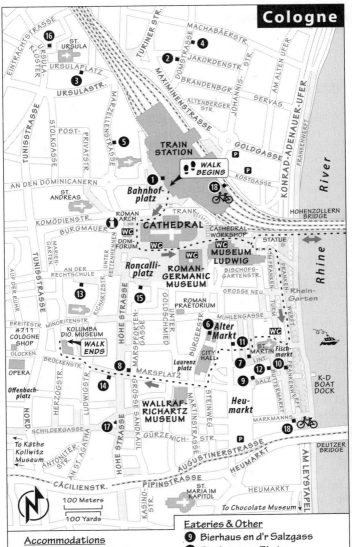

Cologne

COLOGNE & THE UNROMANTIC RHINE

Accommodations

1. Hotel Ibis Köln am Dom
2. Hotel Domspitzen
3. Classic Hotel Harmonie
4. Hotel Domstern
5. Station Hostel
6. Stern am Rathaus
7. Lint Hotel
8. Hotel Engelbertz

Eateries & Other

9. Bierhaus en d'r Salzgass
10. Bierhaus am Rhein
11. Papa Joe's Klimperkasten
12. Papa Joe's Jazzlokal
13. Holtmann's im MAKK
14. Café Eigel
15. Früh am Dom
16. Schreckenskammer
17. Grocery
18. Bike Rentals (2)

koelnerkarneval.de). Cologne's annual **Kölner Lichter** festival lights up the sky on a mid-July weekend, with fireworks, music, and lots of boats on the river (www.koelner-lichter.de). It's part of the Rhein in Flammen regional festival (see page 128).

Bike Rentals and Tours: Convenient bike rental is available at two branches of the friendly **Radstation** (€6/3 hours, €12/day; tel. 0221/139-7190, mobile 0171-629-8796, www.radstationkoeln.de). One branch is tucked under the train-track arcade (long hours daily, ID and €50 deposit required; from the station, exit out the back by track 11 to Breslauer Platz, turn right, cross the street, and look toward the train tracks). The other is along the river a 10-minute walk from the station, on Markmannsgasse (daily April-Oct 10:00-18:00, leave photo ID as security deposit, 100 yards upstream from the K-D Line dock). Consider biking the path along the Rhine River up past the convention center *(Messe)* to the Rheinpark for a picnic.

Radstation also offers German/English guided city tours by bike (€22.50, 3 hours, April-Oct daily at 13:30, includes bike rental, about 10 people per guide, reservations smart).

Cologne Walk

Cologne lends itself to a fine orientation walk, worth ▲▲. The old town, towering cathedral, and most of the sights cluster near the train station. Starting at the train station, this self-guided walk takes less than an hour and provides a good introduction. The main sights on this walk—the cathedral, Roman-Germanic Museum, Museum Ludwig, Wallraf-Richartz Museum, and Kolumba Diocesan Museum—are described in more detail later, under "Sights in Cologne."

Bahnhofsvorplatz: Stepping out of the train station, you're confronted with a modern hodgepodge of post-WWII architecture and the towering icon of Cologne, its cathedral. The city feels rebuilt—because it was. The Allies bombed Cologne hard in retaliation for Germany's bombing of London. Your gaze is grabbed by the cathedral. While it was built according to the original 13th-century plans, and the left (east) part was completed in the 13th century, the right half wasn't built until after German unification, in the 1880s.

• *Climb the steps and circle right, to the people-filled square facing the cathedral.*

Roncalliplatz (Roncalli Square): In centuries past, a clutter of half-timbered huts crowded around the cathedral. They were cleared out in the late 1800s so the great building would have a suitable approach; in the late 1960s the plaza was pedestrianized.

This has been a busy commercial zone since ancient times. The Roman arch was discovered nearby and set up here as a reminder of the town's Roman roots. This north gate of the Roman city, from AD 50, marks the start of Cologne's nearly 2,000-year-old main shopping street, Hohe Strasse.

Look for the life-size replica tip of a spire. The real thing is 515 feet above you. The cathedral facade, while finished in the 1880s, is exactly what was envisioned by the original church planners in 1280.

• *Continue around the right side of the church, passing modern buildings and public spaces. Step up to the window of the **Roman-Germanic Museum** to see a...*

Roman Mosaic: Through the Roman-Germanic Museum's generous window, you can get a free look at the museum's prize piece—a fine mosaic floor. Once the dining-room floor of a rich Roman merchant, this is actually in its original position (the museum was built around it). It shows scenes from the life of Dionysus...wine, women, and song, Roman-style. The mosaic is quite sexy, with several scenes showing a satyr seducing and ultimately disrobing a half-goddess, half-human maenad. First he offers her grapes, then he turns on the music. After further wining and dining—all with an agenda—the horny satyr finally scores. The cupid on a lion's back symbolizes the triumph of physical love.

The mosaic is at the original Roman street level. The tall monument above and left of the mosaic is the mausoleum of a first-century Roman army officer. Directly across from you (at eye level, beyond the mosaic) are beautifully carved stone reliefs—an indication of what a fine city Roman Cologne must have been.

• *Walk 20 steps beyond the mosaic farther along the cathedral and look down to see the...*

Cathedral Workshop: Any church of this size is a work in progress, requiring constant renovation, repair, and care. Sandstone blocks are stacked and waiting to be shaped and plugged in wherever needed. The buttresses above are the church's showiest, because they face the bishop's palace, city center, and original entrance (south transept). For 500 years, the church was left unfinished, simply capped off midway. You're facing the functional part of the church, where services were held from the 1300s until the late 1800s.

• *From the cathedral, walk past the **Museum Ludwig** and continue left onto the...*

Hohenzollern Bridge (Hohenzollernbrücke): This is the busiest railway bridge in the world (30 trains an hour all day long). A classic Industrial Age design from around 1900, the bridge was destroyed in World War II and later rebuilt in its original style. These days, the bridge is a landmark for its "love locks"—couples come here, mark a little padlock with their names and the date, chain it to the bridge railing, and throw away the key as proof of their everlasting love.

• *Walk back in the direction of Museum Ludwig, then head down the stairs toward the river.*

Riverfront: The statue (to your left) honors Kaiser Wilhelm II, who paid for the Hohenzollernbrücke (named after his family). Stairs lead down to a people-friendly riverside park. This is urban planning from the 1970s: Real and forward-looking. The riverside, once a noisy highway, is now a peaceful park. All that traffic still courses through the city, but flows unnoticed below you in a tunnel. A bike-and-pedestrian path follows the riverside in each direction, and families let their children frolic in the fountain.

Turn right, and walk away from the bridge for a few blocks along the Frankenwerft, Cologne's riverside restaurant district, until you are even with the tower of the Romanesque church. (Cologne's famous chocolate museum is a five-minute walk farther downstream.)

Notice a strip of sockets for a metal flood wall (on the inland side of the grassy stretch; an eight-foot-high structure can be erected here when needed). Locals see a definite climate change: They say that "floods of the century" now happen every decade, thunderstorms are 10 times more prevalent, and for the first time, this part of Europe has witnessed small tornadoes.

• *At the foot of the church is the Fischmarkt, a tiny square.*

Fischmarkt and "Old Town": Right below Great St. Martin Church, this little square—once the fish market—faces the river. It's ringed by medieval-looking buildings from the 1930s. In the early 20th century, Cologne's entire old town was a scruffy, half-timbered slum where prostitutes and their clients mingled. To the disgusted Nazis, prostitutes were human dirt. Their vision for old towns all over Germany: Clear out the clutter,  boot the riffraff, and rebuild in the clean, tidy, stone-and-stucco style you see here. After World War II, Cologne decided to rebuild in a faux-medieval style to approximate what had once been. This square and the streets around the church are from that period.

• *Walk inland, circling around the right (downstream) side of the church. From the church's front door, a passageway leads away from the river directly to Alter Markt (Old Market Square).*

Alter Markt and City Hall: The ornate City Hall tower symbolized civic spirit standing strong against the power of the bishops in the 15th century. Circle around the tower to see the City Hall's fine Renaissance porch—the only historic facade left standing after the 1945 bombings. Its carvings stress civic independence. The busts of emperors bring to mind Cologne's strong Roman past; the lions symbolize the evil aspect of church authority. If it's viewable, look above the door to see the mayor killing the lion (thus establishing independence from church government for his city). This scene is flanked by Biblical parallels: the angel saving Daniel from the lions (on right), and Samson fighting lions (on left).

In front of City Hall, an archaeological site has uncovered both Roman ruins and the remains of Cologne's old Jewish quarter.

• *Head back down the steps and turn right to walk around the modern side of the building, looking out for flying rice—the City Hall is often busy with civil wedding parties. Turn right again, passing the Wall-raf-Kollwitz Museum. Continue up Marsplatz until you reach Hohe Strasse.*

Shopping, Church Art, and Eau de Cologne: Look left and right to see the hustle and bustle of the town's main pedestrian shopping street. **Hohe Strasse** thrived during the Middle Ages, when Cologne was a major player in the heavyweight Hanseatic League of northern European merchant towns. The street was rebuilt after its complete destruction in World War II and was Germany's first pedestrian shopping mall. Today it's a rather soulless string of chain stores—most interesting for its seas of shoppers (the big MediaMarkt electronics store, Germany's version of Best Buy, is a couple of blocks down to the right).

Continue straight ahead on Brückenstrasse to the modern white building, set atop the ruins of a bombed-out Gothic church. This is the **Kolumba Diocesan Museum.** Inside, from the corner, you can grab a free peek at what was the church interior.

Across busy Tunisstrasse stands Cologne's circa-1960s **Opera House** (a big deal in Germany when built). And across the street from that, on the right, is a historic building at **Glockengasse 4.** When Cologne's houses were renumbered in a single series during the Napoleonic era in 1796, this building was given the number 4711—which the perfume-making firm based here later adopted as its trademark. A shop on the ground floor has Cologne water running in a fountain by the door—sample this year's new fragrances for free at the counter. A small, free exhibit is upstairs (Mon-Sat 9:30-18:00, closed Sun, tel. 0221/2709-9910, www.glockengasse. de).

Sights in Cologne

▲▲▲COLOGNE CATHEDRAL (DOM)

The Gothic *Dom*—Germany's most exciting church—looms immediately up from the train station in one of the country's starkest

juxtapositions of the modern and the medieval. The church is so big and so important that it has its own information office, the Domforum, in a separate building across the street (described later).

Cost and Hours: Free, Mon-Sat 9:30-11:30 & 12:30-16:30, Sun 12:30-16:30; closed to tourists during services (generally Mon-Sat at 6:30, 7:15, 8:00, 9:00, 12:00, and 18:30; Sun at 7:00, 8:00, 9:00, 10:00, 12:00, 17:00, and 19:00; confirm times at Domforum office or at www.koelner-dom.de).

Tours: The one-hour English-only tours are reliably excellent (€8, Mon-Sat at 10:30 and 14:30, Sun at 14:30, meet inside front door of *Dom*, tel. 0221/9258-4730). Your tour ticket also covers the 20-minute English video in the Domforum directly following the tour.

❷ Self-Guided Tour: If you don't take the guided tour, follow this seven-stop walk (note that stops 3-7 are closed off during confession Sat 14:00-18:00, and any time services are underway).

❶ Cathedral Exterior: The cathedral—the most ambitious Gothic building project north of France in the 13th century—was stalled in the Middle Ages and not finished until 1880. Even though most of it was built in the 19th century, it's still technically a Gothic church (not "Neo-Gothic") because it was finished according to its original plans.

• *Step inside the church. Grab a pew in the center of the nave.*

❷ Nave: If you feel small, that's because you're supposed to. The 140-foot-tall ceiling reminds us of our place in the vast scheme of things. Lots of stained glass—enough to cover three football fields—fills the church with light, which represents God.

The church was begun in 1248. The choir—the lofty area from the center altar to the far end ahead of you—was inaugurated in 1322. Later, during the tumultuous wars of religious reformation, Catholic pilgrims

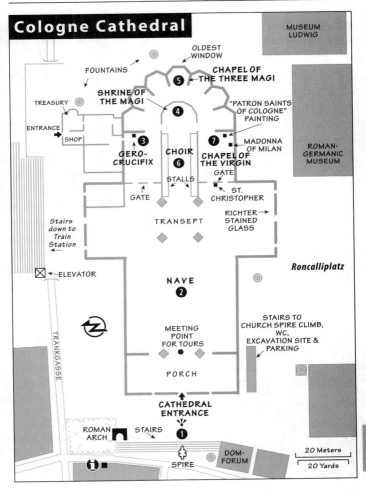

Cologne Cathedral

MUSEUM LUDWIG

OLDEST WINDOW

FOUNTAINS

CHAPEL OF THE THREE MAGI

⑤

SHRINE OF THE MAGI

④

TREASURY

"PATRON SAINTS OF COLOGNE" PAINTING

ENTRANCE

SHOP

❸

GERO-CRUCIFIX

CHOIR

⑥

❼

CHAPEL OF THE VIRGIN

MADONNA OF MILAN

ROMAN-GERMANIC MUSEUM

STALLS

GATE

GATE

ST. CHRISTOPHER

Stairs down to Train Station

TRANSEPT

RICHTER→ STAINED GLASS

◇ ◇

Roncalliplatz

⊠ ←ELEVATOR

NAVE

❷

⌀

MEETING POINT FOR TOURS

STAIRS TO CHURCH SPIRE CLIMB, WC, EXCAVATION SITE & PARKING

TRANKGASSE

◇ ● ◇

PORCH

↑ **CATHEDRAL ENTRANCE** ↓

❶

ROMAN ARCH

STAIRS

DOM-FORUM

20 Meters

20 Yards

🛈 ■

SPIRE

stopped coming. This dried up funds, and eventually construction stopped. For 300 years, the finished end of the church was walled off and functioned as a church, while the unfinished nave (where you now sit) waited. For centuries, the symbol of Cologne's skyline was a huge crane that sat atop the unfinished west spire.

With the rise of German patriotism in the early 1800s, Cologne became a symbol of German unity. And the Prussians—the movers and shakers behind German unity—mistakenly considered Gothic (which actually originated in France) a German style. They paid for the speedy completion of this gloriously Gothic German church. With nearly 700 workers going at full speed, the church was finished in just 38 years (1842-1880). The great train station was built in the shadow of the cathedral's towering spire.

The glass windows at the east end of the church (in the chapels and high above) are medieval. The glass surrounding you in the nave is not as old, but it's precious nevertheless. The glass on the left is early Renaissance. Notice the many coats of arms, which depict the lineage of the donors. One of these windows would have cost as much as two large townhouses. The glass on the right—a gift from Ludwig I, grandfather of the "Mad" King Ludwig who built the fairy-tale castles—is 19th-century Bavarian. Compare both the colors and the realism of the faces between the windows to see how techniques advanced and tastes changed over the centuries.

While 95 percent of Cologne was destroyed by WWII bombs, the cathedral held up fairly well. (It was hit by 15 bombs, but the

skeletal Gothic structure flexed, and it remained standing.) In anticipation of the bombing, the glass and art treasures were taken to shelters and saved.

The "swallow's nest" organ above you was installed to celebrate the cathedral's 750th birthday in 1998. Attaching it to the wall would have compromised the cathedral's architectural integrity, so the organ is actually suspended from precarious-looking steel wires.

The guys in the red robes are cathedral cops, called *Schweizer* (after the Swiss guard at the Vatican); if a service is getting ready to start, they hustle tourists out (if you'd like, you can stay for the service if you're already inside).

• *Leave the nave to the left and step through the gate at the far end (beside the transept), into the oldest part of the church.*

As you enter, look down at the 19th-century **mosaic** *showing a saint holding the Carolingian Cathedral, which stood on this spot for several centuries before this one was built. Ahead of you on the left is the...*

❸ **Gero-Crucifix:** The Chapel of the Cross features the oldest surviving monumental crucifix north of the Alps. Carved in the 970s with a sensitivity 300 years ahead of its time, it shows Jesus not suffering and not triumphant—but with eyes closed...dead. He paid the price for our sins. It's quite a twofer: great art and power-

ful theology in one. The cathedral has
three big pilgrim stops: this crucifix,
the Shrine of the Magi, and the *Madonna of Milan.*

• *Continue to the front end of the church,
stopping to look at the big golden reliquary
in the glass case behind the high altar.*

❹ **Shrine of the Magi:** Relics
were a big deal in the Middle Ages.
Cologne's acquisition of the bones
of the Three Kings in the 12th century put it on the pilgrimage map and
brought in enough money to justify the
construction of this magnificent place.

By some stretch of medieval Christian logic, these relics also justi-
fied the secular power of the German king. This reliquary, made in
about 1200 of gilded silver, jewels, and enamel, is the biggest and
most splendid I've seen. On the long sides, Old Testament prophets
line the bottom, and 12 New Testament apostles—with a wingless
angel in the center—line the top. The front looks like three stacked
coffins, showing scenes of Christ's flagellation, Crucifixion, and
Resurrection.

Inside sit the bones of the Magi...three skulls with golden
crowns. So what's the big deal about these three kings (of Christ-
mas-carol fame)? They were the first to recognize Jesus as the Sav-
ior and the first to come as pilgrims to worship him—inspiring
medieval pilgrims and countless pilgrims since. For a thousand
years, a theme of this cathedral has been that life is a pilgrimage...a
search for God.

• *Opposite the shrine, at the far-east end of the church, is the...*

❺ **Chapel of the Three Magi:** The center chapel, at the
church's far end, is the oldest. It also features the church's oldest
window (center, from 1265). The design is typical: a strip of Old
Testament scenes on the left with a parallel strip of New Testament
scenes on the right that matches theologically and visually (such
as, on bottom panels: to the left, the birth of Eve; to the right, the
birth of Mary with her mother Anne on the bed).

Later glass windows (which you saw lining the nave) were
made from panes of clear glass that were painted and glazed. This
medieval window, however, is actually colored glass, which is as-
sembled like a mosaic. It was very expensive. The size was limited
to what pilgrim donations could support. Notice the plain, budget
design higher up.

• *Peek into the center zone between the high altar and the carved wooden
central stalls. (You can't usually get inside, unless you take the tour.)*

❻ **Choir:** The choir is surrounded by 13th- and 14th-century art with carved oak stalls, frescoed walls, statues painted as they would have been, and original stained glass high above. Study the fanciful oak carvings. The woman cutting the man's hair is a Samson-and-Delilah warning to the sexist men of the early Church.

• *The nearby chapel holds one of the most precious paintings of the important Gothic School of Cologne.*

❼ **Chapel of the Virgin:** *The Patron Saints of Cologne* was painted around 1440, probably by Stefan Lochner. Notice the pho-

tographic realism and believable depth. There are literally dozens of identifiable herbs in the grassy foreground. During the 19th century, the city fought to move the painting to a museum. The Church went to court to keep it. The judge ruled that it could stay in the cathedral—as long as a Mass was said before it

every day. For more than a hundred years, that happened at 18:30. Now, 21st-century comfort has trumped 19th-century law: In winter, services take place in the warmer Sacrament Chapel instead. (If you like this painting, you'll enjoy the many other fine works from the School of Cologne at the Wallraf-Richartz Museum.)

Overlooking the same chapel (between the windows), the delicate ***Madonna of Milan*** sculpture (1290), associated with miracles, was a focus of pilgrims for centuries. Its colors, scepter, and crown were likely added during a restoration in 1900. The reclining medieval knight in the cage at the back of the chapel (just before the gate) is a wealthy but childless patron who donated his entire county to the cathedral.

Pass through the gate and look back above the tomb with the cage to find the statue of **St. Christopher** (with Jesus on his shoulder and the pilgrim's staff). He's facing the original south transept entry to the church. Since 1470, pilgrims and travelers have looked up at him and taken solace in the hope that their patron saint is looking out for them.

As you head for the exit, look into the transept on your left. The **stained-glass windows** above you are a random and abstract pattern of 80 colors, "sampled" from the church's more-historic windows. The local artist Gerhard Richter designed these windows to create a "harmony of colors" in 2007.

• *Go in peace.*

More Cathedral Sights
Church Spire Climb (Dom-Turm)

An exterior entry (to the right of the church as you face the west facade) takes you into a modern excavation site, where you can see an arch and the foundations from the cathedral's predecessor (free), and pay to climb the cathedral's dizzying south tower. For a workout of 509 steps, you can enjoy a fine city view. From the belfry (*Glockenstube;* only 400 steps up), you can see the *Dom*'s nine huge bells, including *Dicke Peter* (24-ton Fat Peter), claimed to be the largest free-swinging church bell in the world.

Cost and Hours: €4, €8 combo-ticket with treasury, daily 9:00-18:00, closes earlier off-season.

Treasury

The treasury sits outside the cathedral's left transept (when you exit through the front door, turn right and continue right around the building to the gold pillar marked *Schatzkammer*). The six dim, hushed rooms are housed in the cathedral's 13th-century stone cellar vaults. Spotlights shine on black cases filled with gilded chalices and crosses, medieval reliquaries (bits of chain, bone, cross, and cloth in gold-crusted glass capsules), and plenty of fancy bishop garb: intricately embroidered miters and vestments, rings with fat gemstones, and six-foot gold crosiers. Displays come with brief English descriptions; the little *Cologne Cathedral* book sold inside the adjacent cathedral shop *(Domladen)* provides extra information.

Cost and Hours: €6, €8 combo-ticket with spire climb, daily 10:00-18:00, tel. 0221/1794-0530.

Domforum

This helpful visitors center, across from the cathedral's entrance, is a good place to support the Vatican Bank (notice the Pax Bank ATM just outside), or to take a break from the crowds. The staff offers plenty of cathedral info, and the welcoming lounge has inexpensive coffee and juice. The English "multivision" video about the church starts slow but gets a little better.

Cost and Hours: Visitors center-free, Mon-Fri 9:30-18:00, Sat until 17:00, Sun 13:00-17:00, may close for special events, clean pay WC downstairs; video-€2, included with church tour, runs Mon-Sat at 11:30 and 15:30, Sun at 15:30 only, 20 minutes; tel. 0221/9258-4720, www.domforum.de.

Kolumba Diocesan Museum

This museum contains some of the cathedral's finest art. Built around the Madonna in the Ruins church, the museum is conceived as a place of reflection. There are no tours or information or noise. It's just you and the art in a modern building built upon the rubble of war. The daring modernist rebuild is a statement: We lost the war. Just accept it.

Cost and Hours: €5, Wed-Mon 12:00-17:00, closed Tue; on Kolumbastrasse, which runs between Minoritenstrasse and Brückenstrasse, a few blocks southwest of the cathedral; tel. 0221/933-1930, www.kolumba.de.

NEAR THE CATHEDRAL
▲▲Roman-Germanic Museum
(Römisch-Germanisches Museum)

One of Germany's top Roman museums offers minimal English information among its elegant and fascinating display of Roman artifacts: glassware, jewelry, and mosaics. All these pieces are evidence of Cologne's status as an important site of civilization long before the cathedral was ever imagined. Temporary exhibits are on the ground floor. Upstairs, you'll see an original, reassembled arched gate to the Roman city with the Roman initials for the town, CCAA, still legible, and incredible glassware that Roman Cologne was famous for producing. The museum's main attraction, described near the start of my self-guided walk, is the in-situ Roman-mosaic floor—which you can see from the street for free through the large window.

Cost and Hours: €6.50, €9 combo-ticket with Roman Praetorium; Tue-Sun 10:00-17:00, first Thu of month until 22:00, closed Mon; Roncalliplatz 4, tel. 0221/2212-4438, www.roemisch-germanisches-museum.de.

Nearby: The **Roman Praetorium** houses the ruins of the fourth- century palace of the Roman governor in Lower Germania (same hours as Roman-Germanic Museum, tiny entrance off Kleine Budengasse).

▲▲Museum Ludwig

Next door to the Roman-Germanic Museum and more enjoyable, this museum—in a slick and modern building—offers a stimulating trip through the art of the last century, including American Pop and post-WWII art. Head upstairs to find the Haubrich collection. Josef Haubrich managed to keep his impressive collection of German Expressionist art out of Nazi hands (they considered it "decadent art") and eventually gave it to the city. The collection includes works by the great German Expressionists Max Beckmann, Otto Dix, and Ernst Ludwig Kirchner. Their paintings capture the loss of idealism and innocence following World War I and helped take art into the no-holds-barred modern world. Also upstairs is a Picasso collection spanning the artist's entire career. The lower level is mostly contemporary and abstract paintings.

Cost and Hours: €12; Tue-Sun 10:00-18:00, first Thu of

COLOGNE & THE UNROMANTIC RHINE

month until 22:00, closed Mon; audioguide-€3, free WC in entry hall, pricey cafeteria, Heinrich-Böll-Platz, tel. 0221/2212-6165, www.museum-ludwig.de.

FARTHER FROM THE CATHEDRAL
These museums are several blocks south of the cathedral.

▲▲Wallraf-Richartz Museum
Housed in a cinderblock of a building near the City Hall, this minimalist museum—Cologne's oldest—features a world-class collection of old masters, from medieval to northern Baroque and Impressionist. You'll see the best collection anywhere of Gothic School of Cologne paintings (1300-1550), offering an intimate peek into those times. Also included are German, Dutch, Flemish, and French works by masters such as Albrecht Dürer, Peter Paul Rubens, Rembrandt, Frans Hals, Jan Steen, Vincent van Gogh, Pierre-Auguste Renoir, Claude Monet, Edvard Munch, and Paul Cézanne.

Cost and Hours: €8-13 depending on special exhibits; Tue-Sun 10:00-18:00, first and third Thu until 22:00, closed Mon; on Obenmarspforten, tel. 0221/2212-1119, www.wallraf.museum.

▲Imhoff Chocolate Museum (Schokoladenmuseum)
Chocoholics love this place, cleverly billed as the "MMMuseum." Three levels of displays follow the cocoa bean from its origin to the finished product. Local historians, noting the "dumbing-down" of this generation of tourists, complain that this museum gets more visitors than all of Cologne's other museums combined—in fact, it's the only sight in Cologne worth booking in

advance. You'll see displays on the history, culture, and business of chocolate from the Aztecs onward, step into a hot and muggy greenhouse to watch the beans grow, and follow sweet little treats as they trundle down the conveyor belt in the functioning chocolate factory, the museum's highlight. The top-floor exhibit on chocolate advertising is fun. Some find that the museum takes chocolate too seriously, and wish the free samples weren't so meager—you'll have to do your indulging in the fragrant, choc-full gift shop.

Cost and Hours: €11.50; Mon-Fri 10:00-18:00, Sat-Sun 11:00-19:00, last entry one hour before closing; lines—though fast-moving—can be long in high-season, book online in advance; Am Schokoladenmuseum 1a, tel. 0221/931-8880, www.

schokoladenmuseum.de. It's a pleasant 15-minute walk south from the cathedral along the riverfront, between the Deutzer and Severins bridges.

Käthe Kollwitz Museum

This museum contains the largest collection of the artist's powerful Expressionist art, welling from her experiences living in Berlin during the tumultuous first half of the 20th century.

Cost and Hours: €5; Tue-Fri 10:00-18:00, Sat-Sun from 11:00, closed Mon; Neumarkt 18, tel. 0221/227-2899, www. kollwitz.de. From Hohe Strasse, walk west on Schildergasse for about 10 minutes to Neumarkt; go past the Neumarkt Gallerie shopping center to Neumarkt Passage, enter Neumarkt Passage, and walk to the glass-domed center courtyard, where you'll take the glass elevator to the fifth floor.

Sleeping in Cologne

Cologne is *the* convention town in Germany. Consequently, hotels are either jam-packed (rates double or even triple), or they're empty and hungry for guests. An updated list of convention dates is posted at www.koelnmesse.de (choose English, then "Trade fairs and events," then "Trade fairs in Cologne"). Unlisted smaller conventions can also lead to small price increases, and big conventions in nearby Düsseldorf can fill rooms and raise rates in Cologne. Outside of convention times, prices are soft, so ask the hotel for its best offer.

All the options listed here are an easy roll from the train station with your luggage.

NEAR THE STATION

$$$ Hotel Ibis Köln am Dom, a 71-room chain hotel, offers predictability and tidiness, and you can't beat the location—inside the station building—though it lacks personality (breakfast extra, air-con, elevator, Bahnhofsvorplatz, entry across from station's *Reisezentrum,* tel. 0221/912-8580, https://ibis.accorhotels.com, h0739@accor.com).

$$ Hotel Domspitzen is the 30-room sister hotel to the Domstern (listed later). Its convenient location, whimsical wallpapered rooms, and sun terrace with a peek-a-boo view of the cathedral make it a good value (elevator, pay parking; from the train station, take the Breslauer Platz exit by track 11 and walk a half-block up Domstrasse to #23; tel. 0221/998-930, www.hotel-domspitzen.de, info@hotel-domspitzen.de).

$ Classic Hotel Harmonie's 72 business-class rooms include some very small, nicely priced singles as well as luxurious "superior" rooms, which have hardwoods and swanky bathrooms with heated floors. It's plenty pricey during conventions, but becomes affordable on weekends and is a downright steal when business is slow (more expensive rooms have air-con, elevator, limited pay parking, Ursulaplatz 13, tel. 0221/16570, www.classic-hotel-harmonie.de, info@classic-hotel-harmonie.com). It's a five-minute walk northwest of the station: Exit by track 1 and walk straight to the roundabout, then go right on Marzellenstrasse and bear left on Ursulaplatz, toward the church.

$ Hotel Domstern is a 16-room boutique hotel with fresh, pleasant rooms above a colorful lobby with funky furniture, located in a fine townhouse just steps from the station (elevator, pay parking; from the train station, take the Breslauer Platz exit by track 11 and walk two blocks up Domstrasse to #26; tel. 0221/168-0080, www.hotel-domstern.de, info@hotel-domstern.de).

¢ Station Hostel is a five-minute walk from the train station and has a clean and welcoming vibe (private rooms available, breakfast extra, elevator, next-door restaurant, no curfew, tel. 0221/912-5301; exit station on cathedral side, walk along right side of the church one block, turn right on Marzellenstrasse to #44; www.hostel-cologne.de, station@hostel-cologne.de).

IN THE TOWN CENTER

$$ Stern am Rathaus has nine stylish rooms on three floors in a quiet location just around the corner from Alter Markt and the City Hall. The staff and breakfast room are equally cheery (family rooms, air-con, no elevator, pay parking; Bürgerstrasse 6, tel. 0221/2225-1750, www.stern-am-rathaus.com, hotelstern@mailbox.org).

$$ Lint Hotel, a small place with 18 modern rooms and hardwood floors, is comfortably located in a little alley between Fischmarkt and Alter Markt. It's expensive during conventions and in high season, but offers affordable deals at other times (includes breakfast with homemade Bircher Muesli, no elevator, pay parking, Lintgasse 7, tel. 0221/920-550, www.lint-hotel.de, contact@lint-hotel.de).

$ Hotel Engelbertz is a fine, family-run, 40-room enterprise. It's simple and feels dated, but it's clean and in a good location, at the end of the pedestrian mall (RS%, elevator, some rooms with street noise, public pay parking; just off Hohe Strasse at Obenmarspforten 1, coming from station turn left at Hohe Strasse 96; tel. 0221/257-8994, www.hotel-engelbertz.de, info@hotel-engelbertz.de).

Eating in Cologne

The city's distinct type of beer, called *Kölsch,* is pale, hoppy, and fermented in a way more typical of wheat-based beers, lending it a slight sweetness. Beer halls tend to have similar menus but distinguish themselves by which brand of beer they serve (usually Gaffel, Päffgen, Peters, or Früh). Beers come in delicate glasses (by Bavarian standards) and are shuttled around in small wreath-like trays *(Bierkränze).* Cologne's waiters, called *Köbes,* have a reputation for grumpiness, and some beer halls have a sloppy, sticky-tabled feeling, but others have helpful and attentive service and attractive interiors. This is the place to satisfy your cravings for blood sausage *(Blutwurst)* and kidneys *(Nierchen)*...or, for something a little more mainstream, look for the tasty *Rheinischer Sauerbraten* with *Klössen* (dumplings) and applesauce. Pub after pub advertise yard-high beer glasses and yard-long bratwurst.

NEAR ALTER MARKT

The area around Alter Markt, a square a few blocks from the cathedral, is home to dozens of beer halls, most with both outdoor and indoor seating. Wander from Alter Markt through Heumarkt (an adjacent square) and down Salzgasse to Frankenwerft (along the river) to catch the flavor.

$$$ **Bierhaus en d'r Salzgass,** cozy and stylishly decorated, is where locals have been coming for beer since the 19th century. Today it belongs to Päffgen brewery and serves authentic German dishes (Mon-Thu 16:00-24:00, Fri from 12:00, Sun from 11:00, Salzgasse 5, tel. 0221/800-1900). Päffgen's nearby $$$ **Bierhaus am Rhein** has the same menu and offers views of the Rhine and park at Frankenwerft (Mon-Thu 15:00-24:00, Fri-Sun from 11:00, Frankenwerft 27, tel. 0221/800-1902).

If you're more interested in music and beer than in food, check out $$ **Papa Joe's Klimperkasten,** a dark pub packed with memorabilia and live jazz daily (Gaffel on tap, live piano jazz Sun-Thu from 20:00, Alter Markt 50, tel. 0221/258-2132). A couple of minutes' walk away is its rowdier sibling, **Papa Joe's Jazzlokal** (live bands Mon-Sat from 20:30, Sun from 19:30 except closed Sun June-Aug, Buttermarkt 37, tel. 0221/257-7931, www.papajoes.de for jazz schedule—American jazz and Dixieland have a big following in Germany). The pubs on the Frankenwerft, along the river across from the K-D boat dock, tend to be a bit more expensive.

ELSEWHERE IN COLOGNE

$$ **Holtmann's im MAKK,** a museum café with sophisticated locals enjoying light fare, is a good option for a non-*Brauhaus* lunch. If you eat here on a Sunday morning, be sure to sit outside and

enjoy a free organ concert al fresco—the courtyard abuts a church (Tue-Sun 11:00-17:00, closed Mon, on other side of Hohe Strasse from the cathedral in Museum of Applied Arts—Museum für Angewandte Kunst—at An der Rechtschule 1, inside front door and down the stairs, no museum ticket needed, tel. 0221/2779-8860).

$ Café Eigel, just off Hohe Strasse near the recommended Hotel Engelbertz, is a good option for *Kaffee und Kuchen* (afternoon cake and coffee) or for a light lunch (including salads and omelets). In the same location for many years, it's been remodeled in a fresh, sleek, modern style. Enjoy delicious pastries in the airy atrium, and be sure to pick up some homemade chocolates. Order your *Kuchen* at the counter first, then find a table and a server will take the rest of your order (Mon-Fri 9:00-19:00, Sat until 18:00, Sun 14:00-18:00, Brückenstrasse 1, tel. 0221/257-5858).

$$ Früh am Dom, near the cathedral, is the closest beer hall to the train station. Popular with both locals and tourists, it offers three floors of traditional German drinking and dining options. In the adjoining delicatessen on the left, check out a painting of what the city looked like in 1531 (daily 8:00-24:00, Am Hof 12, tel. 0221/261-3211).

$$ Schreckenskammer is a down-home joint and might be the least touristy beer hall in central Cologne. It's located just behind the St. Ursula church, near the recommended Harmonie hotel. The sand on the floor, swept out and replaced each morning, buffs the hardwood and also keeps it clean. The *kammer* is small and cozy, so be prepared to share a table and make new friends over a *Kölsch* or two. Most meals (choose from the *Tageskarte,* or daily specials) start with a complimentary cup of *Brühe* (broth). Don't mistake this as an act of hospitality—it only serves to make you thirstier. This eatery is popular, so arrive early or make a reservation (Tue-Sat 11:00-13:45 & 16:30-22:30, closed Sun-Mon, Ursulagartenstrasse 11, tel. 0221/132-581, www.schreckenskammer.com).

Groceries: For a quick snack or picnic essentials, there's a **Rewe To Go** along the city's main drag (long hours daily, Hohe Strasse 63).

Cologne Connections

From Cologne by Train to: Bonn (5/hour, 30 minutes), **Remagen** (2-3/hour, 50 minutes), **Aachen** (2-3/hour, 1 hour), **Frankfurt** (direct ICE trains almost hourly, most leave from Cologne's Köln-Messe-Deutz station—a 2-minute trip across river by S-Bahn, 1.5 hours; slower, cheaper, less frequent IC trains along Rhine are better for enjoying scenery, 2.5 hours), **Frankfurt Airport** (1-2/hour, 1 hour; trains along Rhine go less often and take 2.5 hours), **Bacharach/St. Goar** (hourly; 2 hours with change in Koblenz,

2.5 hours direct), **Cochem** (hourly, 2.5 hours; most change in Koblenz), **Trier** (at least hourly, 3 hours, some change in Koblenz), **Würzburg** (hourly, 2.5 hours by ICE; also 3/day by IC, 4 hours), **Hamburg** (hourly direct, 4 hours), **Munich** (2/hour, 4.5 hours, some with 1 change), **Berlin** (hourly, 4.5 hours, night train possible), **Paris** (5/day direct, 3.5 hours, Thalys train—requires seat reservation), **Amsterdam** (every 2 hours direct, 3 hours). Night trains are possible to Berlin, Innsbruck, Munich, and Vienna. Train info: www.bahn.com.

The Unromantic Rhine

HIGHLIGHTS
▲Bonn

Bonn was chosen for its sleepy, cultured, and peaceful nature as a good place to plant West Germany's first post-Hitler government. Since the two Germanys became one again in 1989, Berlin has taken back its position as the capital.

Today, Bonn is sleek, modern, and, by big-city standards, remarkably pleasant and easygoing. The pedestrian-only old town stretching out from the station will make you wonder why the US can't trade in its malls for real, people-friendly cities. The market square and Münsterplatz— filled with street musicians—are a joy. People-watching doesn't get much better, though the actual sights are disappointing.

The **TI** is a five-minute walk from the station (Mon-Fri 10:00-18:00, Sat until 16:00, Sun until 14:00, go straight on Windeckstrasse, next to Karstadt department store, tel. 0228/775-000, www.bonn.de).

If you're a classical-music fan, you can stop by **Beethoven's Birthplace,** with its sparse exhibits (€6; daily 10:00-18:00, shorter hours Nov-March; free tours run Mon, Thu, and Sat at 14:30; Bonngasse 18, tel. 0228/981-7525, www.beethoven-haus-bonn.de).

The Unromantic Rhine

Düsseldorf•

Rhine

Cologne•

Brühl•

•**Aachen**   •**Bonn**

Bad Godesberg

Remagen•

30 Kilometers

30 Miles

River

BEST OF RHINE

Koblenz•

Mosel

▲Remagen

Midway between Koblenz and Cologne are the scant remains of the Bridge at Remagen, of WWII (and movie) fame. But the memorial and the bridge stubs are enough to stir the emotions of Americans who remember when, in 1945, it was the only bridge still standing on the Rhine, allowing the Allies to pour across the river and race toward Berlin. The bridge was built during World War I to help supply the German forces on the Western Front. (Ironically, one war later, General Eisenhower said the bridge was worth its weight in gold for its service *against* Germany.) An American unit captured the bridge on March 7, 1945, just after two failed attempts to demolish it (Hitler executed four generals for this failure). Ten days after US forces arrived, the bridge did collapse, killing 28 American soldiers. Today you can pay your respects here and visit the **Peace Museum,** which tells the bridge's fascinating story (€3.50, daily 10:00-18:00, off-season until 17:00, closed mid-Nov-early March; it's on the Rhine's west bank, south side of Remagen town, follow *Brücke von Remagen* signs; tel. 02642/20159, www.bruecke-remagen.de). Remagen **TI:** Tel. 02642/20187.

▲Aachen (Charlemagne's Capital)

This city was the capital of Europe in AD 800, when Charles the Great (Charlemagne) called it Aix-la-Chapelle. The remains of his rule include an impressive Byzantine- and Ravenna-inspired church, with his sarcophagus and throne. Enjoy the town's charming historic pedestrian center and festive Christmas market. See the headliner newspaper museum and great fountains, including a clever arrange-'em-yourself version.

LOWLIGHTS

Heidelberg

This famous old university town attracts hordes of Americans. Any surviving charm is stained almost beyond recognition by commercialism. It doesn't make it into Germany's top three weeks.

Mainz, Wiesbaden, and Rüdesheim

These towns are all too big or too famous. They're not worth your time. Mainz's Gutenberg Museum is also a disappointment.

PRACTICALITIES

This section covers just the basics on traveling in Germany (for much more information, see *Rick Steves Germany*). You'll find free advice on specific topics at www.ricksteves.com/tips.

MONEY

Germany uses the euro currency: 1 euro (€) = about $1.20. To convert prices in euros to dollars, add about 20 percent: €20 = about $24, €50 = about $60. (Check www.oanda.com for the latest exchange rates.)

The standard way for travelers to get euros is to withdraw money from ATMs (*Geldautomat*) using a debit card, ideally with a Visa or MasterCard logo. To keep your cash, cards, and valuables safe, wear a money belt.

Before departing, call your bank or credit-card company: Confirm that your card(s) will work overseas, ask about international transaction fees, and alert them that you'll be making withdrawals in Europe. Also ask for the PIN number for your credit card—you may need it for Europe's "chip-and-PIN" payment machines (see below); allow time for your bank to mail your PIN to you. Also keep in mind that some shops and restaurants in Germany accept only the local "EC" debit cards—not American credit cards.

Dealing with "Chip and PIN": Credit and debit cards now have chips that authenticate and secure transactions. European cardholders insert their chip card into the payment slot, then enter a PIN. (Until recently, most US cards required a signature.) Any American card with a chip will work at Europe's hotels, restaurants, and shops—although often the clerk may ask for a signature. But some self-service payment machines—such as those at train stations, toll roads, or unattended gas pumps—may not accept your card, even if you know the PIN. If your card won't work, look for a cashier who can process the transaction manually—or pay in cash.

Dynamic Currency Conversion: If merchants or hoteliers offer to convert your purchase price into dollars (called dynamic currency conversion, or DCC), refuse this "service." You'll pay more in fees for the expensive convenience of seeing your charge in dollars. If an ATM offers to "lock in" or "guarantee" your conversion rate, choose "proceed without conversion." Other prompts might state, "You can be charged in dollars: Press YES for dollars, NO for euros." Always choose the local currency.

STAYING CONNECTED

The simplest solution is to bring your own device—mobile phone, tablet, or laptop—and use it just as you would at home (following the tips below, such as connecting to free Wi-Fi whenever possible).

To call Germany from a US or Canadian number: Whether you're phoning from a landline, your own mobile phone, or a Skype account, you're making an international call. Dial 011-49 and then the area code (minus its initial zero) and local number. (The 011 is our international access code, and 49 is Germany's country code.) If dialing from a mobile phone, you can enter + in place of the international access code—press and hold the 0 key.

To call Germany from a European country: Dial 00-49 followed by the area code (minus its initial zero) and local number. (The 00 is Europe's international access code.)

To call within Germany: If you're dialing from a phone number within the same area code (for example, from a local landline), just dial the local number. If you're calling outside your area code (for example, from a mobile phone), dial both the area code (which starts with a 0) and the local number.

To call from Germany to another country: Dial 00 followed by the country code (for example, 1 for the US or Canada), then the area code and number. If you're calling European countries whose phone numbers begin with 0, you'll usually have to omit that 0 when you dial.

Tips: Local phone numbers in Germany can have different numbers of digits within the same city or even the same business. Mobile phone numbers start with 015, 016, or 017. Some numbers, typically those that start with 018 (including some train and airline information numbers), are premium toll calls.

If you bring your own mobile phone, consider signing up for an international plan; most providers offer a global calling plan that cuts the per-minute cost of phone calls and texts, and a flat-fee data plan.

Use Wi-Fi whenever possible. Most hotels and many cafés offer free Wi-Fi, and you'll likely also find it at tourist information offices (TIs), major museums, and public-transit hubs. With Wi-Fi

Sleep Code

Hotels in this book are categorized according to the average price of a standard double room with breakfast in high season.

$$$$	**Splurge:**	Most rooms over €170
$$$	**Pricier:**	€130-170
$$	**Moderate:**	€90-130
$	**Budget:**	€50-90
¢	**Backpacker:**	Under €50
RS%	**Rick Steves discount**	

Unless otherwise noted, credit cards are accepted, hotel staff speak basic English, and free Wi-Fi is available. Comparison-shop by checking prices at several hotels (on each hotel's own website, on a booking site, or by email). For the best deal, *book directly with the hotel*. Ask for a discount if paying in cash; if the listing includes **RS%**, request a Rick Steves discount.

you can use your device to make free or inexpensive domestic and international calls via a calling app such as Skype, FaceTime, or Google Hangouts. When you can't find Wi-Fi, you can use your cellular network to connect to the internet, send texts, or make voice calls. When you're done, avoid further charges by manually switching off "data roaming" or "cellular data."

Without a mobile device, you can make calls from your hotel and get online using public computers (there's usually one in your hotel lobby or at local libraries). Most hotels charge a high fee for international calls—ask for rates before you dial.

For more on phoning, see www.ricksteves.com/phoning. For a one-hour talk on "Traveling with a Mobile Device," see www.ricksteves.com/travel-talks.

SLEEPING

I've categorized my recommended accommodations based on price, indicated with a dollar-sign rating (see sidebar). I recommend reserving rooms in advance, particularly during peak season. Once your dates are set, check the specific price for your preferred stay at several hotels. You can do this either by comparing prices on sites such as Hotels.com or Booking.com, or by checking the hotels' own websites. To get the best deal, contact my family-run hotels directly by phone or email. When you go direct, the owner avoids any third-party commission, giving them wiggle room to offer you a discount, a nicer room, or free breakfast. If you prefer to book online or are considering a hotel chain, it's to your advantage to use the hotel's website.

For complicated requests, send an email with the following information: number and type of rooms; number of nights; arrival date; departure date; and any special requests. Use the European style for writing dates: day/month/year. Hoteliers typically ask for your credit-card number as a deposit.

Some cities require hoteliers to charge a daily tourist tax (about €1-5/person per night). This may be included in the room price or may appear as an extra charge on your bill.

In general, hotel prices can soften if you do any of the following: offer to pay cash, stay at least three nights, or travel off-season. To find an apartment or room in a private home, try Airbnb, Booking.com, and the HomeAway family of sites (HomeAway, VRBO, and VacationRentals).

EATING

I've categorized my recommended eateries based on price, indicated with a dollar-sign rating (see sidebar). At mealtime, there are many options beyond restaurants. For hearty, stick-to-the-ribs meals—and plenty of beer—look for a beer hall *(Bräuhaus)* or beer garden *(Biergarten)*. *Gasthaus, Gasthof, Gaststätte,* and *Gaststube* all loosely describe an informal, inn-type eatery. A *Kneipe* is a bar, and a *Keller* (or *Ratskeller*) is a restaurant or tavern located in a cellar. A *Schnell Imbiss* is a small fast-food takeaway stand. Department-store cafeterias are also common and handy.

The classic German dish is wurst. The hundreds of varieties are usually served with mustard *(Senf)*, a roll *(Semmel)* or pretzel *(Brezel)*, and sauerkraut. The generic term *Bratwurst* (or *Rostbratwurst*) simply means "grilled sausage." To enjoy a *Weisswurst*—a boiled white Bavarian sausage made of veal—peel off the skin and eat it with sweet mustard. *Currywurst* comes with a delicious curry-infused ketchup. You'll also find schnitzel everywhere (pork is cheaper than veal). Salads are big, leafy, and good. Germans are passionate about choosing organic products—look for *Bio*.

Ethnic eateries—such as Italian, Turkish, Greek, and Asian—are good values. Shops and stands selling Turkish-style *döner kebab* (gyro-like, pita-wrapped rotisserie meat) are also common.

In Germany, good service is relaxed (slow to an American). When you want the bill, say, *"Rechnung* (REHKH-noong), *bitte."* To tip for good service, it's customary to round up around 10 percent. Rather than leave coins on the table (considered slightly rude), Germans usually pay directly: When the server comes by with the bill, simply hand over paper money, stating the total you'd like to pay. For example, if paying for a €10 meal with a €20 bill, while handing your money to the server, say "Eleven, please" (or *"Elf, bitte"* if you've got your German numbers down). The server will keep a €1 tip and give you €9 in change.

Restaurant Price Code

Eateries in this book are categorized according to the average cost of a typical main course. Drinks, desserts, and splurge items can raise the price considerably.

$$$$ **Splurge:** Most main courses over €20
$$$ **Pricier:** €15-20
$$ **Moderate:** €10-15
$ **Budget:** Under €10

In Germany, a wurst stand or other takeout spot is **$**; a beer hall, *Biergarten,* or basic sit-down eatery is **$$**; a casual but more upscale restaurant is **$$$**; and a swanky splurge is **$$$$**.

Germany has both great wine *(Wein)* and beer *(Bier)*. Order wine *süss* (sweet), *halb trocken* (medium), or *trocken* (dry). For beer, *dunkles* is dark, *helles* or *Lager* is light, *Flaschenbier* is bottled, and *vom Fass* is on tap. *Pils* is barley-based, and *Weizen, Hefeweizen,* or *Weissbier* is yeasty and wheat-based. When you order beer, ask for *eine Halbe* for a half-liter (though it's not always available) or *eine Mass* for a whole liter (about a quart).

TRANSPORTATION

By Train: German trains—speedy, comfortable, and fairly punctual—cover cities and small towns well. Faster trains (such as the high-speed ICE) are more expensive than slower "regional" trains. To see if a rail pass could save you money—which is often the case in Germany—check www.ricksteves.com/rail. If buying point-to-point tickets, note that prices can fluctuate (you can usually save money by booking more expensive train journeys online; tickets are sold up to three months in advance). To research train schedules and fares, visit Germany's excellent online timetable, www.bahn.com.

By Bus: While most American travelers find the train to be the better option, ultra-low-fare long-distance buses are worth considering. The main bus operator is FlixBus (www.flixbus.de). Though not as comfortable as trains, their brightly colored buses are surprisingly well-outfitted and make for a more pleasant ride than your average Greyhound trip. Most offer free Wi-Fi and on-board snack bars and WCs.

By Car: It's cheaper to arrange most car rentals from the US. For tips on your insurance options, see www.ricksteves.com/cdw, and for route planning, consult www.viamichelin.com. Bring your driver's license.

Germany's toll-free autobahn (freeway) system lets you zip around the country in a snap. Autobahns are famous for having no speed limit, but some sections do have posted limits, particularly in urban areas and near complicated interchanges. Sometimes there are signs with "dynamic" limits that change depending on traffic conditions.

Many German cities—including Munich, Freiburg, Frankfurt, Cologne, Dresden, Leipzig, and Berlin—require drivers to buy a special sticker *(Umweltplakette)* to drive in the city center. These come standard with most German rental cars; ask when you pick up your car. A car is a worthless headache in cities—park it safely (get tips from your hotel).

Local road etiquette is similar to that in the US. Ask your car-rental company for details, or check the US State Department website (www.travel.state.gov, select "International Travel," search for your country in the "Learn about your destination" box, then click on "Travel and Transportation").

HELPFUL HINTS

Emergency Help: In Germany, dial 112 for any **emergency**—ambulance, police, or fire. To replace a passport, call the **US Embassy** (in Berlin, tel. 030/83050, https://de.usembassy.gov) or the **US Consulate in Frankfurt** (tel. 069/75350, https://de.usembassy.gov/embassy-consulates/frankfurt). Canadians should contact the **Canadian Embassy** (in Berlin, tel. 030/2031-2470, www.germany.gc.ca). For other concerns, get advice from your hotel.

Theft or Loss: To replace a passport, you'll need to go in person to an embassy or consulate (see above). Cancel and replace your credit and debit cards by calling these 24-hour US numbers collect: Visa—tel. 303/967-1096, MasterCard—tel. 636/722-7111, American Express—tel. 336/393-1111. In Germany, to make a collect call to the US, dial 0800-225-5288. Press zero or stay on the line for an English-speaking operator. File a police report either on the spot or within a day or two; you'll need it to submit an insurance claim for lost or stolen rail passes or travel gear, and it can help with replacing your passport or credit and debit cards. For more information, see www.ricksteves.com/help.

Business Hours: In Germany, most shops are open from about 9:00 until 18:00-20:00 on weekdays; smaller stores generally close earlier on Saturdays, and most stores are closed all day Sunday (shops and grocery stores in train stations often have longer hours). In small towns, shops may take a midafternoon break (roughly between 12:00 and 14:00 or 15:00).

Holidays and Festivals: Germany celebrates many holidays, which can close sights and attract crowds (book hotel rooms ahead). For more on holidays and festivals, check Germany's website: www.germany.travel. For a simple list showing major—though not all—events, see www.ricksteves.com/festivals.

PRACTICALITIES

Numbers and Stumblers: What Americans call the second floor of a building is the first floor in Europe. Europeans write dates as day/month/year, so Christmas 2020 is 25/12/20. Commas are decimal points and vice versa—a dollar and a half is 1,50, and there are 5.280 feet in a mile. Germany uses the metric system: A kilogram is 2.2 pounds; a liter is about a quart; and a kilometer is six-tenths of a mile.

RESOURCES FROM RICK STEVES

This Snapshot guide is excerpted from my latest edition of *Rick Steves Germany,* one of many titles in my ever-expanding series of guidebooks on European travel. I also produce a public television series, *Rick Steves' Europe,* and a public radio show, *Travel with Rick Steves.* My website, www.ricksteves.com, offers free travel information, a forum for travelers' comments, guidebook updates, my travel blog, an online travel store, and information on European rail passes and our tours of Europe. If you're bringing a mobile device on your trip, my free Rick Steves Audio Europe app features dozens of self-guided audio tours of the top sights in Europe—including my Rothenburg Town Walk and Best of the Rhine Tour—and travel interviews about Germany. You can get Rick Steves Audio Europe via Apple's App Store, Google Play, or the Amazon Appstore. For more information, see www.ricksteves.com/audioeurope.

Additional Resources
Tourist Information: www.germany.travel
Passports and Red Tape: www.travel.state.gov
Packing List: www.ricksteves.com/packing
Travel Insurance: www.ricksteves.com/insurance
Cheap Flights: www.kayak.com or www.google.com/flights
Airplane Carry-on Restrictions: www.tsa.gov
Updates for This Book: www.ricksteves.com/update

German Survival Phrases

In the phonetics, ī sounds like the long i in "light," and bolded syllables are stressed.

English	German	Pronunciation
Good day.	Guten Tag.	**goo**-tehn tahg
Do you speak English?	Sprechen Sie Englisch?	**shprehkh**-ehn zee **ehgn**-lish
Yes. / No.	Ja. / Nein.	yah / nīn
I (don't) understand.	Ich verstehe (nicht).	ikh fehr-**shtay**-heh (nikht)
Please.	Bitte.	**bit**-teh
Thank you.	Danke.	**dahng**-keh
I'm sorry.	Es tut mir leid.	ehs toot meer līt
Excuse me.	Entschuldigung.	ehnt-**shool**-dig-oong
(No) problem.	(Kein) Problem.	(kīn) proh-**blaym**
(Very) good.	(Sehr) gut.	(zehr) goot
Goodbye.	Auf Wiedersehen.	owf **vee**-der-zayn
one / two	eins / zwei	īns / tsvī
three / four	drei / vier	drī / feer
five / six	fünf / sechs	fewnf / zehkhs
seven / eight	sieben / acht	**zee**-behn / ahkht
nine / ten	neun / zehn	noyn / tsayn
How much is it?	Wieviel kostet das?	**vee**-feel kohs-teht dahs
Write it?	Schreiben?	**shrī**-behn
Is it free?	Ist es umsonst?	ist ehs oom-**zohnst**
Included?	Inklusive?	in-kloo-**zee**-veh
Where can I buy / find...?	Wo kann ich kaufen / finden...?	voh kahn ikh **kow**-fehn / **fin**-dehn
I'd like / We'd like...	Ich hätte gern / Wir hätten gern...	ikh **heh**-teh gehrn / veer **heh**-tehn gehrn
...a room.	...ein Zimmer.	īn **tsim**-mer
...a ticket to ____.	...eine Fahrkarte nach ____.	ī-neh **far**-kar-teh nahkh
Is it possible?	Ist es möglich?	ist ehs **mur**-glikh
Where is...?	Wo ist...?	voh ist
...the train station	...der Bahnhof	dehr **bahn**-hohf
...the bus station	...der Busbahnhof	dehr **boos**-bahn-hohf
...the tourist information office	...das Touristen-informations-büro	dahs too-**ris**-tehn-in-for-maht-see-**ohns**-**bew**-roh
...the toilet	...die Toilette	dee toh-**leh**-teh
men	Herren	**hehr**-rehn
women	Damen	**dah**-mehn
left / right	links / rechts	links / rehkhts
straight	geradeaus	geh-**rah**-deh-**ows**
What time does this open / close?	Um wieviel Uhr wird hier geöffnet / geschlossen?	oom **vee**-feel oor veerd heer geh-**urf**-neht / geh-**shloh**-sehn
At what time?	Um wieviel Uhr?	oom **vee**-feel oor
Just a moment.	Moment.	moh-**mehnt**
now / soon / later	jetzt / bald / später	yehtst / bahld / **shpay**-ter
today / tomorrow	heute / morgen	**hoy**-teh / **mor**-gehn

In a German Restaurant

English	German	Pronunciation
I'd like / We'd like...	Ich hätte gern / Wir hätten gern...	ikh **heh**-teh gehrn / veer **heh**-tehn gehrn
...a reservation for...	...eine Reservierung für...	**ī**-neh reh-zer-**feer**-oong fewr
...a table for one / two.	...einen Tisch für eine Person / zwei Personen.	**ī**-nehn tish fewr **ī**-neh pehr-zohn / tsvī pehr-**zoh**-nehn
Non-smoking.	Nichtraucher.	**nikht**-rowkh-er
Is this seat free?	Ist hier frei?	ist heer frī
Menu (in English), please.	Speisekarte (auf Englisch), bitte.	**shpī**-zeh-kar-teh (owf **ehng**-lish) **bit**-teh
service (not) included	Trinkgeld (nicht) inklusive	**trink**-gehlt (nikht) in-kloo-**zee**-veh
cover charge	Eintritt	**ī**-trit
to go	zum Mitnehmen	tsoom **mit**-nay-mehn
with / without	mit / ohne	mit / **oh**-neh
and / or	und / oder	oont / **oh**-der
menu (of the day)	(Tages-) Karte	(**tah**-gehs-) **kar**-teh
set meal for tourists	Touristenmenü	too-**ris**-tehn-meh-**new**
specialty of the house	Spezialität des Hauses	**shpayt**-see-ah-lee-**tayt** dehs **how**-zehs
appetizers	Vorspeise	**for**-shpī-zeh
bread / cheese	Brot / Käse	broht / **kay**-zeh
sandwich	Sandwich	**zahnd**-vich
soup	Suppe	**zup**-peh
salad	Salat	zah-**laht**
meat	Fleisch	flīsh
poultry	Geflügel	geh-**flew**-gehl
fish	Fisch	fish
seafood	Meeresfrüchte	**meh**-rehs-**frewkh**-teh
fruit	Obst	ohpst
vegetables	Gemüse	geh-**mew**-zeh
dessert	Nachspeise	**nahkh**-shpī-zeh
mineral water	Mineralwasser	min-eh-**rahl**-vah-ser
tap water	Leitungswasser	**lī**-toongs-vah-ser
milk	Milch	milkh
(orange) juice	(Orangen-) Saft	(oh-**rahn**-zhehn-) zahft
coffee / tea	Kaffee / Tee	kah-**fay** / tay
wine	Wein	vīn
red / white	rot / weiß	roht / vīs
glass / bottle	Glas / Flasche	glahs / **flah**-sheh
beer	Bier	beer
Cheers!	Prost!	prohst
More. / Another.	Mehr. / Noch eins.	mehr / nohkh īns
The same.	Das gleiche.	dahs **glīkh**-eh
Bill, please.	Rechnung, bitte.	**rehkh**-noong **bit**-teh
tip	Trinkgeld	**trink**-gehlt
Delicious!	Lecker!	**lehk**-er

For more user-friendly German phrases, check out *Rick Steves' German Phrase Book and Dictionary* or *Rick Steves' French, Italian & German Phrase Book.*

INDEX

W

Waffenkammer (Rothenburg): 23

Wallraf-Richartz Museum (Cologne): 205

Weikersheim: 45

Weindorf wine festival (Rothenburg): 8–9

Werner-Kapelle (Oberwesel): 147

West End (Frankfurt): 88–89

Wiesbaden: 211

Wieskirche: 50

Wi-Fi: 9, 214–215

Wine and vineyards: 217; Bacharach, 143–144; Beilstein, 184–185; Cochem, 167, 171; Frankfurt, 104–105; Mosel Valley, 166, 167, 171; Oberwesel, 147; Rothenburg, 8–9, 40

Wood Market Tower (Bacharach): 138

World War I: 133, 183

World War II: 191, 197, 200; Remagen Bridge, 211

Würzburg: 53–76; eating, 73–76; helpful hints, 55–57; history of, 54; maps, 56–57, 65; planning tips, 53; self-guided walks, 64–71; sights, 58–71; sleeping, 71–73; tourist information, 54; transportation, 55, 57–58, 76

Würzburg City Hall: 68

Würzburg Welcome Card: 54

Z

Zehnthauskeller (Beilstein): 184, 188

Zeil (Frankfurt): 90

Zell: 171, 186

Zentralplatz (Koblenz): 161

Explore Europe

At ricksteves.com you can browse through thousands of articles, videos, photos and radio interviews, plus find a wealth of money-saving travel tips for planning your dream trip. And with our mobile-friendly website, you can easily access all this great travel information anywhere you go.

TV Shows

Preview the places you'll visit by watching entire half-hour episodes of Rick Steves' Europe (choose from all 100 shows) on-demand, for free.

your travel dreams into affordable reality

Radio Interviews

Enjoy ready access to Rick's vast library of radio interviews covering travel

tips and cultural insights that relate specifically to your Europe travel plans.

Travel Forums

Learn, ask, share! Our online community of savvy travelers is a great resource for first-time travelers to Europe, as well as seasoned pros. You'll find forums on each country, plus travel tips and restaurant/hotel reviews. You can even ask one of our well-traveled staff to chime in with an opinion.

Travel News

Subscribe to our free Travel News e-newsletter, and get monthly updates from Rick on what's happening in Europe.

Audio Europe™

Rick's Free Travel App

Get your FREE **Rick Steves Audio Europe**™ app to enjoy…

- Dozens of self-guided tours of Europe's top museums, sights and historic walks
- Hundreds of tracks filled with cultural insights and sightseeing tips from Rick's radio interviews
- All organized into handy geographic playlists
- For Apple and Android

With Rick whispering in your ear, Europe gets even better.

Find out more at ricksteves.com

*Gear up for your
next adventure at
ricksteves.com*

Light Luggage

Pack light and right
with Rick Steves'
affordable, custom-
designed rolling carry-on
bags, backpacks, day
packs and shoulder bags.

Accessories

From packing cubes to
moneybelts and beyond,
Rick has personally
selected the travel
goodies that will help
your trip
go smoother.

Shop at ricksteves.com

Experience maximum Europe

Save time and energy

This guidebook is your independent-travel toolkit. But for all it delivers, it's still up to you to devote the time and energy it takes to manage the preparation and logistics that are essential for a happy trip. If that's a hassle, there's a solution.

Rick Steves Tours

A Rick Steves tour takes you to Europe's most interesting places with great

with minimum stress

guides and small groups of 28 or less. We follow Rick's favorite itineraries, ride in comfy buses, stay in family-run hotels, and bring you intimately close to the Europe you've traveled so far to see. Most importantly, we take away the logistical headaches so you can focus on the fun.

Join the fun

This year we'll take thousands of free-spirited travelers—nearly half of them repeat customers— along with us on four dozen different itineraries, from Ireland to Italy to Athens. Is a Rick Steves tour the right fit for your travel dreams? Find out at ricksteves.com, where you can also request Rick's latest tour catalog. Europe is best experienced with happy travel partners. We hope you can join us.

See our itineraries at ricksteves.com

BEST OF GUIDES

Full-color guides in an easy-to-scan format. Focused on top sights and experiences in the most popular European destinations

Best of England
Best of Europe
Best of France
Best of Germany
Best of Ireland
Best of Italy
Best of Scotland
Best of Spain

COMPREHENSIVE GUIDES

City, country, and regional guides printed on bible-thin paper. Packed with detailed coverage for a multi-week trip exploring iconic sights and venturing off the beaten path

Amsterdam & the Netherlands
Barcelona
Belgium: Bruges, Brussels,
 Antwerp & Ghent
Berlin
Budapest
Croatia & Slovenia
Eastern Europe
England
Florence & Tuscany
France
Germany
Great Britain
Greece: Athens & the Peloponnese
Iceland
Ireland
Istanbul
Italy
London
Paris
Portugal
Prague & the Czech Republic
Provence & the French Riviera
Rome
Scandinavia
Scotland
Sicily
Spain
Switzerland
Venice
Vienna, Salzburg & Tirol

HE BEST OF ROME

e, Italy's capital, is studded with
an remnants and floodlit-fountain
es. From the Vatican to the Colos-
with crazy traffic in between, Rome
derful, huge, and exhausting. The
, the heat, and the weighty history

of the Eternal City where Caesars walked
can make tourists wilt. Recharge by taking siestas, gelato breaks, and after-dark
walks, strolling from one atmospheric
square to another in the refreshing evening air.

*Pantheon—which
dome until the
2,000 years old
ver 1,500).*

*thens in the Vat-
s the humanistic*

*diators fought
ther, entertaining*

ome ristorante.

Rick Steves books are available from your favorite bookseller.
Many guides are available as ebooks.

POCKET GUIDES
Compact color guides for shorter trips

Amsterdam	Paris
Athens	Prague
Barcelona	Rome
Florence	Venice
Italy's Cinque Terre	Vienna
London	
Munich & Salzburg	

SNAPSHOT GUIDES
Focused single-destination coverage

Basque Country: Spain & France
Copenhagen & the Best of Denmark
Dublin
Dubrovnik
Edinburgh
Hill Towns of Central Italy
Krakow, Warsaw & Gdansk
Lisbon
Loire Valley
Madrid & Toledo
Milan & the Italian Lakes District
Naples & the Amalfi Coast
Normandy
Northern Ireland
Norway
Reykjavík
Rothenburg & the Rhine
Sevilla, Granada & Southern Spain
St. Petersburg, Helsinki & Tallinn
Stockholm

CRUISE PORTS GUIDES
Reference for cruise ports of call

Mediterranean Cruise Ports
Scandinavian & Northern European
  Cruise Ports

Complete your library with...

TRAVEL SKILLS & CULTURE
*Study up on travel skills and gain
insight on history and culture*

Europe 101
Europe Through the Back Door
European Christmas
European Easter
European Festivals
Postcards from Europe
Travel as a Political Act

PHRASE BOOKS & DICTIONARIES

French
French, Italian & German
German
Italian
Portuguese
Spanish

PLANNING MAPS

Britain, Ireland & London
Europe
France & Paris
Germany, Austria & Switzerland
Iceland
Ireland
Italy
Spain & Portugal

Avalon Travel
Hachette Book Group
1700 Fourth Street
Berkeley, CA 94710

Printed in Canada by Friesens.
First Edition. First printing March 2019.
ISBN 978-1-64171-167-8

For the latest on Rick's talks, guidebooks, tours, public television series, and public
radio show, contact Rick Steves' Europe, 130 Fourth Avenue North, Edmonds, WA
98020, 425/771-8303, www.ricksteves.com, rick@ricksteves.com.

Rick Steves' Europe
Managing Editor: Jennifer Madison Davis
Assistant Managing Editor: Cathy Lu
Special Publications Manager: Risa Laib
Editors: Glenn Eriksen, Julie Fanselow, Tom Griffin, Suzanne Kotz, Rosie Leutzinger,
    Teresa Nemeth, Jessica Shaw, Carrie Shepherd
Editorial & Production Assistant: Megan Simms
Editorial Intern: Maddy Smith
Researcher: Rosie Leutzinger
Contributors: Cameron Hewitt, Gene Openshaw
Graphic Content Director: Sandra Hundacker
Maps & Graphics: David C. Hoerlein, Lauren Mills, Mary Rostad
Digital Asset Coordinator: Orin Dubrow

Avalon Travel
Senior Editor and Series Manager: Madhu Prasher
Editors: Jamie Andrade, Sierra Machado
Copy Editor: Maggie Ryan
Proofreader: Patrick Collins
Indexer: Stephen Callahan
Production & Typesetting: Christine DeLorenzo, Lisi Baldwin, Jane Musser
Cover Design: Kimberly Glyder Design
Maps & Graphics: Kat Bennett, Mike Morgenfeld

Let's Keep on Travelin'

Your trip doesn't need to end.

Follow Rick on social media!